LIVING OUT ISLAM

Living Out Islam

Voices of Gay, Lesbian, and Transgender Muslims

Scott Siraj al-Haqq Kugle

NEW YORK UNIVERSITY PRESS
New York and London

NEW YORK UNIVERSITY PRESS
New York and London
www.nyupress.org

References to Internet websites (URLs) were accurate at the time of writing.
Neither the author nor New York University Press is responsible for URLs that
may have expired or changed since the manuscript was prepared.

Library of Congress Cataloging-in-Publication Data
Kugle, Scott Alan, 1969-
Living out Islam : voices of gay, lesbian, and transgender Muslims / Scott Siraj al-Haqq Kugle.
pages cm Includes bibliographical references and index.
ISBN 978-0-8147-4448-2 (hardback) — ISBN 978-1-4798-9467-3 (pb)
1. Homosexuality—Religious aspects—Islam. I. Title.
BP188.14.H65K84 2013
297.086'64—dc23   2013023734

New York University Press books are printed on acid-free paper, and their binding materials
are chosen for strength and durability. We strive to use environmentally responsible
suppliers and materials to the greatest extent possible in publishing our books.

Manufactured in the United States of America

10 9 8 7 6 5 4 3 2 1

Also available as an ebook

CONTENTS

A Muslim is a brother to a Muslim. Let one not oppress
another or betray him. Whoever sees the need of his brother,
God sees to his need. Whoever relieves a Muslim from distress will be relieved by God from distress on the day of resurrection. Whoever protects a Muslim will be protected by
God on the day of resurrection.

~The Prophet Muhammad, in a *hadith* report[1]

In this teaching about empathy, the Prophet Muhammad succinctly
expresses the ideals of Islam. A Muslim should see herself or himself
in every believer in order to overcome egoism and reach out to others with justice and compassion. See, serve, console, and protect others, he tells us—that is the practical demonstration that one worships
God. Struggling to embody compassion and justice is the way to live
out Islam—yet how quickly we forget.

Muslims began their community as vulnerable and despised outsid-
ers. When they became strong enough to impose their will on others,
they all too often lost sight of their Prophet's teachings of empathy,
compassion, and justice. This book shares the voices of some marginalized within the Muslim community who call out to be recognized as
fellow believers—sisters and brothers—who are worthy of respect, who
deserve protection, and who demand justice.

Muslims believe that ultimate justice is only received when one faces God directly, for "the Just One" (*al-'adl*) is one of God's ninety-nine names. Until then, while people struggle and stumble in this ever-changing world, justice is demanded of us. Anyone who takes this demand seriously must get used to hearing uncomfortable truths in unexpected voices speaking from society's margins. This book is about such voices, those of Muslim activists who are gay, lesbian, or transgender, as they share their stories, insights, plights, and joys. Interviews reveal how they struggle to form an integral identity, to elicit empathy from their families, to join with others in solidarity, and to live out Islamic ideals even as they face rejection from Muslim authorities.

This book was written for a wide audience. Scholars and students who study social change in relation to gender and religion will find the stories and strategies documented here fascinating and challenging. Muslims who question their sexual orientation and gender identity will find in it resources for their own struggle. Families and friends of lesbian, transgender, or gay Muslims can find in it guidance, for people who first confront someone who belongs to a sexual orientation or gender identity minority often do not know how to react. Lacking information, they may fall back upon stereotypes and moral condemnation. Parents and authority figures need some way to understand and accommodate their loved ones who are gay, lesbian, or transgender, and this book is also for them.

This book is not only for Muslims. It is also for observers who want to understand Muslims as they wrestle with these issues. This book argues that gay, lesbian, and transgender Muslims can reconcile their identity with their religious beliefs, though this reconciliation is a struggle both within themselves and with their community. This struggle is facilitated by support groups built by gay, lesbian, and transgender Muslim activists. This book presents the lives, struggles, and insights of some of these activists.

To meet these activists, I received a two-year research fellowship at the International Institute for the Study of Islam in the Modern World (ISIM at the University of Leiden). This institution's support—both intellectual and financial—allowed me to carry out this project and I am grateful to scholars at ISIM who helped me with insightful discussion and debate, such as Khalid Masud, Asef Bayat, Martin van Bruinessen, and Abdulkader Tayob. During my tenure at ISIM, I met transgender, lesbian, and gay Muslim activists from five nations on three continents, attended their conferences and spiritual retreats, and learned about their lives and struggles. Their stories reflect the experiences of countless others who do not have the courage to speak up or who never survived coming of age. Each person interviewed was so sincere and forthcoming with me; I thank these open-hearted people deeply for sharing with me their stories, which is an act of bravery and generosity.

When I began this project, I was teaching at Swarthmore College, and colleagues there encouraged me greatly. At Emory University where I now teach, my new colleagues create an environment that is secure yet provocative, and I am especially grateful to Rkia Cornell, Vincent Cornell, Roxani Margariti, Benny Hari, Joyce Flueckiger, and Gordon Newby for their camaraderie and guidance. Two special students at Emory deserve my thanks: Ayisha Ashley al-Sayyad helped me to reorganize the manuscript and Jessica Lambert proofread it tenaciously. Jennifer Hammer, my editor at NYU Press, was encouraging and exacting, and I am obliged to her along with Dorothea Stillman Halliday and the whole staff.

Writing a book is a unique opportunity to give thanks and there are many friends, comrades, and beloved ones who encouraged me. I am deeply grateful to Ben Hekkema, whose friendship made Amsterdam my home while I wrote this book, along with friends like Hans Veenhuys and Sami Abu Rayhan. In South Africa, my gratitude goes to Sa'diyya and her family, and to Fayrose and Ilham. Many in the United Kingdom were generous with me, including Farah, Mujahid, Ubaid, Faiz, and Faizan, and I still long for their company. My admiration also goes to those whose courage to speak has shaped this book—those few whose interviews are quoted here and the many others who are not quoted or not interviewed, but who have shared experiences with me. They remind me of one of my favorite songs, a *ghazal* by Asadullah Khan Ghalib, the great poet of Urdu.[2]

> I'm not parked here forever on your doorstep
> To hell with a life spent waiting! I'm not, after all, a stone
>
> Why this eternal revolving that bewilders my heart?
> I'm a human being—I'm not, after all, a cup of wine

O Lord, why does time move to obliterate my every trace
On the tablet of the universe I'm not, after all, a misspelling

There should be a limit to torment of your punishment
I may be a simple sinner but I'm not, after all, an infidel

In closing with Ghalib's poem, I acknowledge my teachers in the Sufi order to which Ghalib, too, belonged.

Introduction

> If I'm going to end up in hell then I'm going
> to end up in hell, but God is the judge and not
> human beings.
> > ~Fatima, a transgender volunteer with Imaan
> > in London

> Now this is very bizarre, but through gay life I
> came closer to Islam.
> > ~Rasheed, a gay volunteer with Habibi Ana
> > in Amsterdam

The voices of Muslims who are gay, lesbian, and transgender are rarely heard. Their voices have been silenced in the past. Now if they speak, they are expected to express contrition. Yet they stand up against those who denounce them. The quotes above capture the tenor of the voices of activists who volunteer to run support groups for lesbian, gay, and transgender Muslims. They strive to live out Islam even as they acknowledge their sexual orientation and gender identity. The fact that they speak is surprising to some. What they say will startle many.

This book presents interviews with a range of gay, lesbian, and transgender Muslim activists, weaving their voices together to offer a composite picture of their struggle. Theirs are voices of an oppressed minority group within its religious community, a group which struggles to achieve liberation from oppression. Their struggle has psychological, social, political, and spiritual dimensions. Their experiences arise from diverse circumstances but are unified in reclaiming Islam as their own

religion. Their voices are brought together here to offer an "oral history" of the nascent movement to assert their rights and insist on their
dignity. This movement is not about being "out" as opposed to being "in
the closet." Rather it is about finding ways to live out one's Islam with
dignity and integrity by reconciling one's sexuality and gender with
one's faith.

This volume argues that gay, lesbian, and transgender Muslims can
reconcile their sexual orientation and gender identity with Islam. But
this reconciliation requires active struggle, struggle that is sustained
only by camaraderie with like-minded individuals and the solidarity of
support groups. Activists working with such support groups employ a
variety of strategies to promote social change at many levels, from personal transformation to political assertion to religious reform. Activists'
efforts through such support groups can flourish in societies with strong
systems of legal protection for individual rights, such as in countries
with democratic constitutions. The activists we will meet in this book
all live in countries with democratic constitutions and social systems
with a "secular" separation between political rule and religious belief:
the United States, Canada, the United Kingdom, the Netherlands, and
South Africa.

Muslims constitute a small religious minority in these countries.
These nations' democratic constitutions grant lesbian, gay, and transgender citizens access to certain rights and protection from oppression,
allowing them the freedom to think, speak, and organize. This freedom allows them to critically engage with their religious identity, family authorities, and community norms in ways that are not possible in
many Muslim-majority countries. This context allows these activists to
make full use of their multiple social positions: they are members of a
minority religious community and ethnic group, but also members of a
minority defined by sexual orientation or gender identity, even as they
are citizens of a secular state. Their modes of activism reveal how they
strive to balance these competing demands and find in this complex
situation resources and opportunities for protecting their rights and
fostering their welfare.

This book documents these strategies or "modes of activism" as
they are made manifest in the life stories of gay, lesbian, and transgender Muslims who volunteer with support groups. These "modes of

activism" are patterns of action, decision, and compromise. They reveal the underlying identity formation of gay, lesbian, and transgender Muslims in the context of belonging to minority Islamic communities in secular democratic states. Before we proceed to engage with their experiences, however, a number of terms need to be clarified, even those that seem basic—such as activism, subjectivity, sexual orientation, gender identity, and Islam.

Modes of Activism and Theories of Subjectivity

One goal of this book is to demystify the term "activist." Activists are ordinary people who strive to change the social relationships around them to achieve some modicum of justice. Some of those whose stories are related here are leaders while others are supporters, seekers, or healers. Some ways of struggling are more visible than others, but activism is not limited to those who appear in the media, organize protests, confront politics, or raise funds. A lesbian Muslim who struggles to attain an education and economic independence from her family is an activist. A transgender Muslim who insists on being able to pray in her mosque despite an imam's disapproval is an activist. A gay Muslim who strives to succeed in a secular profession while being open about his identity is an activist. Anyone who actively struggles with her or his existential plight is an activist.

This book identifies "modes of activism" through which such activists approach identity formation, religious loyalty, and social change. These modes are strategies through which they approach a complex problem; yet unlike strategies that are rationally adopted after calculation, these modes of activism are intuitive and from the gut. Those interviewed may not rationally think about their modes of activism or identify them as strategies for identity formation and social change. They are patterns of thought-and-action rather than plans of action. This book identifies six major modes of activism:

Engaging religious tradition
Challenging family and community
Adapting religious politics
Adjusting secular politics

Forging minority alliances
Journeying toward individual identity

Though they are listed separately, these modes are not mutually exclusive. Activists combine them according to their personality and situation.

This book is divided into six chapters, each of which focuses on one
mode of activism, analyzing the lives of those whose struggles and decisions illustrate that mode. It shows how these modes of action combine and interweave as the activists make sense of their lives and activities. The everyday struggles of the social activists documented in this
book contribute to the ongoing debate about sexual orientation and
gender identity in Muslim communities. In the academy, this debate
has become even more heated with the publication of Joseph Massad's
Desiring Arabs, which analyzes the discourse of sexuality and civiliza-
tion in Arab societies after colonialism. Massad contends that gay and
lesbian identity is imposed upon Arab and Middle Eastern societies as
part of a "gay international agenda" of American neoimperialism in the
region. His contention is polemic and he accuses Arab lesbian and gay
activists in Muslim-majority countries like Egypt and in the West of
succumbing to false consciousness foisted upon them by Western interests that exploit them in the guise of protecting their rights. This book
documents the lives of the kinds of activists whom Massad denounces,
intervening in this ongoing scholarly and political debate. This intervention aims to restore humanity to activists who are struggling to live
dignified and integral lives as gay, lesbian, or transgender Muslims,
even as they are silenced by Islamic authorities and denounced by intel-
lectuals like Massad, who appear more concerned with ethnic solidarity
than with insuring the security and welfare of vulnerable members of
the ethnic groups he purports to defend.

Massad's scholarship is important in this debate because he claims
the place of the much lauded Arab cultural critic, Edward Said. In *Ori-
entalism,* Said mobilized the theories of Michel Foucault to argue that
Western colonial powers engineered the creation of knowledge about
Arab and Middle Eastern societies in order to dominate them not just
in terms of political power but also cultural production, artistic imagination, and discursive interaction. Everyone working in the fields of
Islamic Studies and Middle Eastern Studies is indebted to Said, though

he has been justifiably critiqued for selectively using Foucault's ideas while constructing an ahistorical binary opposition between Western powers and Eastern peoples. Massad claims the mantle of Edward Said, yet instead of listening to critiques of Said and learning from them, Massad has exaggerated Said's theoretical errors. *Desiring Arabs* claims to follow in Said's footsteps, but it jettisons the theoretical concerns of Foucault in order to sketch a Manichean struggle between postcolonial Arabs and the Western imperium driven by American military interests and UN declarations.

This study of gay, lesbian, and transgender Muslim activists—some of whom are Arabs—complicates Massad's contentions. It returns our attention to Foucault by raising issues of subjectivity and agency in the lives of Muslims who belong to sexuality minorities. There are several scholars working on Islamic and Arab communities whose engagement with Foucault is much more useful than that of Massad. This volume is theoretically indebted to Saba Mahmood and Talal Asad, and the life stories of gay, lesbian, and transgender Muslim activists it documents should be read within the context of their engagement with Foucault. Mahmood and Asad try to preserve the best of Foucault's theories while shedding his Eurocentric bias and restoring a humanistic concern about the rights of vulnerable persons and communities.

From Talal Asad's work, this book adopts the idea that religious practice and secular participation—in national politics or human rights advocacy—are not contradictory loyalties. Asad's discourse analysis of secularism finds religious concepts and concerns deeply enmeshed with secular politics from the early-modern era to contemporary times.[1] His work informs the analysis here of Muslim activists who question religious custom from the viewpoint of human rights and who simultaneously critique their secular nation for not embracing ethnic and religious minorities. These activists' strategies of complex identity negotiation cross and recross the assumed barrier between religious and secular commitments, forcing the one to dialogue and be accountable to the other.

From Saba Mahmood's work, this volume takes up a renewed engagement with certain parts of Foucault's theory about subjectivity and ethical formation. Foucault stresses that subjectivity is not a private space of self-understanding, but that it forms in response to formative practices, social constraints, and moral codes that exist prior to the individual, such that subjectivity is best understood as a modality of power. Foucault calls "moral subjectivization" the process of "developing relationships with the self, for self-reflection, self-knowledge, self-examination, for the decipherment of the self by oneself, for the transformations that one seeks to accomplish with oneself as object."[2] Many scholars use Foucault's theories to emphasize the overdetermined nature of subjectivization—that subjectivities are formed by power relations set up by discursive formations in society, a process in which individuals have little choice or agency. Joseph Massad's work is an example of this kind of scholarship.

But Mahmood shifts the discussion to underemphasized parts of Foucault's theory that allow subjects to exert agency as they react to moral codes and transform social relations. She writes, "For Foucault, the relationship between moral codes and modes of subjectivization is not over-determined, however, in the sense that the subject simply complies with moral codes (or resists them). Rather, Foucault's framework assumes that there are many different ways of forming a relationship with a moral code, each of which establishes a particular relationship between capacities of the self (will, reason, desire, action and so on) and a particular norm."[3] She explains that these ways of forming a moral subjectivity are manifest in everyday life, through bodily comportment, spiritual exercises, and daily routines. This book draws from her theoretical approach. The interviews with gay, lesbian, and transgender Muslim activists presented here show how everyday life constitutes the formation of ethical subjectivities that are beholden to social structures and moral codes while also challenging their norms.

This volume investigates agency and subjectivity formation through the concept of identity, which is both given and contested. However, it does not dwell on social theory, but rather focuses on lived experience. The modes of activism that it documents are specific practices and communal activities through which subjects come to understand themselves, exert themselves, express themselves, and fashion an effective subjectivity that fosters their flourishing in sexual relationships, family life, social connections, and political rights. Religious values, rituals, and ideals are intimately tied to all these fields, which are more commonly divided into private and public.

Interviews, Methods, and Limitations

Those interviewed for this book are all members of support groups for transgender, lesbian, and gay Muslims. There are, of course, many others who participate in these support groups who were not interviewed. As noted above, the reader should not assume that those interviewed are exclusively leaders or that the support groups documented are exhaustive. These groups are all located in constitutional democracies where Islam is a minority religion and Muslims act within a democratic political and legal framework. This specificity gives this study focus but it also creates limitations.

I interviewed activists from support groups with which I was familiar. These activists were volunteers who have shaped those groups. I employed a "qualitative method" of inquiry, a social science technique that emphasizes personal narratives for use in interpretative analysis (rather than a "quantitative interview" to gather specific information for use in statistical analysis). The interviews were open-ended and encouraged those interviewed to articulate their narrative of life and conflict resolution. I asked each activist about issues such as family history, youthful experiences of gender and sexuality, religious education and theological views, romantic relationships, and activist involvement. Those interviewed revealed their process of identity formation better when allowed to narrate their own stories freely, so I kept my questions spontaneous to spur each person to tell his or her own story in depth. The interviews left me with hours of recorded conversation that I transcribed and sent in textual form to those interviewed, asking for clarification and permission to use their words in this book. I asked whether I should change their names or those of persons mentioned in the interview; some requested names to be changed for personal safety or to protect family members from harassment. Some names in this book are thus not the actual names of those interviewed.

This book presents interviews with fifteen activists residing in South Africa, the United Kingdom, the Netherlands, the United States, and Canada. These nations are home to the earliest established and the longest-running support groups. The interviewees are diverse: four are lesbian women, nine are gay men, and two are transgender persons (one transitioning female-to-male and one identifying as male-to-female).

Eight are South Asian, three are Arab, one is Berber, one is African American, and three identify as "mixed ethnicity" (known in South Africa as
"Coloured"). Despite this diversity, all those interviewed share much in
common. They are Muslims as defined by personal identity or spiritual
faith. Many of them strive to practice the rituals of Islam in their daily
lives to the extent and depth possible in their personal circumstances.

The activists interviewed are a minority of a minority but they are a
very insightful few. They have struggled deeply with their consciences,
against their religious tradition, and with their families. Since the early
2000s, their thoughts have become increasingly cohesive due to an
international network of support groups. New technology allows these
groups to organize, share experiences, and compile information. This
network of support groups aims to build a community of gay, lesbian,
and transgender Muslims and to represent their concerns to their larger
Muslim community, their nation, and the wider world of concerned
citizens. For this reason, their voices reveal more than their own stories;
they reveal common patterns of identity formation, shared modes of
activism, and intensifying connections between communities that are
separated in space but united in intention.

The voices of these activists are the heart of this book, but it is written from my point of view as a participant-observer.[4] I acknowledge that
any person or group's apprehension of the truth is always partial, yet
no truth is apprehended without the risk of commitment. My commitment to this movement of Muslim gay, lesbian, and transgender support
groups is this: their voices are valuable, their experiences are irreplace-
able, and their struggles are admirable—whether one agrees with their
opinions or not. Therefore, I chose to write this book in a way that lets
them speak for themselves. I have asked questions, elicited responses,
sought clarifications, and made comparisons. While this book analyzes
these activists' accounts and their theological insights, and contextu-
alizes their political struggles, I have tried to keep my own beliefs as a
Muslim aside in order to better appreciate the diversity of views offered.
My own views are highlighted in other writings, especially in *Homosexuality in Islam*, which discusses in detail the Qur'an, *hadith* reports of
the Prophet Muhammad's teachings, and the *shariʿa* developed by Muslim jurists in medieval times. In that book I reflect theologically upon
the issues raised by lesbian, gay, and transgender Muslims. Readers who

are interested in theology can turn to that volume; this book highlights the lived experience which makes such theology necessary.

This book has limitations. It does not present interviews with activists who identify as "bisexual."[5] Its interviews are only with transgender, lesbian, and gay activists. They work with support groups for Muslims who belong to the wider community of different people who identify with some part of the LGBTQIQ continuum (the acronym stands for Lesbian, Gay, Bisexual, Transgender, Queer, Intersex, and Questioning). I hope this book will contribute to establishing a firm foundation for understanding that wider group with all its variations. I encourage researchers to focus on bisexual, intersex, and queer-identified Muslims to deepen the work that I offer here. The same tools and techniques of research that this study has employed can be applied to others to create a fuller picture of Muslims who belong to the minority group defined by sexual orientation and gender identity.

The fifteen activists interviewed volunteer with support groups for lesbian, gay, and transgender Muslims, groups which hold that religious belief and practice are important for their members. This fact sets this book apart from others, such as *Illegal Citizens* by Afdhere Jama, which offers snapshots of a wide diversity of "queer Muslim" lives globally, and Pepe Hendricks's edited collection of stories of "queer" personal narratives from Cape Town entitled *Hijab: Unveiling Queer Muslim Lives*. These two books are admirable but they do not focus intensively on reconciling sexual orientation and gender identity with Islam, as this present book does. This book also differs from Brian Whitacker's *Unspeakable Love*, which describes the lives of sexuality and gender minorities in the Middle East, including Jews and Christians as well as Muslims. By interviewing activists involved in support groups, this book tells a different story. The experiences of these activists showcase a sustained struggle to reconcile religious belonging with alienation because of sexual orientation and gender identity.

Identity Formation

The interviews presented here each capture something of the unique personality of the activist interviewed while also highlighting themes that many have in common. This interaction between person and situation gives rise to identity formation, which is the groundwork for organizing support groups. Identity takes shape in the interaction between forces at four different levels: individual psyche, family relationships, community defined by religious tradition, and citizenship defined by national belonging. Distinguishing between these four levels can help us to understand identity formation, though in reality forces at all four levels interact as an organic whole in one person's life. The interviews demonstrate how these forces interact in the life trajectory of each person. Their interaction is particularly dramatic for those whose lives are characterized by social conflict rather than conformity, as are the lives of many gay, lesbian, and transgender Muslims. Conflict manifests at each different level: as internal conflict within one's own psyche, as disagreement over family expectations, as dissonance with the community's norms, and as argument over national citizenship that confers legal rights.

Even as this book illuminates wider patterns and repeated motifs, it rests on the foundation of interviews with individuals with distinctive situations, unique motivations, and singular life choices. These individuals have consciously resisted the pressure to conform. Their will to resist is rooted in their individual psyches before it can be expressed in family, community, or nation. All the interviews highlight how a person discovers her or his inner personality and conscience and each demonstrates how erotic awakening is an integral part of this process of discovery which is both exciting and dangerous, especially when sexual attraction leads in directions that family and community prohibit.[6]

While the interviews foreground the crucial role of individual psyche in identity formation, the importance of family should not be overshadowed. The individual exists in relation to the family that nurtures her or him. Therefore, the second level at which identity formation takes shape is that of the family, as one comes to understand one's self in relation to parents, siblings, and relatives. As all children do, lesbian, gay, or transgender Muslims have very complex relations with their parents. Parents provide positive models for emulation and parents also serve as negative figures against whom to define one's own individuality. The interviews reveal a wide variety of ways in which gay, lesbian, and transgender Muslims relate to their parents. This finding should dispel the notion that homosexuality and transgender behavior are caused by a particular configuration of parent-child relationship; examples of such suggestions are the myth of the overbearing mother, the stereotype of the father who really wanted a son, or the Freudian simplification that an absent father causes a homosexual son.

One pattern in these interviews that may surprise readers is the loving appreciation that transgender, lesbian, and gay children often feel toward their parents, despite the intense disagreements or coercion that they endure. This should caution us against seeing the formation of homosexual or transgender identity as a rejection of the family itself or as repudiation of one's parents. To the contrary, the interviews reveal that many transgender, lesbian, and gay Muslims feel deep and abiding affection for their parents and a profound desire for their parents' blessing, even if they are rejected, threatened, or ostracized by their families.

Other family members play crucial roles, and in several interviews grandparents were decisive figures in the identity formation of gay, lesbian, and transgender Muslims. This is only to be expected in cultures where extended families are valued and generational continuity is cherished. Often, grandparents substitute for parents who are absent due to practical contingencies or emotional distance. Sometimes grandparents represent figures of intense spirituality. Many of those interviewed for this book claim their grandparents—rather than their parents—as their role models for healthy spirituality.

Because Muslim families are often widespread and close-knit, aunts and uncles can also play important roles as substitutes for parents, providing relief for a child struggling against a parent's personality. Some of those interviewed found support with aunts or uncles even if their parents rejected them. But the extended family can also cause difficulties, as a young family member has to deal with not just a mother and father but also a host of adult authorities who observe, criticize, and control what they see as norm-breaking behavior. In this way, Muslim families often extend seamlessly into the wider Muslim community. The family often acts to control its members to preserve family honor, reputation, and standing in the community (which is often valued more than an individual family member's own identity or welfare).

The third level at which identity formation takes place is community, which refers primarily here to religious community. For most Muslims, individual belief and family affiliation compel them to understand

themselves as being part of an Islamic community. While in most cases
this is not a membership that one chooses, one must choose how to
practice it. The interviews reveal a great variety of experiences. Some
gay, lesbian, and transgender Muslim activists were enthusiastic members of an Islamic community in childhood: praying in mosque, studying in *madrasa* (Islamic school or seminary), preparing for celebrations, and volunteering for charities shaped the identities of many of
those interviewed. Many of them mourn the loss of participation in
the Islamic community if they are ostracized for being lesbian, gay, or
transgender. Ostracism can be more severe if they had held authoritative positions such as *imam* (prayer leader) of a group, as teacher in a
madrasa, as counselor in a spiritual community, or as leader in a student organization. The risk of losing such valued connections to the
wider Islamic community often restrains Muslims from coming out or
engaging in public activism.

Whether or not they play a leadership role in the community, all
gay, transgender, and lesbian Muslims struggle with Islamic discourse.
The interviews show how transgender, lesbian, and gay Muslims have
internalized Islamic discourse and therefore experience conflict over
whether their sexual orientation and gender identity are against their
religion. They question whether behavior based on these identities is
immoral. They do not need family members or religious leaders to
engage in debate, for this debate is already heated within their individual conscience. All the activists interviewed have engaged in debate
through Islamic discourses both within themselves and also with others as members of a community. This debate persisted, often for many
years, before they ever considered joining a support group or taking an
activist stand.

Those interviewed struggle to forge an identity as Muslims while
they live as citizens, for identity formation takes shape also within a
fourth context, that of the nation. Every nation has a distinctive historical chronicle, legal framework, and set of civic values; through these
elements one comes to understand oneself as a responsible citizen.
Nations offer varying frameworks within which citizens exercise political rights and recognize civic obligations. This is especially true with
regard to minority groups defined by gender identity and sexual orientation, because legal norms vary widely from nation to nation even

within the realm of secular democratic states. While gay, lesbian, and transgender Muslims are national citizens, they are also members of minorities defined by ethnicity and religion. Most of those interviewed are also visible members of a minority because they are immigrants or descended from immigrants deemed "of color" in nations that are largely of European ethnicity commonly denoted as "white." Their difference in terms of sexual orientation or gender identity is less immediately visible, though it is no less important in defining their identity. Their struggle to form an identity depends crucially upon how the nation as a collective faces ethical challenges such as mitigating racial prejudice against ethnic minorities, negotiating the status of religious minorities, or fostering legal reform within a constitutional framework. The interviews presented here show that lesbian, transgender, and gay Muslims strive to maintain a delicate balance between solidarity with their religious minority group and their demand for full citizenship and legal protection in the nation. This balance is difficult to support, especially when their community is perceived to be under threat as an ethnic or religious minority. The third and fourth levels at which identity formation takes place—religious community and nation—intersect in novel ways for Muslims who are citizens of secular democratic states.

Clarifying Terms about Islam, Gender, and Sexuality

As Arabic and Islamic terms are mentioned, they are explained in the text or in the glossary at the end of the book. Yet some elements of Islam need to be clarified now. Gay, transgender, and lesbian Muslims participate in Islamic discourse whether or not they play leadership roles in Muslim communities. The term "Islamic discourse" refers to the foundational texts, shared symbols, legal decisions, and style of argumentation through which Muslims collectively enact their religious identity. This discourse motivates Muslims' actions and mediates their conflicts. It orders the words, images, and thoughts through which Muslims generate their communal self-understanding.

Islamic discourse is defined by scholars, spokesmen, and jurists. Nevertheless it filters down into individual lives through community gatherings, family norms, and ritual practices—in some forms that are traditional and ritualistic and in others that are modern and technological.

Therefore, it deeply affects individual identity and group formation among Muslim subcultures. The interviews reveal how Islamic discourse impacts the activists' lives. Most Islamic communities uphold patriarchal values and justify them by reference to religious texts. Therefore, anyone opposing patriarchal norms must confront these texts and dominant interpretations of them. One can confront these interpretations by direct refutation, by counterinterpretation, or by appealing to contradictory texts within the same Islamic discursive tradition (such as countering *hadith* texts with Qur'an or countering *fiqh* legal texts with Sufi teachings). *Qur'an* is the Islamic scripture, defined as God's speech revealed to Muhammad in the Arabic language that was orally memorized by his followers and later compiled as a book after Muhammad's death.[7] *Hadith* are teachings of the Prophet Muhammad—through his words, deeds, or silent approval—that were observed, recalled to later generations, memorized, and eventually recorded in copious volumes as a guide to proper Muslim behavior. *Fiqh* texts are writings by Muslim jurists in the early medieval era who tried to codify proper conduct in all fields—from belief to ritual to commerce to family relations and sexual life. Sufi teachings are spiritual insights from the Islamic mystical tradition, whose advocates saw it as the "inner dimension" of Islam in contrast to the "outer dimension" of conduct regulated by jurists.

Lesbian, gay, and transgender Muslims argue through Islamic discourse against conventional Islamic interpretations, and do so with a variety of discursive agents. "Discursive agents" are people who exert power by invoking a discourse. Agents of Islamic discourse can be family or community; even lovers can be discursive agents, if one has a Muslim partner who refers to Islamic discourses to discuss or regulate one's relationship. The most important discursive agents are religious functionaries: people who hold an official office or serve a public function related to Islam. Religious functionaries include a mosque's imam, a *madrasa* instructor, a *mufti* (authoritative jurist) via the Internet, or a council of *ulama* (religious scholars).

This book explores how Muslims deal with diversity in sexual orientation and gender identity, so these terms need clarification. One must distinguish between sex, gender, sexuality, and sex acts. Sex refers to one's anatomical genitalia, through which one is classified as male or female. Gender refers to one's expression of social behavior organized by norms classified as masculine or feminine. Sexuality refers to one's consciousness of sexual desire and expression of intimacy and pleasure, which includes not just one's "sexual orientation" (whether one desires sexual contact with a person of the opposite sex or someone of the same sex) but also more subtle issues like intensity and focus of sexual desire.

Sexual orientation is one crucial element of sexuality. Orientation refers to the class of person to whom one is attracted for sexual pleasure. A person attracted to those of the same gender is "homosexual" and one attracted to those of the other gender is "heterosexual." One who is attracted to both genders is "bisexual" and one who feels no attraction is "asexual." In many modern societies, English terms are gaining international currency to describe such people. Gay is used as a self-description for men who are exclusively homosexual in orientation, while lesbian is used for women who are exclusively homosexual. The terms gay and lesbian refer not just to a clinical psychological state (homosexuality) but also to a self-conscious identification with a subculture.

Sex, gender, and sexual orientation define important components of one's personality but they say nothing about specific sex acts. One should never assume that a person characterized by homosexual orientation performs particular sex acts (or any sex act at all). A homosexual woman might never practice sex acts with a person of the same gender, but her sexual orientation would still be homosexual. Similarly, a man might practice sex acts with another man but not be homosexual: the sex acts might be caused by coercion or necessity rather than satisfaction of yearning for emotional fulfillment. Stereotyped associations of sex acts with certain kinds of people may not actually accord with the lived experience of those people.

When we analytically use these terms—sex, gender, and sexual orientation—we find that in society most people are "heteronormative." They identify with their ascribed gender and fulfill their sexual desires in heterosexual relationships. But we also find that there are people who are not like this: they are unusual in terms of being statistically rare but they are routinely present in a given population. Diversity in gender identity and sexual orientation is a social fact. Some societies recognize them and give them valued roles, while other societies stigmatize them. Patriarchal societies in particular tend to treat gender and sexuality minorities harshly, perceive them as threating moral order, and try to suppress them.

Patriarchal societies assert that gender is determined by sexual anatomy, but in fact this is not true. A person who appears like a woman to observers—whether family, medical doctors, or people on the street—may identify as a man and feel like a man inside; further, this person may ardently desire to be seen by others as a man, to such an extent as to alter appearance, dress the part, or even elect for hormone therapy and sexual realignment surgery to become biologically male. There are such people whose sense of gender is ambiguous, who feel that they are neither "male" nor "female" but rather are both or neither. All such persons can be said to have "gender dysphoria" or a profound feeling of disharmony between their assigned gender (as imposed by others) and their own gender identity (as perceived by the self).[8]

Transgender is used as a self-description for those who do not identify with the gender that is socially ascribed to them, but rather feel that they are actually of another gender in terms of their inner psyche. Trans is a Greek term meaning "moving across." Transgender indicates a person who "moves across" from the gender into which he or she was socialized to the gender with which he or she identifies. If transgender persons alter their physique, hormonal balance, or sex organs to match their inner psychic gender identity, they become "transsexual" persons. Transsexual means a person who "moves across" from the sex organs with which he or she was born to the sex organs with which he or she feels comfortable because such organs express his or her gender identity. One can be a transgender person without becoming a transsexual if one chooses not to alter one's body to conform to one's gender identity.[9] In this sense, all transsexual persons were first transgender; they felt like a person of the other gender even before they acted to change their body to conform to that internal feeling and identity.

Both transgender and transsexual people are distinct from hermaphrodites, a term commonly applied to them. Hermaphrodite is a term applied to persons who naturally bear both male and female anatomical features (genitalia or secondary sex features that develop with puberty). However, this term is now seen as a derogatory popular term. In the scientific literature, such people are described as "intersex," meaning that a person has anatomical features associated with both sexes, female and male. Some intersex people undergo surgery in order to become either male or female since many societies offer no ambiguous middle ground. Some transgender people deliberately inhabit this ambiguous middle ground and they retain features commonly identified as both male and female; such people are commonly called "androgynous."

Transgender, transsexual, and intersex describe the variable positions that people can take with regard to gender as an internal identity manifested in bodily appearance. These clinical terms help us to describe variable patterns of gender identity and mutability. These terms are relatively recent inventions of sociology, sexology, and clinical medicine. New terms have become necessary, especially as hormone therapy and sex-realignment surgery techniques have been invented and improved, allowing physical alteration of the body in ways not possible only a generation ago.

Sexual orientation is often confused with gender identity in Muslim communities. The families of Muslim gay men often understand them to be acting like or thinking like women; similarly they may understand lesbian women to be thinking or acting like men.[10] Often issues of sexual orientation are treated by Muslim communities as problems of gender behavior, much to the detriment of lesbian or gay Muslims who understand themselves as women who love other women or men who love other men.

Though the terms for sexual orientation and gender identity are new, the patterns of behavior they describe have existed since long ago. Muslims may be familiar with indigenous terms from their own local cultures for people who do not conform to a binary division between male and female. Islamic history has witnessed at least three classifications of gender-ambiguous persons: the castrated man (*khasi*), the effeminate man (*mukhannath*), and the nonman (*hijra*). These categories are discussed in detail because they come up in interviews with Muslim activists. These premodern categories shape how Muslims perceive lesbian, gay, and transgender members of their community.

The eunuch is a person who was born with male sex organs and raised as a boy until castrated (usually when enslaved).[11] Eunuchs did not become female: rather they inhabited an in-between position—they were legally and socially of neither gender. In contrast, the effeminate male (*mukhannath*) is a person born with male sex organs and raised as a boy who displays effeminate behavior in speech, gesture, gait, or possibly dress. The term does not explicitly describe sex, sexual orientation, or sex acts. Rather it describes feminine behavior on the part of one who is known to be male; it describes transgender behavior or transvestite display rather than implying any homosexual orientation or practice of same-sex intercourse. However, in medieval times and later, the term came to be associated with men who accepted a passive role in anal intercourse (an association which is not essential to the category's definition).[12] A parallel category of *mutarrajulat* existed for women who behaved like men in speech, gesture, gait, or dress.[13] These "emmasculine women" did not necessarily have a homosexual orientation or engage in same-sex acts.[14]

Finally, a third indigenous category of the nonman or *hijra* exists in Islamic societies in South Asia (in Pakistan, India, and Bangladesh). The *hijra* is a person born with male sex organs and raised as a boy who, after the onset of puberty, feels that he is a woman. Cultivating inner identity with a woman, he abandons the category "man" and takes on female behavior, name, and dress, and voluntarily undergoes a ritual castration to remove both testicles and penis. Society conceived of the *hijra* as neither man-nor-woman but rather as inhabiting an acknowledged third gender, that is "neither-nor" and therefore "in-between." *Hijras* leave their families to live in highly structured communities with their own dialect of speech.[15] South Asian observers mistakenly call them "eunuchs" because both *hijras* and eunuchs have undergone castration. However, the psychological motivation of a *hijra* (who voluntarily undergoes castration after maturity through a ritual and with initiation into a subculture) is completely different from that of a eunuch. The *hijra*'s status and social role is therefore distinct from that of eunuchs in premodern Islamic societies. Because the *hijra* feels like a woman in the body of a man, *hijras* come closest to transgender (male-to-female or MTF experience as described by modern terms. In premodern times without contemporary medical therapies or reconstructive surgery, the *hijra* could not physically alter the body to become a woman, though the *hijra* could remove the genital organs associated with men and take on features associated with women, like wearing women's clothes and adopting female names.

There is some overlap between contemporary transgender people and categories already established in Islamic societies in the premodern period, but there is no easy equivalence to modern terms. The category transgender describes both men who feel that they are women and strive to become women and also women who feel that they are men and strive to become men. This category depends upon the new reality that medical techniques can actually engineer the transformation, such that the transgender person can become transsexual, often to the point that one is no longer recognizable as belonging to the former gender in which one was originally socialized.

Familiarity with these terms is crucial for listening to the voices of the activists interviewed for this book. I have not used "queer" to describe in one label all varied identities that question patriarchal heterosexuality. In the interests of making this book accessible, I persist in using the terms gay, transgender, and lesbian because these terms are more recognizable to general readers than the term "queer." Queer is a recent label developed in activist and scholarly discourse to refer to all these varied kinds of people as one single group—those defined as "different" due to sexual orientation and gender identity—in an overtly politicized way to which not all members of those groups subscribe.

Some sociological writings use the term "nonheterosexual" as a clinical label to refer to lesbian, gay, bisexual, transgender, and queer persons.[16] This inclusive list of different identities is often reduced to the acronym LGBTQ (and it sometimes extends as LGBTQIQ to include intersex and questioning persons). It is admirable to include all these people in one "umbrella" term but the acronym itself is cumbersome. In contrast, "nonheterosexual" has the merit of being a single-word term, but it has the limitation of being defined as a negation. There are no actual people who self-identify as "nonheterosexual." To do so would suggest that they strive to be everything which heterosexuals are not, which is not an accurate description of transgender, lesbian, or gay people. This book tells of their struggle to assert their common humanity, religious affiliation, and spiritual aspiration while also affirming their difference. The term "nonheterosexual" does not accurately depict the trajectory of their struggle.

I have limited the use of terms and acronyms that might reduce this population's humanity or make them appear irreconcilably different from their heterosexual family members and coreligionists. To further emphasize their humanity, I have employed recited verses and song lyrics to open each chapter, verses that were mentioned by those interviewed as inspirational. The aspirations of gay, lesbian, and transgender Muslim activists are grounded in the same human hopes that all share—security, health, self-sufficiency, love . . . and perhaps even salvation. With this background, we can turn to the voices of these activists and listen in earnest to their narratives that they strive to live out Islam.

1

Engaging Religious Tradition

Remember when you were few and oppressed to the ground
And feared that people would carry you off by force
But God gave you shelter, aiding and strengthening you
And provided for your welfare, that you might give thanks

~ Qur'an 8:26

An integral aspect of being a Muslim is protecting the vulnerable and helping the downtrodden. This Islamic teaching is both a spiritual discipline and a political imperative. The Qur'an reminds Muslims to *remember when you were few and oppressed.*[1] Muslims revere the prophets who are sent by God with the theological mission to persuade people to worship the one single God. But the prophets were sent with the political mission to remove oppression. Through the risks they took and the consolation they provided, the Qur'an says, *God gave you shelter, aiding and strengthening you and provided for your welfare* such that those who dwelt in sorrow are recompensed with joy and those who suffer in alienation are given integrity. All Muslims commemorate the early days of Islam when they were oppressed as a marginalized few, threatened, and vulnerable to persecution. Yet when they became a dominant group, Muslims forgot their former marginalization despite this reminder by the Qur'an. Many Muslims ignore vulnerable minorities within their community like the poor, the youth, and disadvantaged women . . . and also Muslims who are gay, transgender, and lesbian.

To remind their community members of this, lesbian, gay, and transgender Muslims turn to the Qur'an for a symbolic affirmation of their humanity and worth. This is an example of activism in a mode that can be called "engaging religious tradition." The activists interviewed in this chapter demonstrate strategies to engage the Islamic tradition—especially the Qur'an. Two of them are from South Africa where volunteers have formed support groups in Cape Town and Johannesburg. The third activist comes from the United Kingdom, where several support groups coexist with different but overlapping missions. One activist interviewed is a gay male, another is a transgender male-to-female, and the third is a lesbian female.

In presenting their lives and struggles through intimate interviews, this chapter focuses on how Muslim activists who are lesbian, gay, and transgender confront their religious tradition, find consolation in it, and challenge some of the theological propositions that were deemed normative by many Muslims in the past. Let us listen to the voices of a few activists, from Cape Town and elsewhere, as they engage their Islamic tradition to encourage fresh interpretation around the issues of gender identity and sexual orientation.

Muhsin: The Original Nature of Truth

Muhsin is one of the organizers of the first support group in South Africa for lesbian, transgender, and gay Muslims. Founded in 1998, Al-Fitra Foundation organized monthly get-togethers, lectures on sexuality and spirituality, weekly group discussions, and *dhikr* circles. It also utilized the Internet, providing spiritual and social counseling that allowed unprecedented anonymity. Muhsin served not just as an organizer, but also as an informal spiritual advisor to those who joined the group or reached out for help. He took on this role due to his Islamic education and profound spiritual orientation. While in his twenties, he dedicated himself to Islamic study and endeavored to earn a degree in Arabic and Islamic Studies at the University of Karachi. He later reflected, "I thought if I threw myself into my religious studies then I would forget about [being gay] or that I would change. . . . So after six years, I realized it didn't work. I thought more about being gay—what does it mean to be gay and are there more people like me around? I was shocked to find that, yes, in my very own community there are so many. I realized that I'm not alone—these people are going through the very same things that I'm going through. But I've managed, because of my in-depth relationship with God, to reconcile the two. I was completely comfortable saying to the world that I'm gay and I'm Muslim. I wanted to help other people to get there. So that's how I became an activist."[2]

Muhsin decided early on to become a religious leader in his community. In explaining his decision to pursue a calling as a religious leader, he reflects, "I think it was very personal and also [due to the fact that] I come from a very religious family." He clarifies that his family was both religious in the social sense and also intensely spiritual in a more mystical sense. "My grandfather was the imam of the community where I stayed. My mother was the teacher in the *madrasa*. My father was a spiritual healer. . . . So I come from a fairly spiritual family." His father passed away when he was twenty-one, before Muhsin could learn the details of his spiritual healing techniques that were granted to him by being in a Sufi order (*tariqa*). However, important spiritual lessons were passed along; when asked what was the most important thing his father taught him, Muhsin answers without a moment's hesitation: "Love for mankind." Muhsin counts his father as an inspiration for him. "My father never had any enemies. He never followed up his debtors. If people failed to pay him, he never worried. He said, 'We'll sort it out on the day of judgment.'"

Muhsin never had a chance to talk with his father about being gay but admits, "I think he suspected, because one day I wanted to go and work on the building site with my father—my father used to build houses. But then obviously I didn't do a good job on the building site, so my father came home and said to my mother, 'Halima, I think you must keep this one in the kitchen!'" Muhsin notes that homosexual orientation among children and adolescents is largely invisible and hard to articulate, so it is often displayed in gender behavior. Muhsin took up "feminine" activities and hobbies, which his father largely accepted; this Muhsin sees as his insight into a son's latent homosexuality. "I used to sit and crochet with my mother. . . . A normal father would have discouraged his son from doing really feminine stuff. But he didn't." His uncles and aunts on his father's side of the family were also supportive with an open and tolerant style of Islamic devotion that did not impose strictly gendered behaviors on Muhsin.

His mother was also a religious authority in the community, as a teacher of girls and women at the local *madrasa*, leading Muhsin to declare—"I was virtually born in a mosque. . . . My mother was teaching already at the mosque by the time I was born. My mother used to carry me to mosque in a basket. So I've heard Qur'an since the first day I could hear, and I could memorize Qur'an and *hadith* since the age of five." Muhsin's interest in religion conformed to his family environment steeped in scriptural devotion and spiritual healing, but it also challenged religious authority. He explains, "I grew up with the Qur'an. I think that is why I started, early on, challenging certain things about Islam because it just didn't make sense to me. . . . Why do I have to play with boys when I like playing with girls? [We children were] not segregated exactly, but it was socially expected that boys only play with boys. So I was teased a lot as a child, called all sorts of names, because I was very effeminate as a child . . . our community was just like that. It didn't have anything to do with Islam." On the one hand, his effeminate nature meant staying close to women in the family and absorbing their religious devotion. But on the other hand, it meant risking the social stigma of not being a "normal boy" who would grow up into a "real man."

Within this tension, Muhsin grew up empowered by Islamic learning to question the customs of his community. His comment that the norms of boys' and girls' behavior have nothing to do with Islam but rather reflect community custom shows his critical perspective fueled by studying Islam. His ambition was to become a religious scholar or *'alim*. He seized the opportunity when The Call of Islam, a branch of the Muslim Youth Movement that actively embraced the antiapartheid struggle, sponsored students to pursue *madrasa* training in Pakistan. The Call of Islam selected Muhsin as one of the six to be trained as imams.[3]

Intense devotion is a common pattern among transgender, gay, and lesbian Muslims, especially in the period before they acknowledge their inner difference. The devotion is fueled by expectation that prayer will be a "cure," and out of desperate hope that ritual will keep one distracted

from acts that are a "sin." However, beneath either of these extremes is a
spiritual depth in Islam that is real and authentic. As Muhsin expresses
it, "Homosexuality is not just about sex. We have very spiritual people among us. I pray five times a day, read the Qur'an, fast, and attend
mosque regularly."[4]

The very name of the group he helped to establish, Al-Fitra, reveals
an emerging theology of liberation among Muslims who are transgender, gay, or lesbian. *Fitra* is an Arabic term meaning one's "essential
nature." It is used in the Qur'an to describe how God created all things,
distinct in their individuality yet making up a harmonious whole. *So
set your face toward the moral obligation in a true way, according to the
essential nature granted by God, upon which God fashioned people, for
there is no changing the creation of God! That is the original and steadfast
moral obligation, but most of the people do not understand* (Q 30:30).
Most Muslim theologians read such a verse dogmatically, to assert that
Islam is the "original and steadfast" religion, *al-din al-qayyim*, which
uniquely conforms to the requirements of human nature that is the
same for all people. However, lesbian, gay, and transgender Muslims
read it differently—though just as literally—to assert that God creates
each being with an original nature that cannot be changed, and that the
"original and steadfast" religion is to return to God in harmony with
one's own nature. They hear the Qur'an affirm this, even if living and
worshiping in accord with their inner nature contradicts the surrounding society, for *most of the people do not understand*. Most Muslims
from these minority groups assert that their sexual orientation and gender identity are essential components of their personality. It is an innate
quality they were born with or an unalterable characteristic from childhood before rational cognition.[5]

Muhsin affirms that he was born with a same-sex sexual orientation and realized he was different from the age of five. "I was sixteen
before I realized they called it gay, and came out of the closet years later,
at twenty-nine." His story confirms a common pattern of a disturbing
feeling of difference that sets one apart in childhood long before it can
be recognized in concepts, articulated in language, or accepted in one's
heart. "Because of my sexuality, I became withdrawn as a teenager. I
spent a lot of time crying and resenting myself for who I am. I could
have used that time constructively. I lost my teenage years because of

that. There is a positive side to it, though. If I had not had that experience, I would not have had the desire to save other teenagers from the agony of resenting themselves for who they are." For lesbian, gay, and transgender Muslims, then, spiritual growth is about stripping away the accumulated layers of "false self" (imposed by family, society, and religion but through which they survived childhood, adolescence, and often the first phases of adulthood) in order to free a "true self" that had long been buried but through which they can sincerely turn to God. The inner drive to recover this true self from under a family and social life that feels like constant lying is so important that some risk coming into open conflict with their surrounding society. While some keep this search for a true self hidden out of fear, others cannot accept dishonesty and face the difficulty of a bewildered family and hostile community. Muhsin explains that his intense engagement with Islam increased the pressure on him to marry; he relented to this pressure and fathered three children at a young age. But Muhsin relates that by age twenty-eight, "It was very hard, but the conflict within me was so great that I had to tell them the truth." He tells that his mother fainted, while his wife was shocked.

That truth was very difficult to grasp while he was growing up, even though its existence as part of his character was so deeply rooted as to be unavoidable. In Cape Town's "Coloured" communities, where most Muslims lived, there was a subculture of effeminate men called *moffies* who expressed a local variant of gayness. Moffies lived openly and were an accepted part of the community, especially in fashion design and wedding planning. Muhsin recalls their role as he was growing up: "It was an honor to know a moffie, actually, because they're pretty entertaining. The sexual part of it they never questioned—I guess the community never wanted to know of it." The element of homosexual orientation was not emphasized, but rather subsumed under the more overt display of gender-inverting behaviors. Moffies were common in preapartheid Cape Town, and persisted even after "Coloured" communities were broken up and resettled. In his local culture there was recognition of different roles focusing on gendered behavior, but there was no explicit acknowledgment that this involved same-sex acts.

However, for Muhsin growing up, same-sex acts were important and had a great impact upon his self-understanding. "I had sexual contact

with boys since the age of five, but I thought that these are just playing. . . . 'Let's play house-house—you be the mommy and I'll be the
daddy, and we have to go to bed now.' I didn't think it was anything
bad." However, by the age of twelve, his childhood was ending and he
began to feel attracted to another boy at school, attraction both sexual
and psychological with romantic depth to it. When asked if he realized
during this experience that he was "different," Muhsin answered, "Yes,
I did realize it then, at age twelve. [I thought], 'Oh, this is something
wrong because this is something that only girls do—girls fall in love
and talk about boys.'"

This period of realization coincided with a deepening of Muhsin's
religiosity. When asked how he coped with the slowly dawning realization that he was attracted sexually to boys and drawn in friendship toward girls, he answered that he studied hard and became very
religious. "I threw away all my jeans and sweaters and started to wear
only *kurtas*. After age twelve, I became very religious. I was like a her-
mit. . . . My mother actually encouraged it. She thought I was going to
become some great imam." This withdrawal was actually a new kind of
engagement. It allowed Muhsin to connect with his mother, the parent whom he felt was more distant and judging, with a new intensity.
"That was the time when I opened up my own *madrasa*. Actually, my
mother had her first heart attack when I was twelve. I was very close to
my mother and thought, 'Oh my God, my mother is going to die and
she has so many responsibilities' . . . she prepared people for the hajj
and gave *fiqh* (Islamic law) classes to adults during the night and during
the day she would teach the children. So I took over, and told her, 'Don't
worry, I will teach the class for the children.' I had about thirty students.
Then after a year, it [grew to] fifty students. . . . [I was] helping children
to read the Qur'an and memorize, and also *fiqh*—about how to pray,
make *wudu'* (ablutions) and *istinja'* (purification after using the toilet)."
Deeper religiosity also allowed Muhsin to interact with other boys in a
structured and safe environment.

His love of teaching and his immersion in religious learning deepened when Muhsin attended higher training at the University of Karachi's program in *shari'a* studies. Upon completion of the six-year course,
one is named an *'alim* (religious scholar). Muhsin completed four years
of the training before returning to South Africa. His time in Karachi

was complicated by his relationship with his wife, who was unhappy far from home. It was also complicated because Muhsin fell in love with a man in Karachi, a relationship that was fulfilling but frustrating. Between his wife's unhappiness and unsettling memories of his love affair, it became difficult to remain in Pakistan to complete his course.

Despite not completing the full course, his studies gave Muhsin high status and respect when he returned to Cape Town. He took up teaching positions at two *madrasas*, and was known there as *mawlana* (our master), a title of respect for one of learning and piety. But this increasing social status led to increasing inner tension around his sexual orientation. "They used to call me *mawlana* at school. I used to hate that title. . . . Then they called me *imam* (leader) when I was at the other *madrasa*, and I thought, 'No, if you guys knew who I am, you would not want to call me imam.'" Despite this tension between how he saw himself and how others in the community saw him, Muhsin poured his heart into teaching, drawing up Arabic syllabi for the schools, organizing plays for children, even cooking for *madrasa* functions.

Muhsin was walking a delicate line between pursing his religious devotion and accepting his homosexual nature, his inner *fitra*. It took many years to reconcile his outer community status and his inner life. However, Muhsin eventually decided to divorce his wife and "came out of the closet" as a gay man. As he spoke out about being both a gay man and a pious Muslim, *madrasas* terminated his employment. He relied upon his own resources to make a living as a tailor and dress designer for weddings. With this independence, he intensified his activist commitments to create an alternative community for lesbian, gay, and transgender Muslims. "What was important for me [to address] is that people were getting sucked into this gay culture and subsequently losing their Islamic identity."

To understand this concern, one must remember that this was 1996, soon after the fall of apartheid and the very year that South Africa formally adopted its new progressive constitution. Under that new dispensation, prior criminalization of homosexual acts was dramatically lifted. Protection against discrimination on the basis of sexual orientation became a basic inalienable right. Mainstream lesbian and gay institutions flourished—in human rights fields and in nightlife venues—and Cape Town earned itself the reputation of being a cosmopolitan city

and the "gay capital" of Africa. But beneath all the glitter, gay and lesbian life was predominantly for the "white and prosperous." In contrast,
Muslims (mainly from the "Coloured" and "Asian" communities—as
they had been classified under apartheid) were only slowly emerging
from the ghettoization imposed upon them. In general, Muslims were
exploring cautiously how to participate in the now-open environment
of democratic South Africa. Those with secular and professional education took positions in government, the universities, and civil society.
Those with less education or more religious loyalty were hesitant, concerned that secular opportunities would destroy communal solidarity
and Islamic piety. At the same time, issues like drug use, alcohol abuse,
and sexually transmitted diseases like HIV were receiving increasing
media attention and generating public fear. Muhsin, like many others,
was fearful that in "coming out of the closet," gay and lesbian Muslims
would be swept into a secular and profligate lifestyle that was attractive
but dangerous and that ultimately would not lead to a spiritually fulfilling life.

He and the others who first discussed instituting a support group for
lesbian, transgender, and gay Muslims wanted to assert their independence and rights as gay and lesbian people, while keeping firm their
communal loyalties as Muslims. They intended to foster the internal
sense of well-being that can only come through spiritual growth. Muhsin had returned from Pakistan to find that apartheid had fallen, but
now "[Muslims were] going to clubs, Muslims were starting to drink,
taking drugs, the incidence of HIV among Muslims [was increasing],
people [were] sleeping with one another without being moral about
it. I just thought that these are not the qualities that the Prophet came
with—these are not qualities that make you a Muslim. So I felt that my
cause is to help people to understand that they can be Muslim and can
be gay and can be moral as well." He was equally concerned that igno-
rance and homophobia among Muslim communities was driving people away from their own religion. Gay and lesbian Muslims were turning to secular institutions, Christian churches, or entertainment venues
because their own religious community allowed no space for them.

By 1997, Muhsin and a small group of friends created Gay Muslim
Outreach and had about one hundred members in Cape Town.[6] This
first informal organization grew. Leadership positions were formalized,

but all the activists who ran it were volunteers and became tired, while many people were content to join its activities without taking up any responsibilities. It lapsed into inactivity after a year. Then in 1998, Muhsin and others revived the organization under a new and more Islamic name, Al-Fitra Foundation. Muhsin explains why the term was chosen from the Qur'an as the name for the revived support group: "The message then was to let people know that [homosexuality] is not a pathology, that it is [one's] nature—you were either born that way or even if you were conditioned to be that way through society, it was when you were too young to have a decision in that. So it is part of your *fitra*—your nature. That's why we called the group Al-Fitra. . . . We chose an Arabic name [because] it was closest to being Muslim. Instead of calling us the Gay Muslim Support Group, we wanted to Islamize it a little bit. So we chose an Arabic word. Also there was no equivalent word in English to describe the nature of a person. Al-Fitra was the perfect word."

Al-Fitra continued to evolve along its first steps and continued to operate in Cape Town until 2000. That year, a small group of gay Muslims in Johannesburg opened a chapter there, in South Africa's bustling metropolis. However, the Johannesburg chapter devolved into a social club rather than a support group, and many who joined were reluctant to address Islam within the group or engage with the wider Muslim community. This organization in Johannesburg, which had called itself Gay Muslim Outreach, soon dissolved, but it had brought together a small band of serious people in that city. Soon they regrouped and joined with the Cape Town project, Al-Fitra, under the umbrella of a new name, The Inner Circle. This support group continued Al-Fitra's focus on developing an Islamic spirituality for gay and lesbian Muslims through structured discussion of the Qur'an, but balanced this with more informal social gatherings. Muhsin explains this delicate balance: "I think it's important to have some forum where people can just feel that they can be their own people, because they can't be themselves outside. You need a place where you can be gay and you can be Muslim at the same time. But what was very important is to know God—to be responsible, to know your responsibility toward God and toward your community and toward yourself, to build your self-esteem and to know that you belong somewhere, that you have a place in Islam and a place in this world. That is more important than your sexuality. Your sexuality is just a facet of who you are, it is not you . . . and we have to realize that we are going to leave from here [this world] one of these days. We are not going to stay here forever. So are we accommodating that journey forward? That was the message of The Inner Circle."

The group that evolved into The Inner Circle had chosen an Arabic word selected from the Qur'an as its name—*al-fitra*. This symbolic move caused some resistance from gay men from Muslim backgrounds who refused to join the group; they disagreed with its message that one could be both gay and Muslim. These objectors would go partying and live a secret gay life while insisting that Islam condemns homosexuality and objects to gay Muslims building a support organization for themselves. Though Muhsin and others dismiss this as false consciousness and hypocrisy, the issues are clearly complex. The very existence of a gay and lesbian Muslim support group is threatening for those who lead double lives or who do not want to confront the narrowness of religious orthodoxy.

These issues, of course, center upon one's interpretation of the Qur'an. Many Muslims, whether hetero- or homosexual, do not read the Qur'an personally. They may recite it for prayer but they do not read it for meaning. Those who do read it personally often do not feel authorized or empowered to interpret the Qur'an deeply. Muhsin, among others, feels that it is the responsibility of each Muslim to read and interpret, from her or his own perspective and experience. Anything less is shirking one's duty.

Muhsin believes that the Qur'an does not directly address homosexuality. It neither condemns nor approves of homosexuality in explicit terms. It does speak about male assault and rape of other men in the story of the Prophet Lot (at Sodom and Gomorrah), but it does not address homosexuality as sexual orientation or homoerotic relationships as expressions of emotional commitment and care. Such homosexual relationships are something new for which precedent is not found in the Qur'an or in the Prophet Muhammad's example. Therefore, principles must be drawn from the Qur'an to guide one's behavior in homosexual relationships, just as principles are drawn out to apply to any host of new situations that Muslims now confront. "There were lots of things that we have now that were not in [existence at] that time. So, maybe the case [of a loving homosexual relationship or same-sex marriage] was not presented to the Prophet at that time. So we don't have a clue as to what the Prophet would have done in that case. The clues that we can take are that there was no persecution of gay people, gay people were working in the house of the Prophet at that time, and the Qur'an speaks about *ghayr uli al-irba min al-rijal* [a phrase from Q 24:31] recognizing that there were people [men] who were not attracted to women." In this statement, Muhsin makes reference to three little known facts about Islam. The Qur'an makes reference to men who are not attracted to women, allowing such men access to the women's quarters of Muslim homes, a reference that might refer to gay men. In addition, the Prophet Muhammad allowed such men to visit or serve his wives in his home.[7] Muhsin also refers to the fact that there is no known incident in the life of Muhammad when the Prophet punished any woman or man for homosexual orientation or same-sex acts.

Not all lesbian and gay Muslims want to hear this message. Some want to avoid religious discussions, believing that Islam condemns them and cannot change as a tradition. Others feel that Islam is what their families do, which in most cases excludes and threatens them. Muhsin admits that many people who could benefit from the support group do not come out of fear of the word "Islam." In response, he argues, "We are saying [the group] is not religious, it is rather using spiritual tools toward personal development." Thinking of Islam as a set of teachings for personal development certainly challenges narrow perceptions of Islam, which are just as common among homosexual as they are among heterosexual Muslims.

"If people can understand what true Islam is," insists Muhsin, "they would want to come back to it." But what is true Islam? "It is that personal relationship with your Creator: your responsibility toward [God] and toward your fellow human beings. [It is] having values and morals, knowing that there is a journey ahead back to God. [It is] knowing that Islam is progressive and not dictatorial or dogmatic, but that ritual has a meaning in Islam." With his emphasis on ethics and principles, Muhsin resists reducing Islam down to arguing about the *shari'a* or classical Islamic law. He sees the *shari'a* as having failed to evolve, and therefore betraying the progressive dynamism of Islam. As a post-apartheid South African, he says proudly that "I think our constitution is more Qur'anic than the *shari'a* is!" It is his mission to help himself and other Muslims to free themselves of narrow interpretations and see the Qur'an's universal message in its depths. Seen in this way, it gives guidance for the development of gay and lesbian Muslims, just as it does for heterosexual Muslims, goads them to overcome fear, inspires them to care for themselves and others, and ultimately includes them in its announcement of God's unlimited compassion.

This is Muhsin's conviction, and it is also the message of the support group that he helped to establish. This message meets resistance from within the wider Muslim community. In South Africa, there are strong currents of "progressive Islam" which were energized by the multiple oppressions of apartheid. In Cape Town, there are mosques which are organized around progressive spiritual and political interpretation of Islam, like the Claremont Main Road Mosque. Yet not everyone there is willing to extend a progressive interpretation to inclusion of gay and lesbian Muslims. Furthermore, there are many Islamic institutions which openly reject any progressive interpretation in the name of "defending the *shari'a*." Some such institutions have gone on the offensive against the support group that Muhsin helped to establish. An Islamic community radio station, The Voice of the Cape, invited Muhsin to participate in a broadcast "dialogue" about Islam and homosexuality. However, the dialogue was a diatribe, since before he was even allowed to speak or answer questions, Muhsin was introduced on the program not as an *'alim* (one who has knowledge about Islam) but rather as a *zalim* (one who is an unjust oppressor). On the air, Muhsin was subjected to abuse and ridicule, but in retrospect Muhsin concedes that the invitation was a trap into which he willingly stepped. Yet to spark a genuine dialogue, one sometimes has to bear abuse and suffer oppression. When asked what verse of the Qur'an resonates most with him, Muhsin answered, "Yes, my favorite is *Summon them to the way of your Lord with wisdom and good counsel, and argue with them by means of what is more wholesome* (Q 16:125). It speaks about not getting angry or involved too much when you try to convince people about what is appropriate. If somebody argues with you, you try to show him better rather than get angry [in retaliation]." When asked if he is able to achieve such restraint, he laughs, "Yes, after years of practice!"

Muhsin's story is one of personal courage and religious conviction, through which he was able to negotiate with his family. He lives in Cape

Town with his male partner, having left Johannesburg to be closer to his teenage children and family. Not all are blessed with such inner courage to face a hostile family and community, and certainly some families are more hostile than others. Of other members of his support group, Muhsin reports, "One lesbian committed suicide because her family did not accept her. We have a few married men in the group who fear reprisals if they should come out." The wall of fear and intimidation is very dense. Lesbian, transgender, and gay Muslims confront the attitudes of parents, family, community, and religion that are all interwoven. In their life stories, fear of "going to hell" for being homosexual or transgender is juxtaposed upon fear of disappointing parents, fear of being disowned or attacked by siblings, and being shunned and shamed by their community. The strength that Muhsin has to overcome prejudice within his family and community comes from his early involvement with the Muslim Youth Movement (MYM) and his later role as a community member and educator at the Claremont Main Road Mosque in Cape Town, which was deeply shaped by MYM visionaries.

The Claremont Main Road Mosque became a center for antiapartheid activities in the 1970s under the inspiration of the MYM and Qibla movements. It also reorganized the division of space to promote gender justice and the greater participation of women, encouraging a more comprehensive sense of religious inspiration for social activism on all fronts of injustice.[8] The Claremont Main Road Mosque adopted English as the language of sermons and engaged in democratically open debates about scriptural interpretation and ritual norms.[9] Its members saw themselves as a vanguard institution willing to take risks to stand up for what it sees as the progressive spirit of the Qur'an against the authority of custom: it came under "tremendous criticism for the creative and innovative manner in which it addressed a range of social issues . . . result[ing] in a self-awareness of being a unique mosque leading the way, not only for mosques within the country but also for mosques throughout the world."[10] Muhsin perpetuates this sense of courage, even after he was asked to leave the Claremont Main Road Mosque, which judged his being a visible gay Muslim to be too risky. The Inner Circle community embodies this courage on a communal level, drawing strength not only from Muhsin but also from each and every member.

At The Inner Circle's annual retreat in March 2005, I was privileged to meet thirty members of the organization and to conduct interviews with them. Listening to their stories places the legal and theological issues in much-needed depth of human experience that others, both non-Muslim and nonhomosexual listeners, can understand. One of the participants, whom I call Nafeesa, was raised as a male but identifies as a female—she is therefore a male-to-female (MTF) transgender person. Nafeesa was not working toward medical therapy to alter her body to replace male tissues and characteristics with female ones. Rather, Nafeesa is content to "act" the part of a woman through speech, gesture, and dress. Nafeesa is satisfied for others to see her and treat her as a female, without feeling the need to physically alter her body. From her own perspective, Nafeesa also demonstrates the strategy of engaging religious tradition.

Nafeesa: True Self or Made-Up Life

Though Nafeesa belongs to the same community as Muhsin and volunteers with The Inner Circle, she takes a more sarcastic and humorous approach to her Islamic religious tradition. She does not see herself as a religious reformer. Yet as a community member she has some important insights into religion, insights which arise from her organic social experience of conflict with her religious tradition and the community authorities that uphold it. Nafeesa's identity developed considerably since puberty, when she—as a boy—first felt attracted to other boys and thereby came into conflict with her Islamic upbringing. A person raised as a boy might feel sexual attraction to other males because he, deep down beneath all socialization, feels the self to be female and not male. This analysis refers to Nafeesa as "she" because this is how she refers to herself, despite the fact that her family raised her as a boy named Muhammad. She grew up in an intensely Islamic environment though now, in her early twenties, she does not take religion so seriously. She shrugs off the obsessions of her fellow Muslims with a laugh. Nafeesa wears her religious identity very lightly, enjoys poking fun at "orthodoxy," and is content to practice Islam in her own way without much concern for communal norms.

For Nafeesa, Islamic identity is something she inherited from her family and imbibed from her "Coloured" community in Cape Town. Her "Islamicity" owes nothing to Arabs and the ideological reform movements so active in Arab communities. Nafeesa is very outgoing and theatrical, always cracking jokes both at herself and at what she sees as the hypocrisy of others. This is not surprising, since her daily social interactions center on convincing people that she is a stylish woman, despite an appearance that she admits is ambiguous. When I asked to conduct an interview with her for this study, her face lit up—"Oh, my whole life is an interview with everybody who can lay their hands on me! It's always strange . . . well . . . interesting meeting me. And then you are eager to know me, because this is so new for you, because I'm carrying it off so well. People say, 'Wow, she's so natural! How does she do it?' And they want to know why and how!"[11]

Striking people as "natural"—looking and acting as much like a feminine woman as possible—is her goal. She enjoys the challenge of having to persuade rather than simply having people assume. In her mid-twenties, Nafeesa works freelance as a make-up artist. Her love of theater is not surprising, considering that her whole childhood and adolescence consisted of radical role-playing, with reality never being what everyone else assumed it to be. Nafeesa explains, "I was a typical little girl trapped in a boy's body. I was very close to my mom . . . because I'm the only son. . . . Well, I was the only son—rephrase that, please! I have three sisters—two older and one younger. . . . They both see a lot of each other. I won't say I'm an outcast, of course, but I'm very distant. I tend to keep to myself. I don't go back home much to visit. There was a time when I didn't go at all, but then they came to apologize for not accepting me for who I want to be." Nafeesa refers to an incident when, at age nineteen, she was thrown out of her parental home. "I was given an ultimatum: 'Either you make use of the door or you stay and follow my rules in this house!' It was more my mother sitting on my father's head. She forever wants a son. And till this day, she'll probably pray for me to be [a gay man]. Unfortunately, it's not working. . . . She says she accepts me for being gay, but she doesn't understand why I had to wear female clothes. So she doesn't mind me being gay, she just wants me to look like a boy, so she can say, 'That is my son.' At this point, she can't say that. She can only say, 'That's my OTHER daughter . . . that's my son-daughter.' But she doesn't say that—she still insists, 'Oh no, that's my son,' and very nonchalantly. But she'll tell people she's got a son who lives like a woman!"

Despite her failure to live up to basic expectations of her mother, Nafeesa insists that since birth she has been different—in her words, "queer." The process of discovering the dimensions and depths of that feeling of difference took some time and painful experience; the search for terms to conceptualize it took even longer. However, her identity formation happened early in her life, which might be due to her fearless character or to her effeminate behavior that she could not or would not hide. "When I was very young, I always knew that I was gay—that I was interested in males. At fourteen, I was still in denial. At sixteen, I decided to accept myself. At eighteen turning-nineteen, I came out to my parents. I was starting to cross-dress at that time and to go clubbing. . . . At an early age, I was very mature and had to distinguish between pleasure and work. So at work you have to look like somebody who's working and because you're a boy you have to look like a boy. That's what I thought then, but now it's another story." But before she worked outside in society and had the liberty to dress as a woman, Nafeesa played the part of a conventional Muslim boy.

In childhood, Nafeesa worked at a mosque as the only son of the caretaker, her father. After secular school came Islamic school in the same mosque where her father worked, followed in the evening by helping her father during *dars* (sessions of adult religious education) or *dhikr* (sessions of group meditation) late into the night. Her life was divided between the sphere of family-work-community—where she had to behave like a boy—and the theater of friends-parties where she could experiment with dressing and behaving like a girl. As she matured and gained confidence, she began to assert that the secret world, out of view of her parents and the Muslim community, was her real world. It was expanding to crowd out the old false world in which she had been raised to perform.

Of course, that led to a dramatic conflict. Her mother insisted that Nafeesa quickly marry a woman in order to become a real man. If she refused, she would be sent off to *madrasa* far from home as both a cure and a type of banishment. In Nafeesa's view, many gay or effeminate men were exiled to *madrasa* as a quick family solution to the problem, or chose to go as a form of pious flight from a difficult reality. "You know, there's always this [dynamic] that when you're starting to 'behave like a little *moffie*' they send you away to *Dar al-Ulum* (*madrasa*) just to take you out of the area, so that you become a straight person." Nafeesa admitted that not all religious teachers in the *madrasa* institutions were gays-in-hiding. She knew several who were, and had faced a family discussion of whether to send her away, too.

Nafeesa resisted being sent to a *madrasa* and then refused an arranged marriage with a loud rebuttal. "When I was eighteen and coming out, my mother just didn't know how to handle it. She wanted to get me an arranged marriage. I said, 'Hell no, darling! Over this dead body! I would rather kill myself.' I'd rather lower my *iman* (faith) and kill myself than do something like that. I said, 'You wouldn't like your daughter to be embarrassed, hurt, crushed every second night by her husband who behaves like a [woman] . . . or to catch her husband wearing her own wedding dress!'" She tried to appeal to her mother's sense of outrage, if one of her daughters ended up married to a closeted gay man who lived a lie. In this way, Nafeesa argued that she herself should avoid being the "man" in such a sham marriage.

As Nafeesa tells her life story, she always comes out triumphant with brutal logic and a fabulous witty remark. But reality must have been much more difficult. Marrying just to preserve her family's honor is a sin in her view, as it would cause social discord. Nafeesa compares *fasad* (personal corruption) and *fitna* (social discord) to explain that she is choosing the lesser of two evils, both of which are condemned in the Qur'an and Islamic ethics. "I'm afraid I can't do that [marry a woman]. I would never be able to! You know, there are a lot of males who get married and that would be murder to me. . . . That is not going to work— it's going to be *fitna* (social discord). I'd rather love in *fasad* than cause *fitna*!" She explains that she would rather love in ways that others see as dissolute and corrupt than live a life that consists of lies that harm others and cause social discord. She would rather choose the first even if others would see her as righteous for choosing the second.

Such a discussion shows that Nafeesa, despite her breezy and brash manner, thinks deeply about ethical issues in light of her Islamic education, even if she arrives at conclusions that startle her parents and community. "I'm a very logical person. If the shaykh or the imam were talking nonsense on the *minbar* (pulpit) or in the *dars* (lessons), I will question him afterwards. Or I'll ask one of my *khalifas* (*madrasa* teachers), and bring it up again. If I don't find any clarity in it, then I just don't believe it. . . . And the same with my sexuality—when people were saying to me, 'No, you can't be gay,' I said, 'Bring it to me in the Qur'an! Show me that the Qur'an says being gay is not allowed in Islam!' They couldn't. They brought up Sodom and Gomorrah and I said, 'That was how many years back? That was long before the Prophet's time and the Prophet [Muhammad] is the best—so it was different in HIS time. I'm a follower of the Prophet Muhammad, *salla allahu ʿalayhi wa sallim* (peace and benedictions be upon him) and not of *Nabi Lut* (the Prophet Lot). I'm sorry, so I'm afraid I can't pay attention to that. I do believe Lut was one of the prophets, but I'm not a follower of his.' They said, 'How can you say something like that when you are a Muslim and you're supposed to . . . ' I told them, 'No, because [Muhammad] was the last prophet and I believe he was the last and the best prophet, that's why I'm a Muslim.' They couldn't answer me.'" Nafeesa's point is, from the perspective of Islamic jurisprudence, convincing. Even if one assumes that the Prophet Lot forbade homosexual acts (as most Qur'an interpreters do), it does not follow that an ancient prophet's teachings have legal validity in the Islamic dispensation. This is especially valid since there is no evidence that the Prophet Muhammad ever addressed a case of homosexual acts or behaviors with moral denunciation or criminal punishment.[12]

Nafeesa's *ad hoc* theological arguments may have silenced opponents in a friendly debate, but did not work with her parents. They were less concerned with theology than with upholding cultural norms to avoid public scandal. "In Cape Town, being a cross-dresser means that you are probably going on the road, being a prostitute. That is the assumption, especially the old school—I mean my parents and what they learned from their parents. It was an older generation's knowledge, where if you see a guy dressed up like a female, then he's probably one of 'the girls standing on the road.' It was difficult for my father to see me in female clothes, because he thought, 'This child is a prostitute.' What I had to clarify first was to convince them that, 'Just because I'm cross-dressing doesn't mean that I'm wanting to hurt you. No, it's because I'm comfortable. I was a Muslim boy all that time, so I'll just be a Muslim GIRL now—so there is no difference. It's just that I feel more comfortable in female clothes.' Then they showed me the DOOR!" She was nineteen when she was thrown out of the house.

Facing this social and financial disaster, Nafeesa fell back on Muslim friends whose parents and elders were more accepting of her than her own parents were. Nafeesa turned her personal disaster into an opportunity to assert that she was really a woman. She stayed with a friend and her family: "It was a school friend, a girl, and her family—Muslim people. I stayed with her and her family, and they accepted me. I had to share a room, but it was fine. They were accommodating. I shared a room and a bed with my friend, who was a girl [along with her young brother and her grandmother]. We all slept in one big bed. . . . That went on for a year and a half. I won't say that was difficult, but that was a part of my life when I was really struggling. My faith was very strong at that point." This host family treated her as a girl while integrating her into the family and that boosted her faith. They trusted her to behave like a female in the delicate issue of sleeping arrangements.

Nafeesa lived off the generosity of this family and did odd jobs: sewing and washing clothes, making flower decorations, or cooking for parties. She almost ended up on the street, but she thanks God for the blessing of having people in the Muslim community who sheltered her, otherwise she believes she would have drifted into the party world of clubs or the street culture of gangs. "Because my family was pushing me away, I could do what I wanted to do. Nobody's going to tell me what I'm going to do now, as long as I respect the people's house where I'm staying. . . . But I was a girl with more grace and finesse and style, and with many mentors who would encourage me to become a better person." Despite finding shelter with friends, she did experience violence against her from a public that saw her as different and therefore vulnerable. Once gangsters pointed a gun at her head but she shouted them down. Another time she was abducted and regained consciousness in a police station: "That happened but I'm still alive. I thank God every day for my being."

Nafeesa created what can be called a "found family" in the Muslim community to substitute for her family that had driven her out. She contrasts her choices with what normally happens to young people in her situation. "In the Coloured community in South Africa when guys get thrown out of the house, they go live on the road. They make them-selves a new life. They don't forget that they're Muslim or where they come from but they block it out of their lives. . . . They prefer hanging out with Christian or Hindu or Jewish people than to be with Muslims, their own people. But I [was different]—and I thank Allah—because I had a lot of Muslim friends." It was very important to Nafeesa's identity and sense of dignity to keep her ties with Muslim friends. Even far from her parents' mosque, she maintained her connection to the community, perhaps because so much else about her identity was in flux. "I stayed with friends who were Muslim rather than Christian. [I was] still main-taining a Muslim life. I used to be very fem [feminine]—long skirts, shirts, and scarf. I used to always wear a scarf on my head. When I went to pray at the mosque, I'd always go to the female side. I'd dress that way during the day and at functions and at weddings. People at wedding parties didn't even know, and would just say, 'She looks fabulous!' At first, at the mosque where people knew me, I would go in and stand at the back [of the women's section]. It started in Ramadan when I would go to perform my *tarawih* prayers. I would go in late or wait until it was late just to stand in the back in the female section."

Nafeesa started to attend a new mosque where she found support-ive friends.[13] She was "adopted" by the leader's extended family, who observed her transition into coming regularly as a woman. The lead-ership at that mosque "have a whole Islamic library and are seen very highly. I was friendly with the grandchild [of the shaykh who founded the mosque and community center]. . . . It's a very respected institu-tion. This is a family that runs the mosque and they live on the prem-ises of the mosque. One brother used to maintain the mosque and the eldest brother's daughter was my friend, and I got into their family. Starting out as a male, they met me in male clothes, then sometimes in male clothes with a scarf. It was probably a shock to them the first time, but I was to them the same person, actually. But they dealt with it their own way, and they accepted me for still being me. I was still in my last year of school when I met them, that is why they saw me in male clothes. I had stayed away for a while, then phoned them to explain to them before showing up that this is the way it's going to be. They were not surprised, but just acted like it was normal. They spoke with me about my sexuality. It was never closed, but always an open story!

It was never a problem. [They would say], 'The first thing is to never judge—Allah alone will judge. Why should we push them away? Don't push them away because you're going to push them into *fasad*. Rather, bring them in and bring them closer to the *din*, bring them closer to the religion.'" The family that ran this mosque and Islamic community center accepted Nafeesa and gave her an allowance to keep her from falling into trouble. "At that time, I could have just gone into the streets and had a fab life. Hit the road. Made money. Had a beautiful place. I am beautiful, I can confuse any man. But I said to myself, 'Nafeesa, you are a Muslim girl. That is not what's expected of you. That is not the life that Allah put out there for you. You are a good person, people know you. You are smart, you have brain, and you are not a typical blond. You can become something. You can make something out of this life. Just have faith and hope for the best.'"

The acceptance of this religious family was very important for Nafeesa's maturation. They allowed her to look back with appreciation on the religious tradition in which she had grown up and to find resources in it for guiding her ethical life, even if that life in its outward appearance was far from what her parents would consider Islamic. "You don't know what lies in your future, but you can always go back to your past. That was one of the philosophies of my life. So whatever came into my life, I would accept it and deal with it there and then. If it was [good] for me, I would say *al-hamdulillah* (thanks be to God). You accept it with your whole heart and you deal with it and you learn by it. There was no more *'alim* (religious teacher) in my life, no more mother or father in my life, so I had to be on my own and think. I had to make rational decisions on my own, with no mother and no father, no *'alim*, nobody, just me." For her own moral compass, Nafeesa always returns to Islam as she understands it, rather than as teachers or parents present it. "I am first of all still a Muslim and my sexuality has got nothing to do with my religion. That is something for which I never needed any confirmation. It was an inside thing."

Her parents rejected her because they could not accept that Nafeesa's identity—first perceived as a young gay male and later understood as a transgender female—was her "true self," as she calls it. They saw her as a boy and a young man. But for Nafeesa, living out the role imposed upon her by family and community would be living a lie. She accepts her family's rejection as a consequence of her inner moral decision. Yet the strength to make that decision came from her religious faith and moral principles that were taught to her by family and community, even if they rejected her. She sums up her life by noting, "I was raised to know right from wrong, that they never mix. Like oil and water, it just clashes. I had a lot of friends with the older *murids* (religious students) at the mosque. I was mature for my age because I would sit in on their conversations and discussions and I would talk with them with no experience of life. Like Jesus being with the elders, I would sit there discussing their lives and experiences, learning from their mistakes. Then I was nineteen and on the road. The choice was either being who I am—my true self which I am now—or going to live a life which is a made-up life." For Nafeesa, to live according to her family's imposed norms would be to live a false life of pretending to be a man

Nafeesa's piety is disguised behind her humor and sly mockery. Yet as she tells her own story, Islamic faith plays a crucial role. She voices theological ideas that arise from her own personal experience and existential crises, though she is not a trained theologian. Her Islamic education in the mosque and in her family, acquired through her childhood and early adolescence, informed her later choices as she gradually embraced her identity as a male-to-female transgender person. She confronted her internal sense of being female in a male body, her sexual attraction to males, and her rejection of heterosexual marriage. Yet she confronted these challenges by referring back to her Islamic faith, exhibiting the mode of activism termed "engaging religious tradition." She justified rejecting her family's prescription of her gender role and pressure to marry a woman by saying that she prefers being accused of *fasad* than being a cause of *fitna*. It is better to be accused of being a corrupt individual than be guilty of causing harm or injustice to others, she argues through these Islamic ethical terms. Though her struggle to live with sincerity in her minority gender identity led her to conflict with her family, Nafeesa found support and understanding among other Muslim groups. Her love of Islamic rituals like prayer and *dhikr* helped her to find community among other Muslim families even when her own immediate family ostracized her.

Nafeesa refers to Islamic theology in broad strokes and basic concepts rather than in detailed interpretation of scriptural verses. Her engagement with religious tradition is more organic and personal than it is scholarly and systematic. In this way, her example offers both an echo and a contrast to the more formal theological ideas of Muhsin or Tamsila, who will be discussed below. Tamsila is a lesbian activist in London who offers a third example of activism by engaging religion. Like Muhsin, she is interested in a systematic critique and reassessment of the Islamic tradition. But unlike him, Tamsila approaches Islam as a secularly educated professional who does not boast of formal training in Islamic scholarship. This does not lessen her piety or blunt the insights that she has into the challenge of engaging the Islamic tradition.

Tamsila: It's about the Journey

Tamsila comes from a working-class Pakistani immigrant family in the United Kingdom. She has married her lesbian partner, who is also a practicing Muslim. Tamsila is one of the core organizers of the Safra Project, a support group designed by women to address the specific needs of lesbian and bisexual women from Muslim families. It began in November 2001 among a group who had previously been involved with Al-Fatiha UK (a support group which later changed its name to Imaan). This group felt that a more focused group was needed to meet the needs of Muslim women. The Safra Project was intended to meet this need. It is a support group by and for Muslim women and to provide sustained engagement with Islamic tradition through scholarship and media.

Tamsila derives great satisfaction from her work with youth and women. Constant argument with others in her Muslim community does not seem to wear her down, but rather steels her courage. She has a quiet determination and relentless energy to pursue the ethical principles that she finds fundamental in her life. These principles are derived from the Islamic tradition even if they lead her to contradict the presumptions of many in her Muslim community. What kind of woman would choose such a difficult path and adopt it with self-effacing determination? For Tamsila, the ethical principles that drive her to take up activist work as a Muslim lesbian are those that she learned in her family—lessons about solidarity against injustice.

Tamsila's parents were Punjabi immigrants who worked hard to gain the education that their laboring forefathers did not have (and which their mothers, as immigrant Muslim women, could not gain). Tamsila grew up in a small English town where her family was part of a threatened minority in a racist and politicized environment. For her, fighting against injustice was part of her family and community life—it was a tactic for survival: "As for my faith, it has always kept me going. It has given me the strength to oppose racism, sexism, and all the other *isms*."[14] Solidarity against injustice was ingrained in her as a child. She sees it as a core value of Islam without which the religion is mere hypocrisy. "In my childhood, we would have lots of debates about Islam, mostly within a social class context because we grew up in a very working-class town. We would have our debates with the Qur'an in front of us and at the same time, a copy of *The Socialist Worker* that my father would always buy. So we would always talk about class issues and race issues. Because I came from a town outside London that had a small ethnic-minority population, race relations had a very high priority with us, as did class." The town of Northampton where she grew up had only a 5 percent nonwhite minority population.[15] Tamsila recalls that being part of an embattled minority "had a huge impact on my understanding of Islam, in terms of justice and equality, protecting your rights, and defending the rights of others around you, especially minority rights. Something that has encouraged me with my family, within our debates about race issues, is the idea that a large part of Islam is to protect the rights of the others and to step up when you or others are subjected to abuse and hatred. You don't just stand by and watch it happen—you have to take part. . . . That is often said within my home, that you step up and take part [in the struggle for justice]."

Such sayings were not just rhetoric, for racial violence was common. "My father was very much involved in struggle—if he saw injustice he would get involved and often he did get involved physically. I would see him get involved in fights. I saw him bruised and battered, sometimes as the result of racial violence and sometimes at the hands of the police." The solidarity required for survival cut across religious differences, which was another lesson that would impact Tamsila's sense of morality. "If you heard someone scream, you would go and look to see what was going on and you'd help out. So it was a very tight-knit community when I was growing up. Nowadays it is quite different . . . here are divides now along religious lines, divides between Hindus and Muslims and Sikhs, whereas when I was growing up, we didn't have that divide." The rise of religious ideology and right-wing Islamist groups, along with religious fundamentalists among Sikhs and Hindus, has pulled apart the racial solidarity of Asians that characterized her youth. She sees the swerve toward separatist, reactionary, and ideological under-standings of Islam as a major obstacle to achieving justice for women and sexual minorities in the United Kingdom.

Tamsila dates the rise of right-wing Islamic politics among British Muslims to the mid-1990s, after Margaret Thatcher had ruled as prime minister for over a decade. During those years, solidarity of race and class dominated the political discourse, as Thatcher's conservative poli-tics dismantled socialist policies, liberalized industry, and expanded the gap between the elite and the working class. With Thatcher gone, working-class minorities did not have a "common enemy" and their interests began to fragment; simultaneously, Wahhabi and Salafi ideol-ogy was spreading internationally due to the booming oil economy of Saudi Arabia. Muslim immigrants from Pakistan brought with them a synthesis of socialist-inspired politics and popular Islam, but second-generation Muslims born in the United Kingdom, like Tamsila, began to lose a vision of Islam that allowed interreligious solidarity and some began to adopt pietistic exclusion or radical extremism instead.

In her father, Tamsila had a model of the earlier style of being Mus-lim, based on the working-class values of solidarity and justice. Her father worked as a railway laborer in the United Kingdom. Despite his lack of opportunities for higher education, the railway union promoted a culture of self-education, literacy, and discussion of political topics which greatly influenced Tamsila's home life. "During the Thatcher years, people did identify as working class. . . . You were brought into that union culture, and that was brought home in our discussions and debates." Her family dinner table was the site of political debates, and her parents promoted open discussion of religious topics, which strengthened Tamsila's loyalty to Islam and commitment to diversity of opinion.

Tamsila reflects that her parents brought this culture of religious debate with them from Pakistan. Her father came from a family that runs a large *madrasa* (called Jami'a Islamiyya) in a town outside Lahore. Though he rejected the closed formalism of his *madrasa*-educated family, he retained a strong fidelity to Islam and always considered points of religious belief open to question and debate. Tamsila's maternal grandfather was trained as an Islamic jurist and worked as a judge in the secular court system in Pakistan; her mother learned to mix a secular and religious perspective on questions of Islamic practice. "So when my parents got together, one would be coming from a very Islamic school with a theological point of view, and one would be coming from a sociological Islamic background. They would clash head-to-head so often! This was a great way for me to grow up . . . that is very much the way I try to view Islam."

This potent mix of theology and sociology, as Tamsila puts it, is the backbone of an Islamic liberation theology. This is a term that Muhsin also uses to describe his approach to religion. Liberation theology is a movement that began among Latin American Catholics who taught that God always sides with the poor, the vulnerable, and the marginalized. Liberation theologians taught that religion must be interpreted through the experience of the poor—not through charity but through a struggle for justice. Protestants in South Africa applied this theological method to racial exclusion, and some Muslim thinkers have also taken it up.[16] Tamsila asks, "How did the Qur'an first come about? It came about as an empowerment for the downtrodden, the orphans, the women, and children. That is what I always remember about the Qur'an, that it came about to oppose oppression. That is the purpose of the Qur'an and Islam should continue, in my understanding, along that path of opposing oppression." In Tamsila's view, Islam is capable of continued growth by returning to its founding principles of justice and love. In fact, Islam as a tradition must continue to grow; otherwise tyrants can abuse it to justify oppression in the name of religion.

This perspective renews her faith even as she struggles with her family and community, for her process of coming out started early, lasted long, and involved enduring great pain. She declares, "I'm a Muslim before everything else, I'm a believer and I give my submission to Allah. . . . So I speak to you as a woman of faith, as a Muslim. The Qur'an has come originally to oppose oppression, as a means of empowering people. The basic principles of the Qur'an exist as justice and love, so if you use these basic principles of the Qur'an, anything that comes from it has to be along the lines of justice and empowerment and opposing oppression and tyranny. To say to me that all gay people have to be opposed just because they are gay does not follow the principles of the Qur'an when it first came about." In this way she justifies her being both a lesbian and a Muslim. She sees religious faith as part of the answer to reconciling the potential conflicts that her identity raises, and not part of the problem.

Her family did not accept this argument easily. Tamsila came out as a lesbian to her brother when she was sixteen and to her parents when she was eighteen. "I knew that it would involve a religious debate, because that's the way they are and that's the way I grew up—so I came prepared. I came with my Qur'an, and had it all lined up with the story of Lut and my understanding of it. But they weren't willing to see my interpretation—that I didn't see any contradiction between my being Muslim and my being a lesbian. I never have seen that . . . there was a contradiction because the way I've always looked at Islam is that it is a loving faith. It is accepting of diversity and it is about justice. For me, my sexuality does not contradict any of those things. . . . [The question in my mind] was more to do with community and family, as I knew that I would have to struggle with them. As for my faith, it has always kept me going." Tamsila recalls the debate and how she tried to untangle the web of associations that were fixed in her parents' minds. Like most Muslim families, they asserted that the tribe of Lut consisted of homosexuals who were punished by God for this and so it is forbidden. "It doesn't address women or even homosexuality, for I had already understood by that point that the Qur'an is not talking about homosexual relationships. It is talking about certain acts within a particular context—like promiscuity and bestiality and inhospitality. . . . But this is not anything that they [my parents] have been willing to recognize. . . . They still think I'm going to hell—that I'm going to burn in hellfire."

When argument based upon the Qur'an did not resolve the issue, Tamsila's parents cited *hadith* reports that had been woven into the Islamic tradition. "They went to the Qur'an first, but then they had to resort to the *hadith* because I was there with the Qur'an in front of them. I was demanding, 'Show me where [it condemns homosexuality]!' They said, 'This is what it means,' but I replied, 'But that is not what it says.' Then they started trying *hadith* on me. . . . There is the *hadith* that two women cannot lie under the same sheet or that if you find two women in a room you must separate them, or some *hadith* like that which they would throw at me." The tendency to cite *hadith* reports without discussing their authenticity or interpretation is called "*hadith* hurling" by the legal scholar, Khalid Abou El Fadl.[17] Tamsila uses the same metaphor to describe her experience with her parents.

In her theological reflection, Tamsila questioned the role of *hadith* in Islamic discourse. Discussing the theological study published by The Safra Project, she observes, "We reference primarily the Qur'an itself, and not the *hadith*. . . . We feel that there are a lot of contradictions within the *hadith*. . . . So we state that there are variations and there is a lot of debate about what *hadith* are and which are true *hadith*. . . . Our main statement is that the only true *hadith* is the Qur'an and you take everything from that." The Safra Project advocates the primacy of the Qur'an as the key to reform and renewal in Islam, along with most other progressive Muslim groups. In her words, "We try to look at the Qur'an and to understand the Qur'an from itself" rather than relying upon *hadith* and limiting understanding of the Qur'an to such reports.[18]

Such a reformist strategy was integral to Tamsila's argument with her parents. She deflected their citation of *hadith* reports by insisting on returning to the Qur'an and its exact language. "I said, 'Look, here is the Qur'an and here is the story of Lut—it doesn't say anything like what you are talking about. Look at the words!'" Her parents then turned to two verses in Surat al-Nisa', the Chapter of Women (Q 4:15–16) which discusses punishment for women found doing a lewd act.[19] Tamsila argued against them, saying, "Generally, most people would say that verse is talking about prostitution. Again it doesn't say very specifically what is this 'lewd act' or *fahisha* that is being condemned here. Allah has said in the Qur'an itself that there are no words missing here [in the Qur'an]. So if Allah wanted to [condemn] female-female relationships or male-male relationships, he would have said so quite clearly. But it doesn't say relationships. It talks only about very specific acts of the people of Lut."

Faced with a determined and educated counterargument, her parents gave up arguing. Her mother disowned her and she was thrown out of the house. Eventually they accepted her back, only to coerce her into a heterosexual marriage. "Then my mom disowned me because I had ruined the family's name, had ruined her reputation. . . . She was not happy. But through it all, it was my faith that got me through it, because I knew and truly believed I had true faith in Allah, and that whatever I go through, that Allah has faith in me that I'll get through it—otherwise I would not have been sent this challenge. It is a test of faith that I will stay true to Allah."

With time, the tension has lessened somewhat and a détente has developed between Tamsila and her mother. "When I'm disowned, she falls ills and then I go back home to take care of her and then I am 'her daughter' again." Her brother is very supportive and that is a consolation; he even attends lesbian and gay Muslim conferences with her, to show his care for her and learn more about her situation. Détente with her mother has allowed Tamsila to build her own family. Her first lesbian partner, a Muslim woman from a Pakistani family, had a three-year-old son from a former heterosexual marriage that ended in divorce. Tamsila helped to raise him during their long relationship and considers herself the boy's mother. He is now a teenager, and Tamsila feels that she has passed on the best of her own values to him, despite the fact that her relationship with the boy's biological mother has ended and she is in a new lesbian relationship. Tamsila still sees her son almost every weekend, and finds that "he is very interested in the debates and discussion that we have. Sometimes I think he is not listening, but then I find him arguing with either his mother or one of her flat-mates about Islam and homosexuality. Then I realize that he's been paying attention, and knows all the arguments!" As a lesbian raising a child, she tries to convey to her son all the values by which her own heterosexual parents raised her—faith in Islam, love for the Prophet, firm adherence to justice, and commitment to open debate. Most likely, her son will grow up to be a heterosexual man, but one who does not take heterosexuality for granted.

When same-sex civil unions became legal in the United Kingdom in 2005, Tamsila legally united with her current lesbian partner. She was not content with a secular union under civil law, but rather adapted the Islamic *nikah* ceremony to her lesbian marriage. Muslim activists in several democratic nations are discussing the permissibility and possible form of Islamic same-sex unions.[20] Tamsila argues that although the classical *shari'a* does not grant provisions for same-sex marriage, the purpose of lesbian or gay couples in getting married is the same as it is for heterosexual couples. Therefore, the same principles apply, and the *shari'a* can and should expand to cover new situations like same-sex marriage. These principles are the *maqasid*, the principles and goals of the *shari'a* as distinct from its form and past rulings. "The *shari'a* had to develop into a form, but it began with principles. So we're not saying throw away the principles at all; we're saying use those principles but in the current context of the twenty-first century wherever you may be located. It is to develop and encourage *ijtihad*, basically—*ijtihad* for the twenty-first century or for our generation. I personally feel very strongly about that—it is both possible and necessary. Not just in terms of sexuality, but all issues: inheritance, personal law, legal norms, and business law, everything in society." She notes that most Muslims are willing and eager to conduct de facto *ijtihad* in matters having to do with politics, finance, business, and technology but stubbornly resist *ijtihad* in matters of personal relations, family structure, marriage, and sexual conduct. She argues with Muslims who create a schism between public life and personal life: "You're willing to do *ijtihad* on these issues, but if you're going to do that you may as well do it on other issues as well and bring them into line with each other. Otherwise you're going to have two different forms of an understanding happening simultaneously but totally out of synch with each other. No wonder we have all these conflicts within our communities!"

Tamsila's personal contribution to *ijtihad* consists of volunteering time and energy in helping lead The Safra Project. This support group publishes sociological and theological information to allow lesbian and bisexual women to make better choices and lead more fulfilling lives within the framework of living in Muslim communities. For most this is a long struggle, as it has been for Tamsila. "It is a journey and will continue to be a journey. We all have our own routes to get there, but it really is about the journey. As individuals too, it is about your journey in life and not about the end where you get to—that will be determined by your journey. That's the way we see the project." From this insight the support group took its name, The Safra Project, from the Arabic and Urdu word for journey.

In preparing their theological study, The Safra Project tried to steer a middle course between the needs of a lay audience and the requirements of traditional Islamic scholarship. This is difficult because the women who are their audience have often been denied access to traditional Islamic education at higher levels; they may be more concerned with practical needs like how to avoid an arranged marriage, achieve economic independence, or negotiate divorce and child custody issues. However, these practical affairs are, in fact, deeply influenced by Islamic beliefs, customs, and norms, especially as Muslim women deal first and foremost with their families and immediate religious communities before reaching state institutions like the police, courts, and constitutional rights.

The Safra Project also aims to reach out to mainstream Muslim leaders with its message that there is deep diversity in Muslim communities: that homosexual women are part of their mosques, neighborhoods, and families and deserve to be treated with dignity. While this message is a challenge for many mainstream Muslims, it does not fall on completely deaf ears. The Safra Project has been in dialogue with some imams and local Islamic authorities about homosexuality among Muslim women. "We are trying to talk with individual clerics who may not want it to be publicly known that they are talking to us, but will in private discuss issues with us." Imams may be more open-minded than their mosque communities and therefore do not want it publicized that they have dialogues with lesbian, transgender, and gay Muslim support groups. Yet a quiet dialogue might be the only way to achieve a progressive discussion in the current climate of neoconservative backlash.

Despite her strong convictions, Tamsila and The Safra Project are engaged in a very gradual reform. She confronts her Muslim community's split between public and private life. Integrating these spheres of life is essential to achieving integrity as a Muslim, and The Safra Project urges its constituency to do this slowly while reaching out to mainstream Muslim leaders. Yet Tamsila is not waiting for the rest of her religious community to come to a consensus on this, or for her mother to accept her as a lesbian daughter. She is forging ahead to find integrity at the center of her own Muslim family, as a professional, a spouse, and a mother. It is her faith that gives her the courage to step out and reach toward these goals, despite all odds.

Conclusion

For many lesbian, gay, and transgender Muslims, religion is a potent force in life. Just because they struggle against interpretations that condemn homosexuality or gender ambiguity does not mean that they reject religion outright. Many Western observers and allies assume that transgender, lesbian, and gay Muslims must leave Islam in order to live with dignity and pursue social reform. The interviews in this chapter illustrate that it is wrong to assume this. Many activists retain their loyalty to their religion, pursue deeper knowledge about it, and practice its rituals to the extent of their capacity. Others mine the Islamic tradition for resources for a progressive religious interpretation.

While in South Africa, I was invited by some members of The Inner Circle support group to a *dhikr*, a kind of meditative chant done by many Muslims as part of their spiritual tradition. On this evening, I joined a circle of gay Muslims who belonged to The Inner Circle. Their leader recited a verse from the Qur'an: *If they intend to deceive you, surely God is sufficient for you—the One who strengthened you with divine aid along with the believers, and united their hearts* (Q 8:62). The group then repeated again and again the words, *O Prophet, God is sufficient for you and those believers who follow you* (Q 8:64). This ritual is a way of contemplating the meaning of the words, *hasbuna allah*—"God is sufficient for us"—which is repeated with contemplative melody so that the soul can absorb its transformative power. By using these verses in *dhikr*, gay Muslims of The Inner Circle find a new meaning in them to give consolation to those who are oppressed and threatened with violence. Through these verses, they call upon God to provide inner strength and resolve to face a struggle that is intensely inward but also outward.

Muhsin was the leader of this *dhikr*. His interview, along with those of Tamsila and Nafeesa, provides examples of a mode of activism called "engaging religious tradition." Their lives demonstrate the various ways that activists engage Islam, critiquing patriarchal interpretations that were dominant in the past, and drawing upon resources in Islam for a more progressive practice of the faith. Muhsin has specialized theological training while Tamsila has advanced secular education, but both directly engage the Islamic tradition through its textual sources and interpretive commentaries. Nafeesa provides a counterexample as she engages the Islamic tradition in a more playful and provocative way, based upon her personal experience and community relations.

Those who engage religious tradition have a distinct approach to their identity: they say that being Muslim is primary—above gender, ethnicity, class, or other social markers. Because they perceive faith as primary in their identity, they gravitate toward theological debate when confronting issues of gender identity and sexual orientation. They also value religious practices and rituals very highly; they are not willing to jettison their sense of belonging to Islam, even in the face of rejection by community or family. In their perception, the problem is bias and prejudice among Muslims and the answer lies, at least partly, in the Islamic tradition itself.

Activists in this mode usually value theological knowledge. They attain such knowledge by family background, formal *madrasa* training, or university education (or often a combination of all three kinds of training). They often struggle hard to achieve religious education. They intend to create a reformist discourse that addresses the Qur'an and other sources of Islamic authority, in ways both defensive and constructive. More specifically, they announce that lesbian, transgender, and gay Muslims are among the "downtrodden" whom the Qur'an addresses and urges Muslims to protect. They position their community as a vulnerable minority which has endured oppression and yearns for justice. But they have differing opinions on the best strategy to achieve justice and to advocate for their inclusion in the Muslim community; some focus on dialogue with formal religious leaders (imams, jurists, or scholars) while others stress the need to ally with progressive Islamic thinkers who may operate in more secular institutions like universities, government ministries, and research institutes.

This mode of activism, engaging religious tradition, is one possibility for lesbian, transgender, and gay Muslims. As the interviews above demonstrate, this mode of activism is usually combined with others such as adjusting secular politics to their struggle or challenging family and community. It is wrestling with family ties and community loyalties to which we turn in the next chapter.

2

Challenging Family and Community

Come, let's make a tribe,
    maybe in time, we can make it right
We should be flying high,
    this time will pass, we won't be here for long
        ~Simphiwe Dana, "Let's Make a Tribe"

I traveled to South Africa in 2005 to attend an annual conference of lesbian, gay, and transgender Muslims. While there, I attended the Cape Town Jazz Festival where people of all religions, races, and political persuasions converged, leaving aside their profound divisions over their new nation to celebrate their unique bonds through music. They had survived apartheid. Through collective suffering and great sacrifice, they had transformed a government based on injustice into one that promised a brighter future for all. At the Jazz Festival, a young South African singer, Simphiwe Dana, electrified the audience with "Let's Make a Tribe." Her love song was a political plea and an optimistic prophecy that embodied the buoyant mood of the diverse audience. In the notes to her album that features this song, she offers thanks "to the revolution that gives me integrity . . . to the innocence that kept the faith . . . to the music that made me strong . . . to God, who stays with me."[1] This song captured the mood of her new nation but also expressed something essential about the Muslims with whom I spoke. Simphiwe Dana's lyrics echo the moral challenge that the Qur'an poses to families and communities. *O people, We created you . . . [as] different tribes, so that you should come to know one another, acknowledging that the most noble among you is the one most aware of God* (Q 49:13). Both the singer and the scripture declare that diversity and division have a purpose—to challenge us to overcome our clannish assumptions and acknowledge all that is good in others. But all too often, the solidarity of the group is held up as the highest value, and the family or community asks its members to sacrifice their individual welfare to conform to the group's expectations.

A major struggle for lesbian, gay, and transgender Muslims is to overcome the alienation caused by their family's reactions to their sexual orientation. The family can be nurturing, but it can also be controlling and oppressive—and in some cases violent against its own members. Some activists confront this dimension of the struggle more squarely, often deep within their homes and away from more public roles often associated with the term "activist." Their mode of activism can be called "Challenging Family and Community" and their voices fill this chapter.

Those activists who challenge family and community take up a very intimate struggle. They do not primarily engage the Islamic tradition but rather challenge their family's expectations, norms, and behavior. However, family norms are often perceived to be moral norms, so religious tradition is never far below the surface of family tensions. In fact, many Muslims experience their family's norms as Islamic norms, and it is very difficult to challenge this juxtaposition of authorities. The activists interviewed in this chapter are both lesbian women whose struggle with family is particularly intense. The interviews demonstrate that challenging family and community inevitably leads to debating religious values.

Nargis: Getting out of the Family Trap

Nargis is a shy but articulate woman in her mid-twenties, very educated and cultured, whose profession is psychiatric and behavioral counseling. Her story revolves around feeling trapped in her family, community, and religion. From this captivity, she finds a kind of freedom through her long and loving relationship with a female partner. Her struggle with her immediate family is particularly intense and difficult because her family's attitudes are reinforced by those of the surrounding community. This made it very difficult for Nargis to find resources, help, and support. Her opportunities were severely circumscribed by the overlapping power of family, locality, and religious community. Her story reveals the complexities that face Muslim lesbians: they have to struggle for independence as women in a patriarchal society in general and then as lesbian women more specifically. Nargis's story reflects this reality. Even after the realization of her different sexuality, her freedom of movement and choice were tightly circumscribed by family and community because of her gender.

Nargis is from the Indian community in South Africa, which includes both Hindus and Muslims who arrived after 1860 as indentured laborers and small traders. Categorized as "Asian," the Muslims of Indian background are distinct from the "Coloured" community that predominates among Muslims in Cape Town. Their religious discourse is shaped by Hanafi law and South Asian patriarchal values. In general, trading families control the mosques in Indian Muslim communities, and women have a very circumscribed role and are often excluded from mosques entirely.

Nargis grew up in a religious environment and in a business family, which left her very little room for independence in any sphere of life. She is the youngest of five siblings in a clannish extended family. Her first space of autonomous growth came as she went to university, though she was still living at home and under close family surveillance. At university, she met her partner, a woman her own age. "The whole thing started on campus. I've never been with anyone else and I didn't know I was a lesbian before. I used to make fun of gay people when I was in school, so I didn't know when I was younger. Then I got to campus and met my partner, and that is where it all started. . . . [I thought], 'I'm not going to be a lesbian—it's not normal, it's not right!' It's just weird how Allah sort of throws at you the things you least expect, the things you least want. I would never dream of being gay—I used to think it's wrong, it's not right, and now I am!"[2] A long friendship blurred into love and sexual attraction before it become clear to Nargis that she was a lesbian.

At university, Nargis developed a circle of friends—both male and female—which included the woman who became her lesbian partner. The circle also included a male friend who was sexually attracted to Nargis. "We went out one day with three of my other friends. They were just sitting in the back seat [of a car], laughing and having fun, while I was thinking, 'I want to be there, not here in the front seat with a guy next to me!' Which I couldn't understand, because I didn't realize I was a lesbian then! I just felt that they were having so much fun, while I was feeling trapped with this guy! . . . I just wanted to be free. Then when I was getting involved with her, I didn't ever feel trapped." In Nargis's experience, friendship blurred seamlessly into love and sexual attraction for a woman. This experience gave her a taste of freedom beyond the confines of her family and its expectations.

The development of her sexual relationship was not informed by a concept of being "lesbian" or guided by a theory of sexual orientation. "We weren't quite sure what it was, because there are just those feelings that you get falling in love, but you don't know that you're falling in love. Because my impression was that it was never going beyond this point . . . we're just friends and were just close, you know? But it does go beyond there." As feelings of love developed between Nargis and her partner, accompanied by physical intimacy, her friends began to notice. The noose of community, family, and religious control began to tighten around her. "My family found out. My brothers and my sisters and a few other friends from our friendship circle, they found out and didn't tell my father immediately. They approached me first and . . . threatened to tell my father. But I said, 'OK, just don't tell him,' because I knew that if they told him they might take me out of campus. I said, 'Just don't [tell him]—I will stop with the relationship.' Then we tried to not show it so much, in terms of not showing much affection. But obviously, people see the chemistry or something—you try to hide it but in the end it's just not possible." Rather than trying to understand Nargis better, her friends acted as agents of her family and assumed to know better what is "normal" in society and religion both. Thus began for Nargis a long ordeal of confronting her family and their control over her. The bottom line for Nargis was to avoid being taken out of university and trapped at home. That would mean separation from her partner and abandoning any long-term hopes of a career that might give her independence from her family logistically, economically, and emotionally.

Her story of confronting her family reveals the tight web of power relationships between family, community, and religious authorities in Muslim communities. It also reveals how powerfully Islam is invoked in order to control younger members of the family, without religion actually being a subject of reasoned discussion. Nargis had to face a coordinated assault by her whole family, even before she was armed with the concept of actually being a lesbian: "The whole process of them finding out was in my first year of campus. I was struggling with my studies, then it was my whole thing about coming out . . . not even coming out, I wasn't struggling with that because I didn't even know what it was! To me, it wasn't like I had to come out about anything—I was just in a relationship. I couldn't name it. I could never mention the word 'lesbian' until last year. So I couldn't name it and I couldn't say that this is who I am."

Without a concept and a name that she could accept for herself, Nargis had no way to negotiate with her family. She was overwhelmed by how friends joined ranks against her and reported her to family. "Then my family told my father one night, without even warning me. Everyone was sitting in the family meeting . . . and I just wasn't expecting them to do anything like that. Then he found out and he was quite angry. . . . He didn't know what it meant to be 'gay.' They had to explain the whole concept to him. . . . Then I came in for questioning. So it was a whole family affair: my father, my auntie, my brother-in-law and my sister who's married to him, my sister, my brother, my brother's wife, and one or two of my cousins. It was terrible! Literally, they were all sitting around me and I was sitting in the middle on a stool and they were all questioning me. I didn't know what to expect, and I wasn't telling the truth. I was lying through my teeth, saying, 'No, I don't like her, I'm not in love with her.' I denied that, saying, 'No, I'll stop it, I'll stop it.' . . . Then it was the cross-questioning, and they brought up sexual issues as well. . . . It was just terrible. Issues like, 'Have you slept together?' . . . I said, 'I'll stop it, just send me back to campus.'" Her family threatened to withdraw her from university.

In this family confrontation, men held final say but women took the lead in enforcing patriarchal norms. "My mother hit me a lot. She was the one who beat me up, not my father. It was so bad when she knew what was happening—she was so angry at me. She was the one who hit me. Everyone was sitting around there and she was beating me up! . . . [She was] hitting me with her hand, so that I had bruises all over me. My father was there, and I was just keeping quiet, letting her hit me, because I know she's aggressive. So she was bashing me around my ears. I wasn't talking, I wasn't crying, I wasn't screaming, nothing. Then my father got cross because I wasn't saying anything! 'You're not even saying you're sorry! You're not even asking for *muʿaf* (pardon)! You're not even crying!' I only said it because he said that, so I said, 'I'm sorry I'm sorry, forgive me.' So I basically had to go around and ask my whole family for forgiveness . . . for being who I am."

This show of submission worked for a while. Nargis returned to university and resumed her studies. She avoided seeing her partner but still was in love. Slowly, they came back together in secret. However, Nargis's friends were also close to her older brother and informed him of her daily activities. "They were the spies on campus, so they told my brother everything that happened on campus, if we spoke to each other or anything. Half the Indian community on campus sort of knew, because once one person knows, everyone knows. . . . Then my father found out again, because two male friends of mine on campus saw us together in the chat-room on campus. . . . That got blown out of proportion, because apparently they 'saw us having sex,' which was just not true. So that's how the rumors spread." Her father's behavior reveals how deeply a parent's reaction is colored by fear of shame in the wider community, perhaps even more than concern for the welfare of her or his child.

Nargis sympathized deeply with her father's predicament, when she explained, "My father is a very religious man. Not that he's a shaykh (spiritual leader) or anything, but he's always going to holy functions like *gyarwin* (devotional Sufi gathering) in people's houses. . . . And obviously, he's quite well known. So if anyone knows that 'this man's daughter is a lesbian,' it will be a disgrace. It would be something the Cape Town community would love to talk about, because you know how it goes, the gossip that spreads. Anything that goes wrong in anyone's life, especially anyone regarded highly in the community, if someone finds fault in their family or in their way of doing things, then it's a huge deal because they can throw it back in his face now. I suppose that is the scary part. I mean, he might accept it [his daughter's being a lesbian] but then the community might throw it back in his face. That would make me sad. He's a very proud person as well, and it's really about his pride."

The prospect of community shame drove her father to withdraw Nargis from university and keep her home, cut off from outside society. "I couldn't go out and couldn't even phone anybody, not even my best friends. . . . I felt trapped." Again she swore to her father that she would terminate the lesbian relationship. Her father relented, but only after going to campus to inform Nargis's lecturers about her lesbian partner and soliciting their help in keeping an eye on his daughter to prevent the two of them from meeting. "One lecturer was explaining to me, 'Look, at the moment you are living with your family, so try to do what they need now. Then when you are independent and living on your own you can go out and do what you want.' Because she was white and older, that's what they think. But I obviously wouldn't have been able to." Her white, non-Muslim university lecturers could not understand deeply the family and religious issues that Nargis faced.

In the lull created by her deception, Nargis began to wrestle with the question of religious authority, which is also parental authority, in a more profound way. First of all, she drew great solace from her partner, who was brought up in the Hindu tradition from a Cape Town Indian family. "She is much stronger emotionally. She's OK with who she is, this is who she is and that's how she's going to accept herself the way she is. . . . She's never been in a relationship before—it was sort of her first time. . . . But she was always fine with it, because in terms of her spiritual being [she says], 'God just accepts you the way you are, so why be judged by society? Why worry about society and the way other people feel?' That's always been her motto: that God loves you and it's what's in your heart and not about what you do. And it's not about bodies but about the spiritual soul. So she was able to accept it much better than I. . . . She tells me these things and I agree with her, but I can't believe it because of the background I've been brought up with. I've had so many years of being told . . . that if I don't do this right or if I don't respect my father or do that right, then I'm going to go to hell." It is as if her partner were holding out for her a vision of spirituality—that God accepts people the way they are created even if they are lesbian or gay—that Nargis desperately wanted. She wanted to believe this, but could not accept it as it did not seem to reconcile with the Islamic tradition as it had been taught to her by family, mosque, and community.

That is when Nargis began to deepen her own faith and search for alternate models of Islamic spirituality. She turned to her own community tradition, of Urdu poetry and devotional songs of love for the Prophet Muhammad, called *na'at sharif*, that derive from the South Asian Sufi tradition. Indian Muslims in South Africa often identify with the Urdu language, with its rich legacy of love poetry and devotional literature, as an essential part of their Islamic identity.[3] "I was still struggling with the whole sexuality thing and the whole Islamic thing as well. So I got involved with the Urdu classes and I got real recognition with that. I don't pray five times a day, so I'm not that Islamic in that way, but my source comes from *na'at sharif*. . . . I've always been involved with Urdu, since I was thirteen years old. But I think the past few years, I think almost when my relationship with her was starting, that is when I was getting involved and got better known for it. . . . That's the one thing that has kept me going around spirituality. *Na'at sharif*, yes, that is what I love the most, and the Urdu language. Once a week I go to *na'at sharif* classes. It's really incredible. Yes, that is where my spirituality lies. I suppose that's what has kept me going." For South Asian Muslims, *na'at* poems are spiritually potent. Men sing them communally after Friday congregational prayers, as a way of saying goodbye to the Prophet who they feel is spiritually present with them in the mosque. Women sing or recite them even more poignantly at home or in special gatherings, for in South Asian communities that follow Hanafi law, women are generally forbidden from attending mosques for prayer.

These songs express longing to draw near to the Prophet who lives far off in Medina. The poems evoke love for the Prophet, as an ephemeral person and as an eternal spiritual illumination. They translate scriptural terms into the language of love; they move phrases of orthodox belief into the realm of personal commitment. *Na'at* poems allow the singer and listener to imagine that they are in the presence of the Prophet, even if his home is far away or he died long ago. They allow one to appeal directly to him through longing and admiration. They might also suggest a means to bypass the routine social leaders who claim to speak in the name of Islam, and to have access to the original source of the religion "face-to-face." Routine language cannot allow this existential leap, but poetry and song can. Nargis boasted that though she is not a good speaker, she is blessed with being a great singer. For her, religious knowledge is in the form of songs, and this gave her great solace in the midst of her self-doubts about her deepening lesbian relationship and the conflict it generated with her family.

Nargis began to see the Urdu school principal—from whom she learns to sing *na'at*— and his wife as substitute Muslim parents. However, they are caught up in the same community ethos of shame and reputation as her father, so Nargis doubts that she could ever "come out" to them and remain a respected performer at the Urdu school. "One fear that I do have is losing that knowledge. . . . In my coming out process, I'm breaking away from them. . . . I'm really close to the principal and his wife and am well known in the whole school, so I feel very respected and that's a nice social interaction. . . . But the community is such that the school would get a bad name once people knew. So [people will ask], 'How can *Ustad* (teacher) allow me to go and do that, and be on stage or to recite?' . . . The school itself will get a bad name. No, I don't fear for myself, but rather it's the reputation of the school that I have to protect."

Intimacy with her lesbian partner drove Nargis to search for new Islamic authorities who might provide her with guidance—for her the possibility of "acceptance" was too much to hope for from her religious tradition, so she expected only concrete guidance. "On the one hand I was getting closer to Islamic stuff and on the other I was getting closer to her [her partner] as well. That's when I started battling. I tried going out with a guy as well, so that I could 'come right.' I kept on thinking, 'Yes it's an addiction and yes it's wrong and I can get over it if I want to.'" She recalls that the first person who found out about her lesbian relationship was her best friend, a Muslim woman her own age who had known her since childhood. "When my best friend found out as well, she came and quoted *Nabi Lut* and Sodom and Gomorra. She quoted the whole thing and I didn't bother to go and read it. She said, 'Look, it's wrong—go and look up this verse from the Qur'an because that will explain why it's wrong.'" But Nargis did not explore the Qur'an herself: she did not feel she had the authority. She thought she already knew what the Qur'an said, through the filter of her immediate environment.

When asked whether people in her family use religion, quoting Qur'an and *hadith*, to argue with her about her sexual orientation, she answered, "My father is quite learned in the Qur'an so he . . . he will know more or less what's there. So he'd say, 'This is wrong and this is not OK and the *shari'a* says this.' So I always thought I must listen to him because he knows best and he knows more. That's why it's difficult to argue with him. And he's a very controlling person!" She never explored the Qur'an herself or the *shari'a* discussion of homosexuality—"[I never did] because I didn't think there was any hope. . . . I was told that I was wrong—because that's what everybody says, that Islamically it's wrong, the forces of nature say it's wrong. So I always went by what they said. I never thought of exploring it on my own."

Although her father is not a religious scholar, he has the authority within the family to act like one. His religious authority is reinforced by their family's *murshid* or spiritual guide in the Sufi tradition. He lives in Pakistan but travels to South Africa regularly to minister to those families who accept his charismatic authority. In Sufi Islam, a *murshid* is an elder with religious authority and special insight. It is believed that he has a spiritual connection to the Prophet Muhammad and to God that others do not have, giving him the ability to interpret Islam in ways that will allow them to overcome spiritual or worldly obstacles. "The belief with us is that if you have a *murshid* you need to follow what they say . . . the *murshid* knows what's best for you. They'll sort of guide you along. . . . If you don't go according to your shaykh's will then you'll feel guilty. . . . It's like going against the Prophet's word, because they are connected to the Prophet." Her *murshid* gave her the opportunity to discuss her feelings of anguish over her sexual orientation. But she avoided this, sensing that he was a patriarchal authority who supported her father's opinions. "He came to me and spoke to me alone, and said to me that when he was on his travels he would see my face very often, and I seemed distressed. . . . I didn't tell him that it was about this whole homosexuality thing and coming out. . . . I was struggling with that, but I couldn't tell him that! . . . How do you tell your *murshid* that you're a lesbian?" Like her father and her *ustad* at the Urdu academy, her *murshid* is also a patriarchal male religious authority.

Nargis perceived that all these authorities were concerned with keeping religious custom and social structures intact, rather than fostering her own personal health, spiritual development, and integral happiness. She is so certain that they will consort to get her married that she has tried to preempt them by "curing" herself. After graduating from university, Nargis was confined to the home and was unable to see her partner. Her father had invited a male family friend to stay with them, and Nargis almost fell into the role of married woman. "I had almost become a housewife, because he [the family friend] was living there with us. I was almost falling into a trap, because my family recognized him as a nice person. So I was doing the cooking and cleaning at that time, and they were happy with me. . . . [When the two of them were alone] he did try to get physical and I just couldn't. . . . He tried to sleep with me . . . he literally came on top of me and it was crappy. Nothing happened. I just pushed him off me. . . . That was a bad experience for me—it just confirmed that I really hate men!" Nargis laughed as she said she hates men, but she had survived a situation of attempted rape within her own house. This experience triggered disturbing memories of having been sexually molested by her brothers and provoked within her an uncontrollable anger.

Nargis decided to see a counselor for anger management, and chose one who was a woman. "I spoke to her and told her the whole story, saying, 'This is who I am and I'm struggling because I'm in a relationship with a female and I don't know what to do.' She said I must go for therapy. . . . I specifically chose a Muslim therapist so that she could make me 'straight' and [help me] to come out right. [I thought that] she's a Muslim and will tell me that it's wrong and I'm going to come right because of her. . . . The opposite happened. She made me find myself and I learned to start accepting myself. And I struggled a lot! I struggled with religious issues. . . . She couldn't help me with that, but she did help me find myself and understand my relationship with my partner and make things better there." The secular-trained therapist could not help Nargis to unravel questions of religious tradition, but did help her gain insight into her own nature and needs, and to act confidently upon them.

With the therapist, Nargis was able to negotiate through a question that plagued her: the question of whether homosexuality is a matter of nature or nurture. Because she had been sexually abused by her brothers, she had always feared that this experience in her younger life had caused her to have lesbian feelings, in compensation for feeling sexual and emotional discomfort when intimate with men. "It's the [question of] nature-versus-nurture. That's why I thought when going to therapy—if I get rid of that and get rid of the past issues—that maybe I'm not a lesbian. But it wasn't like that. I got rid of those issues and worked through those issues, and I still am [a lesbian]!" She worked through the anger she had harbored over the hurt the men in her family had caused her, and discovered that she was still a lesbian. At the end of this painful struggle, Nargis felt that the issue was resolved. Even though she had never felt like a lesbian as a child or teenager, she was convinced that being a lesbian was deeply part of her nature. "That's how the coming out process started. . . . I've started telling people and started going to The Triangle Project [a gay and lesbian rights organization], reading books, and coming to The Inner Circle. Just the first few months . . . it's very rare . . . it's like I've just started opening up." She has begun to realize that being a lesbian can be the cause of joyful experiences and not simply the result of pain.

This inner conviction, won through great internal struggle and deep introspection, helped Nargis to survive even more pain at the hands of male Muslim authorities. Although she herself turned to a secular-trained professional who was a Muslim woman to guide her through mental and emotional health issues, her family turned to other authorities. They were close to many *mawlanas*, male Muslim religious authorities who combine scholarly knowledge with "spiritual medicine," often to counter "black magic." Her family was convinced that Nargis was not in her right mind, and blamed her lesbian partner for placing a spell upon her. "I went through all this shit with my family. It's because that's what they believe in, they believe in the *mawlanas*. . . . My mother used to get up in the morning after *fajr* (dawn prayer) and come and scream at me and hit me, telling me I must get up now and make *ghusl* (ritual bath). . . . They just thought I was possessed . . . by a spell from . . . my partner. . . . [Various *mawlanas*] came and would give me holy water and tell me to drink it at this time of day . . . until I just said, 'Enough!'" *Mawlanas* or religious experts were treating her for sorcery or spirit possession with "cures" that bordered on magic. But this treatment did not work, and only served to intensify Nargis's frustration with her family.

Amid these trials, Nargis found a Muslim spiritual healer who nudged her toward self-acceptance as had her secular-trained therapist. "There was only one [who was different]. . . . He was always affiliated with my family, and used to come and take us to *karamats* (tombs of holy people) and do *dhikr* (invoking God in meditation). Then he came to me and spoke to me, and I told him my whole story. . . . The nice thing about him is that he could understand why it happened. . . . He said he could see that I wasn't wrong. . . . I was sort of sexually abused by my brothers, both of them. . . . He asked what happened in my past, about my brothers. So I told him, and he said, 'Oh, have your brothers fucked up your life!' He was the first person who looked at it from my perspective!" This local Muslim holy man suggested to Nargis that she get a sex-change operation and become a man because she desired sex with a woman. Nargis declined because she was comfortable being a woman—her discomfort stemmed from sexual orientation, not from her gender identity. "He came back and said to my family that there is nothing wrong with me, because my family still felt there was something wrong with me. My brothers said, 'Then can I have my sister back?' And he said to them, 'But your sister was always here!' . . . That felt so nice, because he didn't do anything to change me. He was the one learned person who said it's OK [to be] who I am." This Sufi spiritual healer showed her that a pious Muslim could accept her humanity as a lesbian, even if he did not reconcile it formally with the religious tradition.

Along with her female therapist, this Muslim holy man gave her the courage to confront her father once again, by her own choice and on her own terms. Partly this was due to increasing pressure on her to marry, since she had finished her university education and was working at a clinic. But partly it was due to her internal courage and conviction that being a lesbian is an integral part of her personality, not something that she can hide or change. "My family is always pushing me to get married. . . . I obviously said, 'No I don't want to.' Then one night I was thinking, 'Must I do this or mustn't I?'—I was fighting a lot with myself. Then I went to him [my father] and I was literally shaking as I sat there on the chair, and I first told him, 'Look, I want to talk with you and whatever I tell you is regarding my future and that my future is going to be a bit different and that I'm never going to get married.' He asked why, and I asked him, 'Do you know what it means to be gay?' He said yes, he knows that men are gay, but not females. [I told him], 'Well, that is what I am [a female who is homosexual, just as a male can be homosexual]!' That's when I told him, and he was a bit confused. I didn't tell him that I was in a relationship, because he immediately said that I should not be in a [sexual] relationship. He said that I could live without a partner, because females can." Her father was clearly moved by Nargis's voluntary approach to him in order to "come out" once again, because he reacted to it quite differently this time. He thought about what it meant to be a lesbian, rather than thinking of how to silence any discussion of it or change his daughter by force. He could think about her sexual orientation but commanded her to avoid any sexual acts with another woman. "In his eyes, a female doesn't need any sort of sexual pleasure at all. They can live without it. Men might need to be in a relationship but not females. . . . It's a sort of acceptance, in that he's accepted me being a homosexual but not in terms of me being in a relationship." Her father searched through his religious tradition for examples through whom to understand his daughter. He came up with the paragon of Sufi women, Rabi'a of Basra, who refused to marry out of devoted love for God. While there is no evidence that Rabi'a was a lesbian, she was certainly not a typical woman, for she refused to live by patriarchal interpretations of Islam.[4] What she has in common with lesbian women is her refusal to marry a man and be defined socially by her relationship to a husband. Before he could begin to grapple with what it meant for Nargis to be a lesbian, he had to grapple with how she could be an independent Muslim woman.

Indeed, Nargis was becoming independent. She has acknowledged the debilitating pain that her family has put her through, knowing that such an acknowledgment is the first step to moving outside their circle of control. "There was a point when I was in a little bit of depression. . . . I did feel like I needed to kill myself at one stage, because I didn't know what to do, feeling stuck here. . . . Since then, I have been just moving forward. No steps back any more, just moving forward from now on." Moving forward, for Nargis, means taking greater responsibility for herself and better care of others, while facing the possibility of leaving her family and possibly being ostracized by her community. She needs to take better care of her partner, who has supported her through so many trials and is still with her after eight years. At the time of our interview, Nargis was contemplating moving out of her family house and living with her lesbian partner. "I'm going to need to tell [my father] that I'm with my partner and I want to move out. . . . That is my next step. I want to do it soon." Nargis began to tell people at her workplace that she has a lesbian partner, and the response has been supportive. "I feel sort of conflicted in that I want to come out and tell everyone and be open and start The Inner Circle movement and help other people in the process and become open." Despite the fear of losing family and community connections and even of facing violence, Nargis was determined to take on a bigger role in The Inner Circle support group, which to her was like a "found family" that offered her the love, connection, and support that was often lacking in her own biological family.

When I last spoke to her, she expressed the desire to organize a weekly study circle of Qur'an and *hadith* in Cape Town, as The Inner Circle already does in Johannesburg. Such study a circle, called *halaqa*, allows lay Muslims to read scripture together and engage in their own *ijtihad* or struggle to apply its meaning to their distinct living circumstances.[5] Such study circles by activist lay people are crucial for gay, lesbian, and transgender Muslims (as they were for Muslims suffering racial discrimination under apartheid or female Muslims marginalized by patriarchy). Nargis, in her humble way, aimed to encourage this by leading Qur'an study groups for The Inner Circle. Yet she feared for her family's reputation and reaction. "On the other hand, I don't want to come out that much, I just want to tell my father and one or two other people in the community. . . . I'd rather just keep it closeted rather than open because the Muslim community can be quite aggressive and violent. . . . I haven't [experienced violence] except from my family. Aggressive in the sense that they would actually speak up and . . . maybe [resort to] violence as well." Nargis can imagine that her Muslim community might shame her extended family, or name her specifically in sermons as an apostate, leading to stones being thrown at her or her family's house. She even fears that community members might "burn down a person's house."

For Nargis, her family remains her greatest concern and also her greatest obstacle. The mode of activism most appropriate for her is challenging her family and through them the wider community. The Islamic tradition offers her some resources in this struggle, but the tradition itself is not her primary object of concern. Nargis struggled hard against family restrictions and community norms; she compromised greatly for survival despite growing independence from her family. Her story is mirrored in the experience of Tayyaba, a Muslim lesbian in the United Kingdom. Both are women from South Asian Muslim families, which lends their stories a profound commonality despite their very different national contexts in South Africa and the United Kingdom.

Tayyaba: Continually Coming Out

Tayyaba has always felt herself to be a lesbian and a strong Muslim, but the road to reconciling these two identities was not easy. She spent four years in a women's shelter while trying to earn enough to live independently from her parents' demands. Tayyaba's faith in Islam has been a big part of the solution though it was also part of the problem. In her late twenties at the time of this interview, she was living apart from her family, attending university to earn a medical degree, and loving a Muslim lesbian partner with whom she is in a long-term relationship that she considers a marriage (though it is not legally registered as such).

Tayyaba lives in her own apartment after a long struggle with her family. But she lives near her family's neighborhood; though she has forcefully asserted her independence from them, she sees them several times each week and talks with them daily. While she values this contact, she feels that it limits her potential to interpret and practice Islam in a way that is healthy for her as a lesbian in a committed same-sex partnership.

Tayyaba is the youngest of four siblings born to first-generation Punjabi immigrants to the United Kingdom. She admires her mother and father who made sacrifices to become educated. Their sacrifices paid off, and both her mother and father are professionals and served as her role models of a gender-equal marriage as they shared the burdens of work outside the home. But Tayyaba's generation faces new challenges that her parents did not. There are new opportunities but also new pitfalls. "We feel very British but also have a new sense of feeling proud of our roots—proud to be Asian. It is acceptable now to feel that way. . . . We are getting told that the only way to integrate is to [assimilate]—you know, 'Do as the Romans do.' We have these very British feelings of questioning who we are and what we are doing.

Then we have our parents' generation which is not about questioning, but rather about blind faith."[6]

As people in her parents' generation struggled for education and basic jobs, their "blind faith" in Islam supported them in this effort. Tayyaba sees her older siblings as having a different struggle—one against increasing white racism which colored their attachment to Islam. Tayyaba perceives a huge difference between her experience compared to her two older siblings. "We are talking now about going back and questioning Islam or the Qur'an and reading about it [from original sources]. But we [British Muslims] have had so many other things to worry about—I mean baseline struggles! When I look back at my older brother and sister and what they experienced, I just can't believe it; they talk about the Ku Klux Klan, about a society in which if they lived in Asian areas they were totally ghettoized but if they wanted to get ahead they were forced to totally sell out their own character and religion. They had to give up their own culture and religion . . . or they had to decide to stick to their religion and culture and say, 'We won't become professionals.' The choices were very limited." When Tayyaba describes her siblings confronting the Ku Klux Klan, she means white-supremist and anti-immigrant organizations like the British National Front that grew in strength during the Thatcher years. The National Front is a political party, but has vigilante gangs and militant groups who adopt it as a cover for violent intimidation of racial minorities; its ideology and actions are similar to the Ku Klux Klan in the United States.

Tayyaba thinks of her immediate family as "devout-but-modern," while her extended family is "largely uneducated." She feels that her extended family restrains her own parents from accepting her as a lesbian. "My family has always been strongly religious, though modern in a lot of ways. In terms of gender and female independence, my family is very modern. But in terms of religion, they are very traditional." She mainly learned about Islam from home, as her family insisted on going to London's Central Mosque even though it was far from their neighborhood and they refused to attend local mosques: this is because the Central Mosque always has a place for women to attend prayer, in contrast with many South Asian community mosques whose patriarchal custom refuses women entry entirely.

Her family performed a cultural balancing act: they lived in a mainly white neighborhood and their children attended private school, because her parents rejected living in a ghettoized Pakistani community. Yet they also valued Islam and wanted their children to grow up in a setting that taught Islamic virtues. "They wanted us to be part of a community that held our moral and religious values seriously, and in that sense we would go every week to see family and friends who would read *namaz* (ritual prayer), and in that sense we learned [about Islam] from them. But at the same time, they didn't want us to be left behind in any way, so we lived in a different [mainly white] area and went to school in a different area." While her parents emphasized secular education to secure professional careers, they supplemented it with religious instruction. Two or three days a week after school Tayyaba attended Qur'an recitation classes until the age of ten. After that she learned about Islam mainly from family and friends.

Tayyaba looks upon both her parents with affection and asserts that her family life was both very Islamic and also very gender egalitarian. "I think my mom . . . tended to favor the guys but my father was very feminist. It balanced out. My dad would say, 'Let the women speak, let the girls talk, don't put them down or tell them to be quiet. They need to be independent.' My dad always said that it was important for us to get married, but still he's encouraged us to be independent and professional and educated so that we were never controlled by someone else's money." Her parents encouraged her to be self-reliant within accepted norms of gender and sexuality, but resisted those norms being questioned.

Tayyaba first came out to her mother at age fifteen. Over ten years later, she insists, "I feel that I've been constantly coming out. . . . I've suffered somewhat from depression, from going through the highs and lows of coming out." For Tayyaba, coming out was not a singular event but a long-drawn-out process. The initial discussion was sparked by Tayyaba falling in love with a girl at school. "I had to tell [my mother] that I liked someone and it was going out of control. My mom said, 'Well, what do you want me to do about it? Do you want me to send you to gay groups? I'm not going to promote your gayism!' Since then, it has been a series of problems [such as her] not believing me, not appreciating it." Her mother and elder brother knew about her being lesbian, but urged Tayyaba not to speak about it with her father. Her family did not restrict her freedom dramatically after this initial disclosure. "I didn't feel that I wanted to abuse the freedoms that I had been given. So until I was eighteen, I was living at home. I thought, 'I'll deal with this later, and concentrate on my education.'" In reaction to her parents' will-not-to-know, she stayed quiet until she left home for university at age eighteen.

At university, Tayyaba befriended other lesbian women and attended support groups. As she began to assert her identity, there was a severe backlash. The hardest moment was when Tayyaba was twenty and had just started a serious relationship with a woman. "My brother and mother found out about it, and called me up in the middle of the night telling me my father had had a heart attack." Tayyaba rushed home to help, only to find that "it was just a ploy to get me to come back home. Then my family became very restrictive: they took away my credit card, my keys, my wallet and money, and started chaperoning me to university classes and back. That was really difficult for me." Several months of such family control put great strain on Tayyaba and her relationship broke up under the pressure.

At this time, her family coerced her to go with them to Saudi Arabia, for 'umra, a ritual visit to the Ka'ba. She saw this as an excuse for them to interrupt her studies and her potential autonomy. She managed to come back from Saudi Arabia a week before her family, arranged for a place to stay, and announced that she was moving out. "I told them, 'Look, I'm not going to pursue this sexuality thing, I'm just going to study and I need space to concentrate, so I'm getting out of here.'" This semi-independence worked for a year, as Tayyaba concentrated on her studies as the only way to achieve economic and emotional autonomy from her family.

But her mother used Tayyaba's dedication to her studies against her. "When I was facing my post-second exam, my parents—my mother and my older brother who really acted as a parent—said, 'Don't work over summer—we'll pay for you and pay your rent even though you're living away from home, just focus on your studies and stop working.' So I foolishly thought, fine. I didn't take up a job." Soon after she became financially reliant upon her family, they threatened to stop sending her the promised money because, they claimed, she was going out to "gay places." Wracked with anxiety about paying her rent, Tayyaba was unable to study properly for her upcoming exams. "It was a total meltdown. At that point I knew that something drastic had to happen for me to get through to my family." The drastic move was for Tayyaba to completely cut off her ties with her family.

She went to live in a shelter for youth having conflicts with parents. Tayyaba did not inform her mother where she was staying. Their only contact was by telephone: she told her mother, "This is the way I am and if you can't understand that then we just can't move on further— if you don't want me in your life, then just tell me so, but now is the time to tell me that." Tayyaba was fortunate that her lesbian partner was street-smart, for she had also been forced out of her family home. Her partner became her support, both emotionally and logistically, in this time of grave crisis. "She is about five or six years older than me. Her family was a lot more backward in many ways—not educated and there were basic liberties that she did not have, like being able to wear jeans or cut her hair. For her, half of her rebellion was about basic liberties." For Tayyaba, the struggle was quite different. She did not lack educational support or liberties as a woman; her struggle with her family was only about sexual orientation and her identity as a lesbian.

Tayyaba lived in the shelter for six months while negotiating with her mother. "We just talked on the phone, and I was against letting them even meet me 'until you get to that level where you realize what I'm saying and take it on board'—and you have to realize this was a full five or six years after I first talked about it with them." Tayyaba recalls that she must have sounded very harsh with her mother, but inside she was intensely hurt and could show no outer weakness. Emotionally, she was prepared for a total break. Tayyaba asserts that deep down she had been preparing for her family to totally reject her since she was sixteen, and that point seemed to have arrived.

When there seemed to be no other way forward, Tayyaba agreed to meet her mother face to face at a café. "I said to her, 'Look, Mom, this is just who I am and how I am, and if you can't accept it as a Muslim, I understand that. But can you accept me as a mother? Do you even want me to be in your life?' She said yes and just broke down crying, and that was the hugest relief I've ever had." The relief was that Tayyaba could live independently while still being in contact with her family, but this solution brought only détente and not reconciliation. Six years later, her mother still cannot accept Tayyaba as a lesbian daughter. "My mom, when you get to the core of the issue, thinks my being gay is a rejection of or a rebellion against my religion. I think that is at the core of her being. She believes that. So when she sees me being religious, then she thinks that I'm returning to my religion and moving away from being gay. If I then bring up a challenge to certain beliefs that people hold, she just closes up. She just sees that as a kind of attack."

While she cannot have a discussion with her family about reconciling Islam and her sexuality, Tayyaba has turned to other resources. She read more about progressive interpretations of Islam and discussed them with others at the support group, Imaan. These new possibilities manifested for her in coming out to her father, a decision against which her mother and older brother had counseled her for many years. While her mother was always very involved with the daily details of her life, her father was more distant—so much so that her elder brother had stepped in to play the role of controlling male in her relationship with her family. While Tayyaba recalls always having felt distant from her father, in the last few years she had found him observing her tension with the family and reacting with concerned questions. Yet her family conversations were crippled by her mother and brother's reaction to her being lesbian while her father remained ignorant of the situation. "I was having these conversations and I got annoyed in the middle of it, thinking, 'I'm hiding half the conversation just because my dad is sitting with us.' So I turned around and I just said, 'Dad, do you know what? I'm gay. Do you understand what I'm talking about? I'm gay—I like women.' He said, 'What? I'm horrified, that's terrible!' He was very calm about it, and simply launched into the reasons why he thought it was unacceptable: the Qur'an says this, and Islam says this, and that is why I think it is not acceptable. Then he said, 'This is going to ruin the family honor.' Then I felt able to say to him something I had never felt able to say to my mom. 'Actually, Dad, you said that the Qur'an says this. I believe that on some level it does condemn homosexuality, but people have interpreted it in other ways.' I actually sat there and had a rational discussion with my father. That was the point [that amazed me], that he didn't overreact. I found him to be very calm and cool." The results of such conversations were not totally positive: her father doesn't accept her being lesbian and still thinks that she will eventually marry a man, somehow. After a long conversation about religion with no resolution, they have stopped talking about it. However, her father's rational reaction contrasted greatly with her mother's reaction that was an emotional outburst characterized by tears and condemnation.

Her father's reaction made Tayyaba feel that perhaps rational and deliberate discussion about alternative interpretations of religion is possible—if not with her actual family, then with her peer group and educated members of the Muslim community. Tayyaba joined the support group Imaan while searching for ways to reconnect with Islam. While growing up, her activism was more focused on issues of race and gender through groups that did not focus on religion.[7] Support groups for women from South Asian and Middle Eastern backgrounds played a crucial role in Tayyaba's life, as she "came out" as a young woman from a Pakistani and Muslim family. However, social support groups focused more on ethnicity than on religion, which Tayyaba found left important questions unasked. For many years, Tayyaba knew about Imaan but resisted reaching out to join the group. She felt that Islam, at some general level, condemned homosexuality and that the Qur'an in particular forbade it. She accepted this belief, inculcated in her by family, community, and tradition and did not want to hear it challenged, even as she explored her lesbian identity in a social support group for women from South Asian or Middle Eastern ethnic communities.

However, at a certain point in her own growth, she felt strong enough to confront tough questions about Islam. Once she began to attend Imaan meetings, she realized that this group was not as prescriptive in religious topics as she had previously assumed it to be. "Now having been to Imaan, what I appreciate is that . . . they effectively presented another side of the story, an alternative viewpoint, but it was not conclusive and was not saying, 'Actually it is like this.' Rather, they said, 'Actually, there is another way of looking at things.'" Tayyaba was eager to see possibilities in interpretation and explore alternatives, but as a very independent-minded and devout Muslim, she did not want to be told by others what she must believe.

It took her a long time to find a flexible approach to questioning her family and community's interpretation of Islam. She felt strongly that she wanted to stay close to the Qur'an, yet also saw that many Muslim interpreters went far beyond the Qur'an in condemning homosexuality by relying on *hadith*, juridical opinions, and popular preaching. When reflecting on why she initially resisted attending Imaan meetings, Tayyaba admits that in her youth, "I thought that the Qur'an expressly forbids homosexual acts." But now, after extensive reading and discussion, she gives a more nuanced interpretation. "What I had come to accept for myself is that there is this story [of the Prophet Lot] and I felt that the rest of it was out of all proportion. When people say that [homosexual acts] is why the towns—Sodom and Gomorrah— were destroyed, and kept adding to the story, that is where I drew the line. . . . If you talk about Qur'anic interpretations of homosexuality, there must be a separation between the words and people's interpretation of them. If somebody says to me, 'There is a clear sentence in the Qur'an that says men should not practice lusts on men,' I would answer, 'Yes, there is,' and then I would ask about its context. But I find that the problem lies in the extrapolation that people make from that—that all homosexual people are condemned to hell, that whole cities were destroyed because of just that. . . . That is where Islam becomes dangerous, when people don't read for themselves." Tayyaba began reading for herself, but that is not easy. Tayyaba finds that her social position— her relationship to parents, brothers, and sisters, and to her financial dependence—influences how she reads the Qur'an. When she tries to discuss sexuality and Islam, she finds that there is "so much disapproval of people having said, 'No, you can't be like this [lesbian or gay].' We read behind such statements so much disapproval and then we connect that to the Qur'an and to *namaz* (prayer) and we get put off. I often think to myself, 'If I could have a year away from my family where I didn't speak with them, then I would be so much more in touch with myself and my religion and my sexuality, much more than I am now.'"

Tayyaba's newly forming self-confidence is still in tension with her sense of responsibility toward her parents, despite all the conflicts that she has endured with them. She argued with them that she can be both a lesbian and a Muslim woman but still refrains from being open in her parents' own community. "I've done radio and TV interviews, and now I'm out to my family but not to my extended family and their social circle, out of respect for [my parents]. . . . That was not my own decision." She used to feel that her family was the source of her religious identity, but now sees them as an obstacle to her faithful practice of Islam. Muslim friends, both straight and gay, have become her more immediate reference point for discussing Islam and its ritual practice, not only in reference to sexual orientation and gender identity but also to a whole array of issues affecting her generation. She has even found the self-confidence to marry her partner in a private Islamic ceremony in which they took vows to each other over the Qur'an.

Conclusion

As we imagine Tayyaba taking a vow of fidelity with her lesbian partner, the importance of family and community gains new clarity. Her parents were not present to consecrate the vows, but Tayyaba held her hand over the Qur'an as a sign of her pure intention and reaffirmation of her loyalty to the Islamic tradition that she inherited from her parents. For her, Islamic loyalty is not merely about belief and theology; it is also about loving and respecting her parents, family, and ancestors. Even if family members were not present at her same sex-gender wedding ceremony, Tayyaba affirmed their importance to her by using Islamic symbols and rituals. For many transgender, gay, and lesbian Muslims, Islam is more important as a symbol of family cohesion and care than as a religious tradition defined by rituals, texts, or legal customs.

Because of the importance of family for most Muslims, lesbian, gay, and transgender Muslims experience debilitating anxiety due to conflict with their closest family members. Often, the most immediate and intense challenge is to cope with parents, siblings, and extended family who misunderstand or try to suppress their sexuality and gender identity. The interviews with two lesbian Muslim activists in this chapter reveals something important about this conflict. Many lesbian, gay, and transgender Muslims do not simply reject their parents' expectations and their siblings' pressure to conform. They challenge rather than reject their families. They also create new models of family and community as they grow in strength and confidence. Tayyaba's commitment ceremony indicates the space—personal, emotional, and spiritual—that she is carving out for herself independently of her family, but it also shows her deep urge to create new affective ties and invite her family to respect her love and commitment with a same-sex partner.

The interviews in this chapter offer two narratives of struggle with family and community. Tayyaba was thrown out of her family home, but set herself up independently from yet near to them. Nargis struggled against many of the same pressures, but she endured from within the family home while seeking resources through university education. These interviews highlight the bonds of love and affection that members of sexuality and gender minorities within Muslim families feel, and continue to feel, even if they suffer emotional distress or physical violence from family members.

The strategies employed by Tayyaba and Nargis to cope with family can be understood as a mode of activism. It is activism that emerges from within the home and manifests itself in intimate relationships between child and parents or sisters and brothers, before extending outward into the wider Islamic community. "Challenging family and community" is a mode of activism for lesbian, transgender, and gay Muslims that is often hidden from the public. It gets revealed only when people are asked to share their intimate stories and personal histories, as the interviews in this book have asked people to do.

These interviews reveal that for most Muslims religious tradition is inseparable from family relationships. Most experience Islam as the family and understand family as Islam. For most Muslims, then, religious values reinforce the power of the patriarchal family to dictate how its members must behave. For many, the struggle to find a modest degree of independence from the family is the first priority. It is a crucial prerequisite for survival in a struggle that has many layers—from parents to siblings to extended relatives to the wider community. Only later, after some creative distance from family expectations has been achieved, can transgender, lesbian, and gay Muslims rethink their religion beyond the pressure of family to conform.

Yet even when gay, lesbian, and transgender Muslims achieve some independence from family, they still need community. The interviews above show that they often build new communities of friends and colleagues who offer them understanding and support that may be hard to find within the family. A "found community" may come in the form of friends at school or university, or from younger (or more open-minded) members of one's religion, or from a lover's circle of support. Or it could come from belonging to a support group for gay, transgender, and lesbian Muslims like those discussed in these interviews. One of the main purposes of support groups is to provide an alternative community for those who may be estranged from their families.

In yet another variation, young Muslims who feel confused and con-flicted might find valuable community in joining an Islamist move-ment that offers ideological purpose. Tayyaba discussed Islamist move-ments among her university peers and observed that joining them is an increasingly attractive option for Muslim youth growing up in the West. In the same U.K. environment, Tamsila—whose interview was presented in chapter 1—also noted with alarm how some Muslim youth are attracted to Islamist movements because they offer an alternative community when family attachment proves unfulfilling. This option appeals to some young Muslims as they question the authority of family and community into which they were born. Some transgender, lesbian, and gay youth from Muslim families are also drawn to Islamist move-ments, and as they recover from this and derive lessons from it, they express another mode of activism, adapting religious politics, to which we now turn.

3

Adapting Religious Politics

Judge not before you judge yourself
Judge not if you're not ready for judgment
The road of life is rocky and you may stumble too
So while you talk about me someone else is judging you
~Bob Marley, Judge *Not*

All people yearn not to be judged by their appearance. All religions warn against judging others by what one perceives on the surface. The Prophet Muhammad is reported to have taught, "God does not look at your bodies or at your forms, but looks at your hearts and your works."[1] We know intuitively that outward appearance is not the same as inward identity: outward appearance does not determine one's capacities or value in life. This psychological and spiritual reality is almost universally acknowledged when we regard skin color, height and weight, facial features, or bodily disability. But it is often ignored when we consider gender and sexuality.

Judging others is not just an individual problem; it is also a political problem. Groups that organize around religious politics—such as fundamentalist movements—gain persuasive power from judging others through their ideology. Islamist movements are powerful in contemporary Muslim communities because they condemn the ambiguities inherent in modern society and assert clear boundaries of right and wrong, belonging and exclusion, salvation and damnation. These boundaries are maintained by strict codes of dress, behavior, ritual, and solidarity.

Some lesbian, gay, and transgender Muslims get involved in religious politics. Such involvement can be a formative experience. This chapter will focus on interviews with transgender, lesbian, and gay Muslims who are involved in a mode of activism that we can call "adapting religious politics." These activists were at one time involved with religious politics, often with Islamist organizations. The sense of belonging and ideological acuteness that Islamic movements offered is important to their growth. But as they confront the reality of gender identity and sexual orientation in their personal lives, the sense of belonging offered by religious politics becomes hard to sustain. Many of them come to fear exclusion from the group whose solidarity they valued so highly. Such experiences can lead activists to join support groups for gay, lesbian, and transgender Muslims; when they do, they bring a heightened awareness of piety and ideology to these groups. Their participation in two radically different kinds of movements may be surprising to some liberal readers in the West who assume that there is an absolute dichotomy between fundamentalists and the gay rights movement.

The song cited above, "Judge Not," is by the Reggae singer Bob Marley, who is the favorite songwriter of Fatima, a transgender Muslim who lives in London and participates in the support group Imaan. Her interview, featured in this chapter, shows how involvement in a fundamentalist group strengthened her faith in times of need and heightened her sense of purpose in life. But Muslims in this movement threatened to judge her harshly on matters related to sexuality and gender ambiguity. The song advises, "Judge not if you're not ready for judgment . . . 'cause while you're talking about me, someone else is judging you." But all too often, people involved in groups—especially those active in religious politics—are seduced by group solidarity into judging others and forgetting that God alone can judge. For Muslims, the watchful judgment of God can restrain one from acting rashly and can hold one to a norm of ethical conduct. It can also free one from being overly concerned with the shallow judgment of others, because one is deeply aware that only God judges one's soul. Examples taken from the United Kingdom and the United States in this chapter show how Muslim activists grapple with these alternatives.

Fatima: God Is the Judge

Fatima was raised as a woman but has always felt that he is a man. For this reason, this interview refers to Fatima as "he." At the time of his interview, Fatima was thirty years old and worked as a nursery school teacher in London. Fatima is a deeply religious and committed Muslim, who participated in Islamist movements. Fatima joined the support group Imaan to sensitize members to issues of transgender people. Joining Imaan was part of the struggle to confront social stigma and reconcile inner experience with the faith that Fatima feels so intently. After the interview, Fatima began medical therapy to alter his sex, for since childhood he had experienced himself psychically as a male living in the "wrong body" of a female. Fatima offers his story as a highly devout female-to-male (FTM) transgender person who took gradual steps toward becoming a fully transsexual male.

Fatima was born into an Arab family with an Algerian mother, a Moroccan father, and a childhood spent in boarding schools in Europe. The story is complex, as Fatima confronted three existential questions while growing up: am I an Arab or not? Am I a Muslim or not? Am I a female or not? To most people the answers to these questions seem obvious, for ethnicity, faith, and gender are ascribed from birth and never questioned. However, in Fatima's path to adulthood, the answers to these three questions did not come easily. Fatima does not see the self as something given and unquestioned; rather, it is something that each person builds, slowly and painfully, with care and attention to how one treats others under the watchful eye of God. "For me, Allah is merciful, loving, and caring. That is what I want Islam to be, and that is the kind of person I want to be—to be understanding."[2] In the process of becoming an understanding person, Fatima had to question the basic assumptions imposed by family, patriarchy, and religion. "I had to start from the bottom and build myself up. So religion is something that I am just beginning to look at, from [the perspective of] just me—from a different perspective, from who I am, from the person I am building."

Looking at things differently means that Fatima has taken decisions to become male in body, after having struggled for decades with ambiguities of gender identity.

Before Fatima could wrestle with the deepest issue—gender identity—there were the more immediate issues of ethnicity and religion. Fatima had always felt "different" and was treated as unique in his family. Fatima's mother divorced her husband when Fatima was an infant and moved with her child to Italy. When Fatima was ten, Fatima's mother remarried her ex-husband (Fatima's father) and took Fatima to Morocco. "It was a big shock to me. I had had my mother for myself before then. Suddenly I have five brothers and a father and a very big family and a very different culture, which I hated at that time! I hated it mostly because I felt that I had lost my mother." Though Fatima's first language is Arabic, Fatima felt completely out of place in this Moroccan family. Growing up, Fatima was always seen as a "tomboy" and an outsider who had grown up in Europe.

The family arranged for Fatima to stay with an aunt in London. Fatima enrolled in a boarding school for foreigners in the United Kingdom and the freedom of boarding school gave Fatima space to cultivate better self-understanding. "I have to say those were the best days of my life. . . . There was nobody to tell me how I should behave." Fatima could dress and act in more boyish ways there without family pressure. "From a very young age, I felt that I was in the wrong body. It is very simple—simple to say and simple to understand but very difficult to explain to anybody, except if one is in the same [condition]. . . . Basically, I say my soul does not match my body. Others might say their brain doesn't fit their body. But for me, I feel it is my soul. . . . I was very frightened of actually going to anybody and saying how I feel that I'm in the wrong body. . . . I was always put down for being boyish, for being a tomboy, at school, in my family, everywhere. . . . They will try to change my dress and style. They will put me in dresses and make me grow my hair. That was, for me, punishment and torture." Boarding school gave Fatima a respite from the family pressure to conform to girlish dress and behavior.

This feeling of gender dysphoria expressed itself in terms of sexuality. At boarding school, Fatima pursued romantic partnerships with female friends. "I found when I was very young that girls were very attracted to me. I found it very easy to love them back." These youthful romances appear to be "lesbian" because they occurred between two women, but Fatima did not experience them this way. Fatima felt like a male who was attracted in conventional heterosexual ways to females. Fatima felt a male psyche dwelling in a female body. Fatima recalls relationships with girls as not just friendship but "more of romance—there was kissing and some body contact. But I was never comfortable with my body, so I never took things further with girls. I know that I would fall madly in love and I would do anything for that person at that time. But when I had to face it, when that person reacted back to me, I would think to myself, 'But I can't—I'm in the wrong body.' I would be very sad and I would think, 'Why is this happening? . . . So I would just break that friendship, that relationship, even though I loved that person. . . . Even when I was in France and in Morocco, there were always girls. . . . But I would break that relationship, definitely. I would never talk to anybody about it—I just couldn't. I was too frightened." When Fatima turned sixteen and sexual play could actually evolve into a romantic relationship, the crisis deepened. "I remember clearly the headmistress would call me handsome and never call me beautiful, because of the way I would dress. I remember once she said, 'Oh, you look really handsome today!' But that frightened me. That was a recognition, and that was very frightening and I didn't know what to do."

As Fatima joined college, Islam played a greater role. "I felt that I had something in me but I suppressed it. And as I was getting older, I had to suppress it even more. This is why, when I became nineteen, I turned to religion." Fatima decided to become a "practicing Muslim" to escape the overwhelming bewilderment of this situation. Practicing Islam in a rigidly ideological way would give life structure, purpose, and meaning. Turning to religion suppressed the issue of gender identity while providing a tight community, for Fatima joined a student organization run by the *Ikhwan al-Muslimun* or Muslim Brotherhood, one of the largest international Islamist movements.

In college Fatima was trained in childhood education. "My aunt believed that I could do excellent work with kids . . . so she decided I should do a course on nursery [care for preschool children]. . . . I was hoping to be more into sports, something more physical. But that was not encouraged and I didn't feel that I had a choice." The family imposed gender roles upon Fatima, but being in the wrong place actually had its advantages. The college course on childhood education was almost entirely filled with women—romance was possible and homosexuality was openly accepted. "A lot of people here [in London] are more aware of lesbians and gays which I was not. . . . Maybe now, as I'm older, I can think about it and maybe those people who had fallen in love with me were actually lesbians and that is why it was easy for them to [love me]. . . . That is when I decided I would turn to religion. Because I just could not face it. I could not accept it. I didn't know how to say, 'I am in the wrong body.'" Faced with a social environment in which denial was not necessary, Fatima changed direction entirely.

Fatima went for a walk one day and ended up in London's conservative Central Mosque at Regent's Park. She arrived during the celebration of the Prophet's birthday—the *mawlid sharif*. "I went in and there was a lady with her daughter. . . . I told her, 'I am a Muslim—I'm an Arab— but I've never been to a mosque. I don't know what to do. I don't know why I'm here, actually!' . . . I didn't know about prayer. I didn't know anything about anything. So I asked, 'Could you show me?' . . . She took me in, told me about the religion, taught me about the Prophet, about Allah, about the pillars [of the faith], about how it makes one a better person, how you learn a new way of life." Fatima hoped that religion would cure her gender dysphoria. Neotraditionalists at conservative mosques like Regent's Park present Islam as a complete code of life that removes the burden of choice from the practitioner.

For Fatima, this new code promised to remove the existential angst she felt. By informing her how to behave in every facet of life, Islam was a powerful distraction. "[I told myself,] 'Now, I don't have to think about it any more. I don't have to solve it [the gender identity issue]. Now, the Qur'an and the *sunna* will do it for me. There must be a code of life for me that will explain and solve my problem!' . . . From their discussions, I learned that Islam could change you as a person. So I said, 'Well, if I become practicing and prayed and fasted and was a good Muslim, not only would I gain paradise but I will actually better myself. I could change myself. This could be the solution to my problem!'" Fatima embraced Islam for inner strength and guidance and found that in abundance. Fatima wanted clear rules to follow and a sense of deeper purpose in following them. Fatima wanted moral self-improvement and had a firm commitment to spiritual progress. She joined the women at the mosque, a circle of ideologically committed Muslims who were dedicated to higher education, modern professions, and fundamentalist ideals about Islam. "She [the Muslim lady at the mosque] took me under her wing. I would go to attend study circles with her. We would pray together. I found it fascinating—this is how you behave with your mother, this is how you behave with your father, this is how you are to your neighbors. It was all new. I found it easy—[I said to myself,] 'If I carry on this way, I will go to paradise! I want to go to paradise—I don't want to go to hell!' I wanted to understand more, [but] obviously I couldn't find my problem being mentioned at all."

The community Fatima fell in with gave her guidance and rules to follow. "They were looking at me as a Muslim woman, so I had to follow the Muslim woman's way and code of life, because that is what everybody believes I am. . . . I actually decided—because I knew how weak I was and how in need I was of a code of life to make my life simpler—to wear the scarf and keep it on from that day forward." Fatima adopted Islam to stop thinking about the self. Fatima became more religious and wore a *hijab*, but the aunt Fatima lived with opposed this new religiosity, fearing that it was fundamentalist and cultish. As Fatima encountered resistance from her family, her new mentor intervened. "She said, 'Come and live with me and we'll sort you out.' . . . I went and stayed with her. That meant study circles and waking up for *fajr* [dawn prayer]. It was a different way of life. I was happy. I didn't have the time to think about me any more. . . . This gave me practical things to do and I thought that following it would change me, so I followed. I was following the *sunna* of the Prophet." It is difficult to judge whether Fatima's commitment to practicing Islam within an Islamist ideology was an enabling or disabling experience; for a decade Fatima was sincere in being "a practicing Muslim woman" and feels no regret even after leaving the movement's religiously sanctioned gender roles.

Fatima resided at a Muslim-hostel run by FOCIS (Federation of Student Islamic Societies) in the United Kingdom, a students' wing of the Muslim Brotherhood. The organization helps students start Islamic study circles and make prayer spaces in colleges and universities. "This was a Muslim hostel—so there were plenty of Muslim ladies," says Fatima, laughing, but quickly clarifies her sincerity. "My intention was to follow the code that was set up—women with women and men with men. I believed that I was doing what Allah was asking of me. . . . I used to speak very honestly and lovingly about the religion, and people used to want to sit with me and pray with me and do things together with me. . . . In our study circles we would choose a topic and then discuss it in the *hadith* and Qur'an. Also we would do *qiyam al-layl* [all-night devotions] and recite the Qur'an. We could take a *surat* and do the *tafsir* [interpretation of a Qur'anic passage]. . . . Now, I understand that it was run by the *Ikhwan al-Muslimun* [the Muslim Brotherhood]. . . . At that time, I just wanted to be a practicing Muslim and I didn't know the different groups."

Fatima soon discovered that a new religion, a new environment, and a new routine cannot actually change the deepest roots of one's personality. "Amazingly with all of this, I found time to fall in love, despite how active I was. . . . She was a Pakistani girl. She was very practicing and very knowledgeable about . . . memorizing the *hadith* and Qur'an, but we still managed to fall in love. We became closer and closer, and I thought, 'This cannot be happening! Why is this happening to me? I have a scarf and I pray and fast, so why?' Obviously, she developed feelings for me—when you kiss, that says it all. There is no need for words then. We would see each other every night, and she started wanting to talk about this—'This is wrong in Islam and this is not supposed to happen.' . . . I only then realized that there are gays and lesbians from her discussions. She would bring up the *surat* about Lut [the Prophet Lot]. . . . For her, I think, lesbians and gays were basically the same. . . . But I didn't tell her how I felt." Fatima could not articulate the concept of being a man in a woman's body. So Fatima accepted the other woman's diagnosis that this was a "homosexual" affair and did not argue against her citing the Prophet Lot, a citation which has debatable application to homosexuals but even less relevance for transgender persons.

Fatima's confusion with a female lover highlights the intimate but indirect connection between gender identity and sexual orientation. Transgender people experience the stigma against same-sex sexual orientation while they struggle to understand their own nature, coming to the insight that their experience is one of gender identity rather than sexual orientation. What might appear to outside observers as Fatima's "lesbian" experiences—falling in love with other women and desiring them sexually—were not lesbian because Fatima was, in his own self-understanding, a man. Fatima's same-sex acts are not those of a lesbian, but of a transgender man in a woman's body. Fatima's sense of bewilderment at this point is palpable in the interview. "I believed I was wrong and bad, having heard all the things I did from [her]. . . . So I began to hate myself even more, to a higher degree. I thought, 'What is the solution? What can the solution be? What haven't I done in Islam that is supposed to make it better?'"

In the Muslim women's hostel, it was obvious what Fatima had not yet done in Islam. Fatima had to marry a man. "We had a study circle about marriage and how important marriage was. . . . Marriage is the other half of the religion—that first you are practicing and then when you get married, you have completed the other half. There is a *hadith* about it, which I have not memorized. So I thought, 'I am practicing now and trying very hard, but the solution will be when I get married.' . . . I did not want to get married and I had never been with a man before." Despite misgivings, Fatima decided that marrying a man was the only way to fulfill religious obligations and "cure" doubts about gender identity. But the idea of having sex with a man was very difficult to face.

Fatima first accepted a proposal by a very elderly man in the circle of committed Muslims, who was already a grandfather. Perhaps Fatima was looking for a way to be married without sex. "I was looking for something safe and secure. . . . He spoke beautifully about Islam, and he was more into the Sufi kind of Islam. He would read Qur'an very beautifully, and I found that very peaceful. . . . He offered me a lot of security." But Fatima's family objected and her aunt yelled, "First you put that stupid scarf on your head and now you want to get married with somebody three times your age!'" Fatima abandoned that plan, but later met a man of the same age who was a graduate student in science, an Arab immigrant and leader in the Muslim students' movement.

They met when he came to the women's hostel to solve a crisis between several residents. The male student leader was attracted to the personality that stood out from the group of women who attended the crisis meeting. "I asked him why he chose me from that room full of other women. . . . He said, 'First, it was the way you spoke about Islam.

Also the way you were sitting.' I was the only one sitting with my legs open. I don't know why he found that [attractive]—I actually try not to think about that! . . . But I feel that he liked the masculinity in me. That must have been an attraction for him, because everyone else was really feminine and I was the only masculine person. I didn't admit to it then, but I was [masculine]. That was my way. That was just me . . . the way I sit is a more masculine way. I don't think about it, but this is who I am." Fatima used to wear a Moroccan *jellaba* [robe] that men wear but which suits the requirement for covering women's bodies. "I always used to wear the nice white [robe] that men wear. . . . I used to wear it and feel comfortable." Fatima's clothes, style of sitting, and social manner were masculine, but this made the male student leader more comfortable with her.

He later met Fatima again and proposed marriage. This student leader impressed Fatima with his intellect, manners, and deep spiritual commitment. But when faced with a proposal, Fatima thought that he would make a good friend and sincere comrade. "I said, 'OK, he's got clean shoes and seems to be a clean person, so I'll look at the positive things.'" Fatima saw him as someone strong, committed, and reliable, but love was out of the question. "The issue was not about love, it was about Islam! It was about becoming better and becoming stronger. He had all these beautiful plans, and I thought, 'Yes, we are going to do it together!'" Though he talked about having children, Fatima did not think realistically about what being married meant, in terms of sex and reproduction. "I was the first woman he felt comfortable enough to speak to and go out with. . . . So we became like good friends. For me, it was a friendship!"

Yet he saw Fatima as a woman and a wife, not merely as a comrade and fellow believer. He proposed and Fatima consulted with her aunt. "My aunt actually sat me down and said, 'Do you know that you will have to sleep with this man?' I said, 'Umm . . . yeah.' I wish that I had sat down and listened to her. But . . . I believed that I could change. I believed that 'Yes, I could do this.' . . . When I look back, I see that my aunt knew more than I thought she did—there is more to it. But I didn't have the strength to ask her or open up." Despite the aunt's attempt to broach the topic of sex and gender to help Fatima realize the practical consequences of getting married, Fatima accepted the proposal.

They were married at a major mosque in London and planned their honeymoon for Mecca on 'umra (a ritual visit to the Ka'ba). Their first night together was traumatic for Fatima. "That was the first moment when I had to actually face things. I only wore two pairs of pajamas!" Fatima's body could not bear a man's touch and did not easily accept genital penetration—it is difficult for Fatima to discuss even now. "The first time it happened very quickly. I don't think there was any penetration or anything. I don't know. I did bleed. I don't know. It was quick. I cannot say it was a loving experience. I cannot say I was in love. I wasn't. . . . No, this was more like a duty and we just have to do it. [I was thinking], 'It has to be done. There is a reason that we are doing this. I want to cure myself here. I am going to cure myself and go to paradise.'" But intimacy such as kissing him was impossible for Fatima. "Even though he is a nice person and clean, I could not kiss him. I kept using his beard as an excuse—I said that I get a rash. So he started shaving his beard. But that was not the problem."

Fatima's husband began to complain to Fatima's aunt that she ought to educate Fatima on how to be a proper woman. "It was hurtful, and I felt I had to change even more and become somebody that I am not. . . . Even though I was a Muslim woman, there was still something of 'me' there. Now [others were insisting] that, 'No, this is what a Muslim woman should be' . . . in terms of dress, behavior, sexuality, and having sex." Kissing him disgusted Fatima and his fondling Fatima's breasts was traumatic. Fatima does not clearly remember vaginal penetration and avoids speaking about it. Although their sex life was never good—completely detached for Fatima and confusingly brief for the husband—their mutual respect was strong and their marriage was based on a firm foundation of friendship that lasted twelve years.

Even while married, Fatima still felt like a man. In subtle ways the husband, family, and their Islamic community treated Fatima as an exception to rigid gender roles even as they saw Fatima as a woman, wife, and sister. "I was always very different from other Muslim women. . . . [My husband] accepted me that way, because he tried to change many things about me but there are some things that he could not change. And if he pushed it, I would get very sad and I would not be myself any more." Fatima was more independent than other Muslim women in her community and would go out at night alone. But Fatima carefully followed Islamic dress code and did not mix with men—"For me that was not a problem, because I was quite happy mixing with other women!"

In her community of ideologically conservative Muslims involved in religious politics, Fatima feels that others never really treated her like a woman. Fatima believes that they understood the subtle gender identity that differentiated him, even if they could not talk about it. The other Muslim women "took care of me not as a woman like themselves, but more like [a man]. . . . It is funny. They would cook for me, and clean for me . . . they would not understand it, but they treated me differently than they would treat each other . . . because I am different than all the other sisters who were there. . . . Unconsciously they know, but consciously [they don't recognize it]." Fatima observed that men also would treat him as a colleague with male roles in the organization. "If we were organizing things, other Muslim women would stay back and be shy. For me, I thought, 'Be shy? Why?' For me, that didn't make sense. Many times I would find myself in meetings being the only woman there." Fatima's husband observed this with some alarm, advising her to behave more like a Muslim woman and keep a distance from other men in the community.

Even while having marital sex, Fatima was psychically sure that she was in fact male. It was a rude surprise when she became pregnant. "Something in me actually believed that I could not get pregnant. So that was my big shock. . . . Something in my head believed that because I am a man, I can't have babies. That made logical sense to me." Fatima gave birth to four children and was dedicated to raising them in a nurturing environment, though Fatima finds it hard to imagine being a mother. "[My husband] was always very supportive in bringing up the kids with me. I think that without him I could not have done it! I don't have that mother [instinct]. I am very loving with my kids—don't get me wrong. Sometimes when I look at some mothers, I think that I am more loving with my kids than these natural mothers, you know? I used to think that it was going to be a big problem . . . but I think those differences don't really matter—a parent is a parent and love is, after all, love. So I was very loving with my children. But the practical things I found difficult. Breast feeding I found difficult to do." Anything in sexual intimacy or childbirth that reminded Fatima of her female anatomy was disturbing, though loving the children was the highest priority. Fatima and the husband worked out very egalitarian and mutual roles to play in caring for the children.

However, Fatima's autonomy and lack of sexual arousal began to take its toll on their outwardly ideal marital relationship. Fatima compared feeling care toward a husband with feeling erotic and romantic love with a woman, reflecting that, "It was never a very loving relationship, like when you are madly in love with somebody and you want to be [with her] every moment. . . . I would not say that I would pretend, because I did have love for him. But it was not the same kind of love that I would have for somebody with whom I'm in a relationship. It was not erotic. . . . It was not from that love like when the Qur'an says about when you marry somebody you become like a cover for them." Fatima here refers to the verse which says God provides Muslims with spouses in order to be their *comfort and cloak* (Q 2:187). "We did [act as comfort and cloak in marriage] because we protected each other. But I didn't feel [erotic love]. . . . We did protect each other, but the other bit I felt like I didn't connect with." The other bit was erotic love and sex. In their tight community of ideologically committed Muslims, their relationship, which was so unusual from within, was seen as ideal from the outside. "Everybody would come to us for advice about marriage, because we were such a successful couple. . . . We were friends! Our success was in our friendship and our love for each other." The two grew even closer as comrades when Fatima's mother stayed with them while undergoing chemotherapy.

Fatima got to spend precious last moments with her mother as she was dying from cancer. Fatima was able to ask her about lingering issues from childhood with regard to gender and identity. "She told me some stories of when I was born that gave me some peace. I was born in Rabat . . . and my aunties were the ones who were around her [as she gave birth at home]. . . . So when I was delivered, when I came out, my auntie asked my other auntie, 'Is it a boy or a girl?' My auntie answered, 'It's a boy!' At that, my mother fainted, because she was disappointed when she heard that—'Not another boy!' She was having all these boys and then another boy came, and that was disheartening for her. But apparently it was the cord [that my auntie saw and not a penis]. I don't know what happened there! But that story made me feel like, 'Oh, so you thought you had a boy?' . . . It made me feel better for a bit. It didn't solve my problem, it didn't give me a strong [basis] to claim that I was actually a boy, but it was something. Even though I would have loved to, I never had the strength to [talk about feeling like a man]. . . . She did mention that she never believed that I could get married! But again, I didn't question it."

The death of Fatima's mother marked a turning point in their lives. To recover, the whole family traveled to Mecca for the holy month of Ramadan. "All you do in 'umra is make du'a [personal supplication]! . . . There is no running away—you are faced with the Ka'ba and you are doing tawaf [circling the shrine] and the only thing you do is ask for health and wealth and you ask for honesty and being sincere. So you keep on doing it, and the more you make du'a, the more you realize what is important for you. The important thing for me was to be sincere! I wanted to be myself. I kept making du'a that I just wanted to be myself." Upon Fatima's return to the United Kingdom, something in Fatima that had been suppressed for so long surfaced after praying at the Ka'ba. Fatima resolved to no longer run from who Fatima really is. Sincerity is what Fatima calls it. This new sincerity manifested when Fatima met Noor, a woman who had recently joined their Islamic community and school. "The only way I can describe it is that I fell in love with this person. My heart she just stole away. It was a beautiful feeling. I was happy and it brought up feelings that I had not felt in a long, long time. . . . We realized that it was not just a friendship, but that it was a lot more than that. I think that is when I first kissed her. . . . She wanted to understand why we were feeling this way. Was I aware of what I was doing? For me, these questions have never been asked! . . . Nobody ever faced me with it, even though I had kissed other girls. . . . This was the first time that I felt my love—for her—was not bad. I felt that I am not a bad person. My love is sincere and I wanted to be myself, just me. So I told her about how I felt . . . and she said that she had had feelings for other women before . . . but she had never had a relationship with another woman or felt such strong love."

Honest discussion of their love brought up the long-suppressed issue of Fatima's gender identity. "When I spoke about how I felt [as if I were a man], we started looking on the Internet and found out that there are other people like me. There is a name for it. Unfortunately, we have to label ourselves. From her questioning me, I told her that I believed I was in the wrong body, that I didn't feel I was a woman, that I was very uncomfortable with my body. . . . I don't want to say I feel disgust with my own body, but it doesn't fix up with my head, with what's in my mind and my soul. I cannot show her my love in the way that I would want to show it, you know." The care and understanding shown by Fatima's lover helped Fatima to work through the difficult issues of relating to the body and intimacy with another person.

Fatima and Noor grew increasingly committed to each other, and reached out to the support group Imaan for information and help. There, Fatima found other Muslims who had struggled with the interconnected issues of sexual orientation and gender identity. "We contacted the Imaan group at that time. We met with [Imaan members] and also Daayiee. They were very helpful and very caring." However, Fatima did not join the support group openly. First, Fatima had to express sincerity and honesty toward a husband and their children. "I decided to be honest with my husband. For starters, he could see the change. Once I became honest with myself, I could not act. I could not kiss him anyway before and our sex life was very limited. But it became even worse, so I felt I had to tell him. So I told him about how I felt, which was very important, about me being transsexual. I explained to him about how [this feeling] was there from a young age." It was at this crucial moment of honesty that Fatima discovered the limits of understanding and compassion. Fatima found that Islamic theology is not a tangential issue to interpersonal relationships but rather is a crucial part of how Muslims interact.

Fatima's husband saw the issue through a lens combining modern science with Islamic moralism. He consulted a Muslim professional who belonged to his close-knit community of conservative Islamists and an Arab psychiatrist whom transgender patients must consult with in order to receive a clinical diagnosis of "gender dysphoria" to access sex realignment therapy. "My husband brought him for that purpose—to see if I really am a transsexual. By the end of our conversation, his conclusion was that I was 'a very mild transsexual.'" He suggested therapy to alter Fatima's behavior and conform to womanly norms. "When I heard this, I laughed because I said, 'I have been doing this for thirty years of my life!' . . . But he thought he had some methods of making me become a woman and making me accept that I am a woman. To finalize it properly, [he said] that because I am a Muslim, if I decided to carry on and go for hormones and treatment to be the man I feel I am and have a right to be, that I would go to hell." After hearing this Islamist doctor's judgment, Fatima was incensed. "I went to my husband and said, 'This man should not be working in this job! . . . If he believes that such people [transsexuals] will end up in hell then how can he help them? How can he support them if he doesn't believe in the cause of his job? . . . This is what I have been fighting and now you have brought somebody who is making me feel worse—[who tells me] that I'm going to hell.' This is where I decided that if I'm going to end up in hell then I'm going to end up in hell, but God is the judge and not human beings." Fatima realized that after years of building trust and friendship with a husband, ultimately he could not feel compassion for Fatima's position. "I said, 'I am honest with you. If you cannot respect it, then there is nothing else that I can do.'" He blamed Fatima's female lover, while Fatima argued that their worship at the Ka'ba and sincere prayers to God had led to a new resolve to live sincerely.

The husband denied that Fatima's gender identity was genuine, with arguments involving both science and theology since he was an ideological Muslim working toward a Ph.D. in chemistry. "If I went through a hormone test and found that I had more male hormones than female ones, or if I had little proofs that would help me, then Islamically they cannot argue with me—I have the right to go and [change my body and gender]." Fatima referred to Arabic newspaper and magazine articles about transsexuals in Egypt, and argued with the husband about the decisions of an Islamic University, al-Azhar, which found transgender students to be acceptable under certain conditions.[3] Fatima's husband would reply, "Well, you look perfectly like a woman—you had four children. . . . What is your proof? Show me something that tells me you are a male!" Fatima does not believe that gender identity can be reduced to chemistry or summed up in anatomy. Fatima believes that gender identity is ultimately a matter of the psyche, the interface between mind and soul. It is a matter of intuition, and one can recognize it only as a harmony of one's inner and outer dimensions. Fatima referred to a theory of brain-sex that speculates that gender identity resides somehow in the neurology of the brain, independent of bodily tissues or hormones.

Fatima believes that this identity in the mind is the effect of the soul which God uniquely creates in every person.

Fatima's husband decided to divorce and expelled Fatima from their home. He cut Fatima off from their joint bank account, took custody of the children, denied Fatima visitation rights, and sent the children away with his Arab relatives. "He believes this [the United Kingdom] is a *kafir* [infidel] country. He uses the excuse that I will be a bad example for them. . . . I believe that [taking away] the children was actually a weapon used against me, to make me change my mind. But I am holding on. It is the strongest weapon he has used and the most painful one, but I am still holding on because I believe that my children know me and understand me." Fatima's ex-husband argued the issue from all angles for over five years. He denies Fatima rights to visit the children but gradually accepted Fatima's self-assertion as a man. "He doesn't deny that I am different. He doesn't deny that I am a transsexual—he doesn't say, 'No, you are not.' . . . I think he sometimes contradicts himself, because now when he talks to me he addresses me as a man—he says, '*Ya shaykh* [Oh sir]!' So in our relationship, he treats me as a masculine person. He doesn't treat me as a female and in fact he never has, when I think about it now. He believes me and he trusts me to the point that he brought me this article about an Egyptian girl. I cried very much when I read it, because this girl was honest to her parents [about feeling like a boy] at the age of eighteen, and went to a general practitioner. The doctor stood by her and helped her to become a man—Ahmed."[4]

At the time of this interview, Fatima was considering medical therapy to "transition" into becoming male-bodied in order to find harmony with his male persona. Fatima has delayed this decision because of uncertainty over whether the children will be allowed to meet him after the transition. Despite his ex-husband's eventual belief in Fatima's feeling like a man, he simply cannot accept Fatima for who he is. Social convention and religious belief are the ultimate obstacles to compassionate empathy. In the end, the husband believes that God creates all people as either male or female, and that the physical body expresses God's immutable will. In his view of Islam, there is no way for the soul to exert an ambiguous force on the body, and no reason for God to create an apparent contradiction between them. Fatima concludes that in the end, rational argument cannot convince him. "He says, 'I know you are not lying to me and that you are saying the truth, but I cannot accept it.' I don't know if it is because the religion does not accept it, so he believes in that. . . . My proof is only what I feel and my own experience." Fatima's trust in his own experience, combined with his faith in God's wisdom and compassion, is the only proof that ultimately matters.

Daayiee: Courage to Change What One Can

Daayiee is a central figure in the gay and lesbian Muslim movement in the United States. He often acts as imam for those in Al-Fatiha Foundation. In this role, he adapts religious politics to a positive agenda of social change for gay, lesbian, and transgender Muslims. He does so from a progressive political agenda, derived from the U.S. civil rights movement and based upon experiences of religious politics in African American Christian churches as well as the Black Muslim drive toward justice. Daayiee provides a counterexample to the previous interview with Fatima from the United Kingdom, who adapted religious politics from Islamist movements and carried over some important ethical values and strategies into volunteer work with transgender, lesbian, and gay Muslims. Daayiee's starting point is very different, rooted as it is in the progressive religious politics of the African American community from the 1950s and 1960s.

Daayiee is in his fifties and has studied Islamic history and theology in both secular university and in devotional *madrasa* settings, in the United States and the Arab world. Both his education and his mature gravitas inspire members of Al-Fatiha to see him as their imam. The person to whom a community turns for guidance becomes an imam— literally, "one who stands in front." The qualities an imam needs are knowledge of the religion and courage to uphold moral standards in the community. The position is traditionally informal, based on community recognition rather than formal ordination or priestly investment. Daayiee reflects this simplicity when he explains, "I think that once I began associating with Al-Fatiha [Foundation] and writing about homosexual and positive interpretations from the Qur'an . . . people have turned to me for guidance."[5]

In the United States, the position of imam is becoming semi-formalized, because the government hires Islamic "clergy" as ministers in the military and prisons. Several institutes of higher education have established "imam training courses" to offer formal degrees recognized by the government. Daayiee enrolled in such a course at the Graduate Institute of Islamic Social Sciences in Virginia, while he was working as a court stenographer and a lawyer in Washington, D.C. There he studied for two and a half years under the tutelage of Dr. Taha Jabir al-Alwany. In the final year of training at the institute, Daayiee decided to write his final paper on the mores governing sexuality in Islam, Judaism, and Christianity. This set off alarm signals in the Institute and Daayiee was apparently "blacklisted," such that no local mosque would accept him for an internship as assistant imam; he eventually was forced out of the institute without an official degree. "Though I sat at Dr. Taha's right hand, taught an innovative structured summer course on Qur'an, and was encouraged by him to do a Ph.D. in Islamic law, my being a nonheterosexual man placed me in jeopardy. . . . Though my dismissal from the Graduate Institute [of Islamic Social Sciences] was an attempt to limit my 'credentiality' by their institution [which is] partially funded by Saudi money, I had already learned the necessary tools and quality of scholarship to still render foundationally well-versed Islamic theological scholarship on topics that many would never touch."[6]

It is no surprise that Daayiee was forced out of the Graduate Institute of Islamic Social Sciences. The Institute is administered by an older generation of Arab immigrant scholars, men who are politically moderate and perhaps progressive in terms of women's rights. Yet they do not like to have their assumptions questioned by students. Their chauvinism assumes that American converts need to learn what Arab Muslims have to teach and yet they themselves have nothing to learn from their American environment and the life experiences of their students. But Daayiee, having grown up in an African American family during the civil rights struggle, is accustomed to speaking his mind.

Daayiee grew up as the middle of eight siblings in a middle-class, educated black family in Detroit. "My mother was college educated and my father as well, both in Southern colleges. . . . Part of the ritual at home was that at the dinner table we all had to talk about current events. . . . We got to express a wide array of opinions—because the civil rights movement was going on at the time. . . . So we were allowed to discuss issues and what was going on [in politics and society]." His family belongs to a Baptist church and Daayiee is the only member to have converted to Islam. He did so later in life through his education and travels (rather than through the "Black Muslim" movement or the Nation of Islam, which brought so many Americans to Islam).

Daayiee's family upheld the "middle-class American values" of sobriety, diligence, and integrity. He spoke to his parents about being gay at the age of seventeen in 1971. "When I came out and told my parents, my father wasn't shocked. . . . My mother asked me, 'Do you think it was something that we did?' and I answered, 'Of course not! You had nothing to do with it.' After we had a chance to discuss all the questions they had, my mother said to me, 'Well, I gave birth to you and as a child of mine, you have always upheld the standards that we have asked you to uphold: not to lie to us and to be able to stand up in front of your community as a person. . . . You've upheld those standards so I don't see anything wrong with you—you're still my child.' So that was very wonderful for me to hear." Daayiee's father was supportive though he was more hesitant about endorsing his young son's identity. "He said that though he didn't understand it clearly, still he was proud of me. . . . But it also gave me an opportunity to educate them." He recalls, "My personal experience when I came out to my parents was very peaceful and loving." That was a great consolation, because a tragedy impelled Daayiee to speak openly about his sexual orientation. "I had participated in a gay sexual relationship with a boy who was my boyfriend in junior high and high school. The fall before I graduated from high school, he committed suicide, which was a very difficult thing to deal with because I never found out exactly why. . . . How could we have stayed together and made it through the turmoil of same-sex relationships? . . . I hope to keep his memory with me all of my life." This experience of death and grieving prompted Daayiee to speak openly with his parents.

As he was finishing university, he began to travel more widely and met more gay men who in the early 1970s were forging an activist movement in the United States. At that time Daayiee was a Christian, so he got involved with groups—both African American and Christian—that were pushing for community centers and support networks. He met gay activists through the Metropolitan Community Church, an ecumenical Christian community for lesbian, gay, and transgender Christians and their supporters. "We talked about spiritual development and were talking about our relationships in terms of fidelity and marriage—all kinds of concepts that were very positive." Daayiee found a gay community with people who were responsible socially, engaged spiritually, and active in community building. "After I finished school and started traveling on my own, I began to meet more gay people who were thinking, 'Although we are gay we still have moral standards.' It wasn't just going to bars, drinking, and lascivious sex. It was about us as people. I met people who had similar ideas. We got together and started a magazine that was about gay life but was not sexually explicit [and it was published] in Detroit and Chicago called *Diplomat*. . . . We discussed gay issues that were legislative or about health care or about religious concepts, but we had no sexual pictures in it. . . . We were not following [the crowd]. The type of materials that were available at the time talked about disco dancing and bars and freedom of sex. Though we thought that this was one aspect of gay liberation, we felt that there were other people who didn't find that atmosphere appropriate."

Daayiee found a role model in Paul Robeson, the African American lawyer, intellectual, actor, and singer who took a progressive stand during the civil rights movement. Robeson (died 1976) was persecuted in the United States; his passport was revoked because he resisted racial segregation, then he was institutionalized and endured electroshock treatment.[7] Robeson wrote, "'To be free—to walk the good American earth as equal citizens, to live without fear, to enjoy the fruits of our toil, to give our children every opportunity in life—that dream which we have held so long in our hearts is today the destiny that we hold in our hands."[8] Daaiyee recalls of Robeson, "He was one of my major role models. It was his legal training and his international stature [that I admired most]. . . . He stood up against the tyranny of governments." Robeson gave Daayiee a model for how to be a politically active and spiritually grounded African American. But Daayiee also turned to his parents as role models. Even though he was gay, he found a role model in the relationship of his parents, who were married for sixty-three years.

As an adult, Daayiee looked for long-term relationships and was attracted to men who had children from previous marriages and were seriously committed to family life. "I was never one to seek sexual partners without some form of commitment to my partner." After moving to San Francisco, he entered into a relationship with a divorced father. "My partner had two children and they came to visit us one summer. He was so nervous about his kids and how they might accept our relationship. From the first, the kids were fine with it. . . . Though our relationship was never spoken of in front of them, they knew we were closer than friends." However, in the current drift of gay subculture in the United States, it is very difficult to find gay men who are willing or able to sustain long-term and family-oriented relationships.

It was a challenge for Daayiee to sustain the kind of relationship he desired, and his traveling in pursuit of knowledge also created obstacles. He completed his bachelor's degree at Georgetown University in Arabic and Chinese Languages and Literatures and earned his professional degree from the D.C. School of Law in public interest litigation. Later, he earned a master's degree in Middle East Studies at the University of Michigan with a concentration in Islamic commercial law. When he traveled to Taiwan to continue learning Chinese, he befriended some ethnically Chinese Muslims and converted to Islam under their guidance. Unintentionally, he had followed the Prophet Muhammad's advice in a *hadith* report, "Seek knowledge even as far away as China." Many African American Muslims followed Malcolm X or gravitated toward Saudi Arabia for education saturated with Wahhabi ideas. But Daayiee avoided these extremist religious ideologies. He learned his Islam from Muslims in China. He did not adopt Islam with a racial ideology, with Arab cultural prejudices, or with Wahhabi extremism. He insisted on making his own way through his adopted religion, with a sense of self-confidence based upon knowledge confirmed by self-reflection. His religious politics was of a more progressive pedigree. He reached back into the past to find a model of progressive Islamic thought that was older and more grounded than either Malcolm X or the Wahhabis.

During his formal studies of Arabic language and Middle East Studies, Daayiee came in contact with the historical figure of Abu Hamid al-Ghazali (died 1111), an authoritative jurist, legendary theologian, and an accomplished critic of philosophical ideas. Though al-Ghazali was a highly respected teacher in a most prestigious *madrasa*, he left formal orthodoxy to wander in the deserts reflecting on Sufi mysticism. He later came back to orthodox institutions to argue that legal obedience and mystical insight were not contradictory but could be reconciled.

Though he was often rejected during his lifetime, al-Ghazali is now recognized as the greatest thinker of his age who synthesized the best of jurisprudence, ethics, mysticism, and theology into an integral whole, indelibly shaping Sunni Islam. Al-Ghazali became an ideal for Daayiee. "Imam al-Ghazali was able to take what was considered in his own time to be an outside source of Islamic faith—that is, Sufism—and bring it into the fold of Islam. He was able to articulate clearly for Sunnis that Sufism had its value and its validity in its own right, and therefore should be included in the fold of the *umma* [Islamic community]. That is what I really like about him. In similar ways, I'm trying to articulate a clear way in which people who are same-sex-oriented can also be a part of the *umma*. In that way, he is a real role model for me." As Daayiee strives to combine fidelity to Islamic law with spiritual vibrancy and openness toward homosexuality, Imam al-Ghazali is his guide.[9]

Imam al-Ghazali demonstrated the Islamic tradition's openness to sexual pleasure as a gift from God, but he interpreted the divine grace of sexual desire within a heterosexual framework, noting that its major benefit is procreation.[10] He interprets God's creating *all things from water* (Q 21:30) as referring to sexual union and the meeting of ejaculatory fluids. However, Daayiee holds that Imam al-Ghazali's sex-positive outlook does not limit the role of sexual desire and pleasure to only procreative acts. Daayiee urges that al-Ghazali's framework be applied beyond the boundaries of heterosexual relationships. Daayiee sees homosexuality as a part of human experience that potentially enriches Islam.

After completing his formal studies and beginning his career as a lawyer, Daayiee realized that although university education provides a firm basis for knowledge of Islam, there was much more to learn from religious institutions. He decided to study in Saudi Arabia, though he was not a typical convert who goes there to gain quick legitimacy or to bask in romantic ideals of desert simplicity. He was already a university graduate with multiple degrees, a lawyer with professional experience, and a seasoned international traveler. He was also a self-consciously gay man who had reconciled himself to his sexual orientation, though he knew that in Saudi Arabia one could not talk openly about such things. He went there with the intention of deepening his knowledge of Arabic and studying the Qur'an with those more knowledgeable than himself.

He knew that this required him to keep quiet about sexuality while he was there.

Yet in Saudi Arabia, Daayiee's patience was sorely tried even as he gained knowledge. "I was studying with a well-known *imam* in Riyadh. . . . We would have the conversation in Arabic, but sitting with us was another fellow [named Omar] who spoke English as well. . . . So one day I was asking some questions of the imam, and the imam . . . just stopped me and said, 'You know, you ask a lot of questions!' I replied, 'Well, isn't it OK that I ask questions if I'm not clear about something? Especially if this is about my faith, shouldn't I ask if I'm not clear about something to make certain that I understand all the issues as they come up?' He said to me, 'I just think you ask too many questions.' I was taken aback!" His teacher objected to Daayiee's open-minded search for the truth based on principles that were beyond the limits of patriarchal culture's authoritarian demand of obedience. Sexuality was not the issue; rather, culture was the issue. "I said, 'Excuse me, but it seems to me that the issue is not that I ask too many questions but that you don't seem to have the answers. Is that not true?' The imam just looked at me, then stood up and said, 'You cannot study with me any more.' I raised my hand and said, 'Al-hamdulillah [praise be to God] that I've now been removed from a person who cannot take the challenge of understanding that people need to know more! Allah will provide me with the right person!' He walked out really angrily. The other guy Omar told me, 'You shouldn't have said that to this man.' I told him, 'I'll say what I'm going to say—he insulted me.' That is intellectually dishonest and I just don't like that." Daayiee was banished from the study circle for the insubordination of asking too many questions.

Many lesbian, transgender, and gay Muslims have a similar experience in *madrasa* settings, where asking questions is seen as impertinence. As Daayiee's friend Omar tried to defuse a tense situation, it seemed that divine providence turned the situation around completely. "Omar said, 'Just come downstairs and have some tea.' So I went downstairs and not twenty minutes after that, Omar's cousin came in. Muhammad [the cousin] was a great guy in his thirties, computer literate, had graduated first in his class at the School of the Prophet in Medina, and spoke *fusha* [classical Arabic] impeccably. We hit it off, almost from when our eyes first met. I think if he had been gay we would have been lovers! It was that immediate spark between us. . . . He continued my studies in Islam at the *madrasa* attached to his mosque. . . . He taught me so many things."[11] Despite a culture clash over the role of intellect in faith, Daayiee was able to continue his studies in Saudi Arabia.

From his new teacher, Muhammad, Daayiee learned to distinguish between legal rulings shaped by cultural assumptions and legal principles that are universal. Islamic law was formed in a certain environment and was based upon unspoken cultural assumptions; therefore, Islamic law reflects the abiding principles of the religion, but in a limited form that is contingent on the culture of the time. Progressive Muslim thinkers accept that the law can adapt to cultural conditions, which inevitably change over the passage of time and variation in place. In fact, this change in the law is providential. In Daayiee's view, the flexibility of Islamic law based on firm principles is a blessing, not a weakness in the faith. Some resist this by adopting an attitude of *taqlid*—blind imitation of decisions in the past. By clinging to applications of the law based on the past despite changed circumstances in the present, they miss opportunities to draw closer to God's presence by gaining new knowledge, acting more justly, and finding skillful means to care for the needs of others. Reformist Muslim scholars such as Fazlur Rahman make this argument forcefully. Fazlur Rahman (died 1988) was an Islamic modernist scholar and political reformer who was the head of the Islamic Research Institute in Pakistan until he was targeted by fundamentalists and forced into exile, after which he taught at the University of Chicago.

Daayiee has adapted the religious politics of Islamic reformists like al-Ghazali in medieval times and Fazlur Rahman in modern times. Like them, he argues for continuing *ijtihad* or faith-based reasoning about religious norms. Daayiee advocates extending the enduring principles (upon which past decisions were based) into new decisions that seem innovative because the context in which they are made is unprecedented. To do this, one needs firm knowledge of the legal principles (*usul al-fiqh*) combined with insight into contemporary circumstances and compassionate wisdom. With these tools, one can lead others from suffering to a greater sense of integrity, dignity, and security.[12]

Like many before him, Daayiee traveled to the region of Mecca and Medina in search of further knowledge about Islam. But while many

American Muslims who study in Saudi Arabia are indoctrinated with the idea that the way Saudis practice Islam (according to the Wahhabi movement) is universal for all Muslims, Daayiee learned just the opposite. He learned that cultural change in the United States and the West creates new potential for Islam. Islam can and should adapt its legal rulings and ritual customs to new cultural contexts—especially those that promote justice, equality, and social benefit—without betraying its moral norms and theological principles. "[My teacher, Muhammad] would say of certain things, 'This is just a cultural ritual and really doesn't have anything to do with Islam.' He would help me parse out the stuff that was more culture from things that were more Qur'anic. . . . He helped me to understand the Qur'an in a really clear way. To questions I had he was able to articulate answers. . . . [He allowed me] to understand that Islam was much more than the culture in which it exists."

Daayiee learned that the Qur'anic message is eternal precisely because it is an open text. It allows for alternative interpretation and flexible application while demanding from human authorities humility before God and restraint not to "speak in God's name." It is ironic, of course, that Daayiee learned this essential lesson in Saudi Arabia, where Wahhabi ideology treats Islamic scripture as a "closed text" with a single interpretation that precludes reasoned analysis. Daayiee's approach corresponds to the ideas of a progressive legal scholar whom he highly respects, Khalid Abou El Fadl. Dr. Abou El Fadl was raised in a Wahhabi environment in which a conservative religious political movement dictates morality and runs the government. Dr. Abou El Fadl broke from Wahhabi ideology to argue that *ijtihad* must continue based upon juridical principles and scriptural precedents while being attuned to contemporary realities. According to Dr. Abou El Fadl and other reformists, *ijtihad* is the struggle of an individual or community to come to a fuller understanding of God's message; *ijtihad* must continue if Muslims are to act justly in the world and refrain from victimizing the vulnerable to maintain a shallow and rigid sense of group righteousness.

Daayiee often discusses these reform-minded ideals with other Muslims in his lecturing, counseling, and Internet discussion groups. Daayiee argues that Muslims can have faith in the sacred sources of their religion while still upholding flexibility in their interpretation. The

Qur'an is a revelation in a particular language to a discrete community. The *hadith* reports are embedded in distinct historical situations. Muslims must extract universal principles from these sources by separating what is historically accidental from what is ethically and spiritually essential. This process requires continuous and ever-renewed interpretation rather than mere traditionalism and imitation of the past.

Some Islamic fundamentalist groups demand that the Islamic law of the past be applied as national law in the present. Others from Islamic groups justify violence against Muslims who disagree with them, or against non-Muslim neighbors whose presence challenges their ideological vision. More common in Daayiee's milieu in the United States are neotraditionalist Muslims who demand unnuanced and rigid application of the *shari'a* while living in nations where it is not applicable. Such traditionalists often police sexuality without exploring the humanity behind it, suppressing or oppressing homosexual or transgender members of their Muslim communities. In this context, Daayiee advocates a reformist faith that is neither a secularist sell-out nor a traditionalist buy-in.

As Daayiee gives advice over the Internet site "Muslim Gay Men" and through the conferences of Al-Fatiha Foundation, he encounters a great deal of despair. There is resistance from conservative Islamic scholars, mainstream Muslims, and also some gay Muslims. Many members of the discussion groups grow weary in the face of resistance to the acceptance of homosexuality in Muslim communities. Many of them scoff at the idea of same-sex marriages in Islam, an ideal that Daayiee holds out as a possibility and which he has helped to make into a reality for a few bold couples who have approached him to act as *imam* in their wedding (*nikah*). Daayiee sees this resistance as akin to racism in the United States, which was so common and pervasive that many, both white and black, could not imagine their society without it.

Daayiee reminds those he counsels that interracial marriage was illegal in the United States several decades ago. In many places—despite changes in the law—it is still considered unacceptable. That prohibition, Daayiee reminds us, was based on an interpretation of scripture and was conflated with religious morality in the minds of many Christians. "One thing that is very important is that, when you are moving forward and trying to get people to see that there is another way of doing things, the truth of it has to have someone's real face attached to it. . . . It is the same thing as miscegenation fifty years ago. . . . In 1967, the Love case in Virginia made the change to federal law in that regard. So we are only forty years past [the time] when interracial marriages became legal in this country. So the same thing applies here; I think it might be just a few decades down the road when this [same-sex marriage] is going to become a permissible standard, and people will have to deal with it." The civil rights movement in the United States—in which African Americans demanded their constitutional rights despite de facto discrimination—offers a powerful model for other liberation movements such as the movement for gay, lesbian, and transgender rights. Sexuality minorities often compare the status of their communities to that of racial minorities. They argue that the stigma against them is irrationally based on stereotypes and hatred, just as antiblack racism was in the United States or South Africa.

In the United States, lesbian, gay, and transgender people—Muslims among them—ask how they can create the combination of factors that push for progressive social change the way the civil rights movement did. These factors are potentially present in the issue of same-sex marriage. Marriage is highly symbolic as it appeals to religious value systems and demands to be either accepted or rejected by religious authorities, yet it is an action that asserts legal rights that demand interpretation in courts or by legislators; marriage is an institution that combines religious and secular elements. Finally, it is an act so commonplace as to generate great political significance if it is denied to members of a group, much like sitting in the front seats of a public bus or eating at a lunch counter were in the days of Martin Luther King.

Same-sex marriage has become a boundary-defining issue since the start of the twenty-first century. Many liberals who claim to support lesbian and gay citizens balk at extending to them the right to marry, and wonder why "they" can't be satisfied with invisible relationships or civic partnerships without "demanding" symbolic equality through marriage. Many conservatives oppose same-sex marriage as a rallying point for conservative values, accusing gays and lesbians of destroying religious values and threatening the heteronormative family. Daayiee has found in the battle for marriage equality a strategy to adapt religious politics to a progressive social agenda. He takes a constructive—if controversial—position in upholding the right of gay, lesbian, and transgender Muslims to marry.

Daayiee has performed Islamic marriage ceremonies for several Muslim couples, including same-sex couples. He acted as the imam during the *nikah* (witnessing and signing a marriage contract) which Islamic law and custom requires. Islamic communities surround the wedding with celebrations involving the families of the partners and the wider community in different ways, depending upon their local culture. However, these celebrations are not considered part of the marriage proper, which requires only four witnesses to the verbal consent and signing of a contract in which the terms of the marriage are clearly written. *Nikah* ceremonies carried out in mosques, as done for many heterosexual marriages in Muslim communities, do not represent a contract that is legally binding under U.S. law; it merely constitutes a religious custom. The marriage is recognized under law when the partners file legal papers at a state courthouse and submit a blood test. For traditional weddings in Muslim, Christian, or Jewish communities, the religious official is delegated by the state to file papers on behalf of the couple. However, the religious official's role in sanctifying and blessing the marriage is distinct from his role in acting as deputy of the state to contractually wed the couple.

When Daayiee acted as imam in same-sex weddings, he kept the traditional form of the *nikah* ceremony and contract but expanded its application to accord with a nonpatriarchal system.[13] The way that Daayiee carries out the ceremony, the terms of the marriage contract are not specified by the gender of the partners. This arrangement allows homosexual couples to join in an Islamic marriage. It also allows heterosexual couples to get married when one partner is a Muslim and the other belongs to a different religion because, under classical *shari'a*, a Muslim man can marry a woman from other monotheistic religions while a Muslim woman is not allowed to marry a man from these same religions. The rights are defined by gender and are unequal. In the interest of practicing Islam without discriminating against individuals based on gender or sexuality, Daayiee has agreed to perform a *nikah* for couples in which the woman is a Muslim but the man is not.

As of 2005, Daayiee had performed *nikah* for six heterosexual couples and two lesbian couples. Five gay couples have gone through marriage counseling with him but have not gotten married. "I've drawn up my own certificate of contract. I've drawn up a contract individually for each of the couples that have gotten married. . . . In the counseling, I ask them as a couple what things they want in the contract and then I present to them a contract to which each party has contributed and I let them go over it again. There are standard parts of the contract but it is customized for each couple." The situation of each couple is unique. Through a process of premarital counseling for which Daayiee has undergone training, he designs a *nikah* contract which equitably fulfills the rights and expectations of each partner. This is in accordance with the Islamic tradition in which the marriage contract (*'aqd al-nikah*) has standard elements that must be present but leaves room for variable conditions depending on the needs of the couple. The contract also makes provision for divorce. In the case of heterosexual couples whom Daayiee has wed, their contracts are legally binding and are recognized under state law because he is deputized by the government of Washington, D.C., to perform marriages. In the case of same-sex couples whom Daayiee weds, their contracts are not legally binding if state law does not recognize them. Daayiee explains that in the United States, "The religious aspect of [the Islamic marriage] is for their own personal and emotional desire to have it done that way—for instance, their families would not recognize them [as married] if they did not have a *nikah*."

As Daayiee conducts same-sex Islamic marriage ceremonies, Muslims may ask him, "How do you justify same-sex marriage within the religious tradition?" They ask how to justify same-sex marriage in reference to the Qur'an and the Prophet Muhammad's teachings (*sunna*). His answer is not simple. There is no evidence that any Muslims engaged in same-sex marriage in the Prophet's own time; the Prophet seems to have arranged only heterosexual marriages in his immediate community. The Prophet's actions shape the *sunna*, but what about the Qur'an? Daayiee finds the Qur'an to be more universal than the cultural practices of the Arab society in which it was revealed or the Prophet's practice in the early Islamic community. "Though the Qur'an does speak in some instances in heteronormative terms, in other instances it is very allegorical. So there is room for interpretation, to make the claim that same-sex partners can [wed] if they follow the process of getting married. I don't find any problem with it because the Qur'an does state that people are sexual beings and should seek partners in order to have their 'comfort and cloak.'" Daayiee refers here to the Qur'anic verse saying that God provides a Muslim with a spouse in order to be his *comfort and cloak* (Q 2:187). The image of one's marital partner clothing one is a metaphor for intimacy, both sexual and emotional; a partner molds to fit one's body, shielding one from the gaze of others and protecting one from temptation by others. Daayiee argues that a same-sex partner plays the same role—sexually, psychologically, and socially—as a heterosexual marriage partner. "When two people find love between them, the purpose of a marriage is to further that love. Though this has been interpreted by people as being between people of the opposite sex, I don't find that the Qur'an limits it to two people of the opposite sex only. So in my inclusive understanding of how the Qur'an works, two people who find love with each other and are willing to make the sacrifice of spending time together and making a contract between themselves and before Allah with two witnesses, they have met the same standards that are applied to opposite-sex couples. The real judgment will be made by God."

Only after a struggle for social change can same-sex marriage be accepted in national law. For such a marriage to be endorsed by religious custom, a further struggle will have to take place because religious authorities resist even if the secular legal system changes. However, in Daayiee's eyes, same-sex couples who wish to join together in marriage can wait for neither judges nor imams to endorse their commitment. The only way the system will change is for some people to choose to do things differently and take responsibility for what they are doing, no matter what the reaction of others. As an imam, Daayiee takes responsibility for performing same-sex marriages with all the formality of a *nikah*. "The way I explain it to the same-sex couples whom I have married is to tell them, 'The only change I make to the *nikah* contract is to change one pronoun in each of the commitment statements that I ask them to repeat—such that he with she becomes he with he or she with she.' To me this is 99.99 percent the very same *nikah* [as applied to heterosexual couples]. So I don't see a very great difference between them. . . . When people can put their same-sex relationship on the same standard as a heterosexual relationship and see that there is nothing different except the sex of the partners, I think that then there really is no difference. They will have to accept that even if they disagree with it because the status is the same. Eventually, people are going to say, 'Well, if my daughter had married a man, it would have been done the same way . . . so where is the big difference?'" For same-sex couples who have so far wed, this change is a small one in language and custom that reflects the comfort they find in each other and the commitment they offer to each other. Regardless of opposition, Daayiee is content to be of service to those who express the sincere love and intent to join together, to "clothe" each other with the comfort of marriage.

Daayiee Abdullah sees this as only one small change in Islamic law to bring the *shari'a* closer to the egalitarian principles of the Qur'an and the universal spirit with which it was first revealed. This requires interpreting the divine message beyond the limiting historical contingency of the patriarchal Arab society in which it was revealed. In Daayiee's humble apartment in Washington, D.C., hangs a small poster that says, "God, give me serenity to accept the things I cannot change, the courage to change the things I am able to, and the wisdom to know the difference between these two." His courage none can dispute, though some fellow Muslims might doubt his wisdom.

For Daayiee, the proposition that God's eternal message speaks only to some, thereby empowering them to dominate or exclude others, is a perversion of God's message. As he understands it, the Qur'an speaks equally to all believers—to female and male, to heterosexual and homosexual, and transgender people alike. It calls each to strive, through *ijtihad* of the mind and *jihad* of the body, to take full responsibility for one's place in the world and become God's vice-regent on earth (*khalifa*). Imitating past generations would be shirking the demands of justice, ignoring the call of wisdom, and forfeiting the opportunity of serenity that comes only with trust in God against all odds. This is the essential message of Daayiee's progressive Islamic stance, which adapts religious politics to the goal of liberation from oppression.

Conclusion

Harnessing religious beliefs and values to an agenda of political change is called "religious politics." It is a familiar strategy in modern times, as movements for political change find that secular strategies are not persuasive among many populations. In the United States, the civil rights movement engaged in religious politics by adopting the charisma, songs, and ideals of various African American churches; through such strategies, the civil rights movement appealed to the religious beliefs of a white majority in order to change popular perceptions of racial segregation. Among Muslims, religious politics is also a familiar strategy.

This chapter highlights how some transgender, lesbian, and gay Muslims engage in activism by "adapting religious politics." They take the strategies and motivations found among religious political movements and adapt them to secure homosexual and transgender rights and welfare. This mode of activism may strike some observers as strange, since many assume that Muslims who engage in religious politics are from "Islamist" movements that are fundamentalist, authoritarian, and conservative. Certainly, Islamist movements are the most evident illustration of Muslims adapting religious politics: examples range from the rise of the Muslim Brotherhood and the rule of Wahhabi cliques among Sunni populations to the Iranian Revolution and Hizbullah among Shi'i groups. Less well known (but no less important) are liberal or progressive Islamic movements which also adapt religious values, rituals, and symbols for an agenda of social reform and human rights. Observers with a more intimate acquaintance with Islamist movements realize that the boundary between conservative and progressive is very permeable in Islamic religious political groups.

The interviews presented in this chapter reveal important points about the intersection of religion and politics. Some lesbian, gay, and transgender Muslims get involved in Islamist groups in ways that influence their personal growth and self-awareness. They explore the possibility for social solidarity and moral maturity through involvement in these movements, even as they find heterosexual normativity imposed upon them. Involvement in these movements often inspires them to become activists even if they eventually leave the group or are driven out due to their sexual orientation and gender identity.

The interviews in this chapter reveal what a formative role involvement in Islamist groups played for some activists like Fatima, who found that being homosexual or transgender was incompatible with allegiance to a tight-knit and politically assertive Islamist group. Yet such activists take the values and ideals learned in such groups with them after they leave to find involvement and support elsewhere. Most

Islamist groups have a conservative agenda which leaves little room for lesbian, transgender, or gay Muslims. Many Islamist groups actively oppose homosexual and transgender rights as signs of social decay and moral perversion, and use stereotypes and scapegoating techniques to galvanize popular support for their ideology. Yet Islamist movements are not inherently conservative and authoritarian in this way. Progressive Islamist movements are possible if they see the "fundamentals of Islam" as religious ideals that promote political equality, social justice, and protection for the vulnerable. Those like Fatima who leave Islamist movements and gravitate toward gay, lesbian, and transgender Muslim support groups find in this new loyalty a progressive version of Islamist activism. In this way, they adapt religious politics to the needs of homosexual and transgender Muslims.

The second interview with Daayiee affirms that not all religious politics are necessarily conservative, authoritarian, and fundamentalist. In the United States, Daayiee is inspired by the civil rights movement whose religious politics, based mainly on Christian values, engineered a profound social change in ways that secular strategies could not achieve. He finds many resources in the Islamic tradition—in its scriptural and legal dimensions that are the heart of "orthodoxy"—for a similar project of progressive politics inspired by Islamic values. Through his life story, we can understand that not all those who adapt religious politics are coming from involvement with fundamentalist groups followed by exclusion from them.

These activists assert that religious beliefs and values can inspire participation in political movements, regardless of whether this is a lesson learned in conservative or progressive movements for social change. But not all activists involved in support groups for transgender, lesbian, and gay Muslims believe this assertion. Some are frankly distrustful of mixing religious values with political rights; rather, they see the separation of religion from politics as serving their interests, since they constitute a small minority of a minority population. Such activists focus their energy on secular politics and its instruments like constitutional rights, legal protections, and party politics. They may have firm faith in Islam but they assert that this is a private affair that should not drive political involvement. Their mode of activism, called "adjusting secular politics," will be the focus of the next chapter.

4

Adjusting Secular Politics

As they talk about us, they try to berate us
We've done nothing to them—still they hate us
As they talk about us, it's insults they shout
It's time this changes so you better watch out
~the Rapper "Raymtzer," *Kut* Marokkanen
(Fuckin' Moroccans)

In the Netherlands, the younger generation expresses itself through rap and hip-hop. These musical genres were taken from America and adapted in Dutch to express the rappers' protest against uniquely European political realities. While the most famous exponents of rap sing in Dutch, they are members of ethnic minorities with Moroccan Dutch men at the forefront. In the troubled multicultural Netherlands, music is one arena in which members of the Arab and Berber minority gain admiration. A whole generation hears in them its own voice, as Bob Dylan observed when rap first emerged: "These guys definitely weren't standing around bullshitting. There were beating drums, tearing it up, hurling horses over cliffs. They were all poets and knew what was going on. . . . The audiences would go that way, and I couldn't blame them."[1]

The Moroccan Dutch rapper Raymtzer, quoted above, speaks as a member of an embittered minority.[2] His verses complain of being excluded, yet in song he speaks back to the powers that be. The refrain of this song complains about the stigmatized treatment North African youths receive by the majority of Dutch: "As they talk about us, they try to berate us. . . . We've done nothing to them—still they hate us." This is both a general complaint and a critique of a political gaffe that revealed the depth of anti-immigrant sentiment, fueled by Islamophobia, among Dutch politicians. In 2003, the speaker of the Labor Party (PvdA), Halbertsma, said in a press conference—when he thought the cameras and microphones were turned off—"those fuckin' Moroccans." His gaffe was caught on record and publicized, causing an uproar among minorities who feel they are discriminated against but rarely have direct proof from the highest echelons of political leaders.[3] It is this incident which gave the ironic title to Raymtzer's rap, as a Moroccan sings about "Fuckin' Moroccans" in order to throw the insult back at those in power. "As they talk about us, it's insults they shout, it's time this changes so you better watch out." For ethnic minority communities, the rapper's voice rings true, and these minority communities include lesbian, gay, and transgender Muslims who listen avidly to its message of standing up to insults and insisting on basic dignity. He speaks about growing up in a minority and finding innovative ways to assert one's place in the rapidly changing urban landscape of Europe. He claims a space of citizenship within the nation and wants his fair share of the secular prosperity that the nation promises.

This chapter will present interviews with Muslim activists who speak for the minority voices within a minority Muslim community. These gay Muslim activists often admire the hip-hop voices that sing of exclusion, even if hip-hop artists often direct hate speech at gay men, women, and other vulnerable groups. These gay Muslim activists appeal to secular ideals of citizenship rights and legal order to better the life potential of those like them who are vulnerably placed at the intersection of ethnic minority, religious minority, and sexual minority. Their involvement in two different support groups exhibits a mode of activism that can be called "adjusting secular politics."

The three activists interviewed in this chapter are gay men, yet they address issues of common concern to transgender people and lesbian women as well. Their interviews highlight how gay, lesbian, and transgender Muslims act as intermediaries between the Muslim community and other citizens. Their voices cause us to reflect upon the law, especially the conflict between national law and the Islamic *sharia* with regard to their status. The interviews come from the Netherlands and illustrate how activist politics works in the ideologically secular democracies of Europe. The Netherlands shares a tradition of secularism with France, Germany, and other continental European nations that were deeply affected by the French Revolution and Napoleonic rule. In these nations, secularism means ardent opposition to any religious practice entering the public sphere of government, education, and civic ethics. This environment creates opportunities for gay, lesbian, and transgender Muslim activists to appeal to secular legal norms, but it also creates deep obstacles for members of ethnic and religious minorities to "integrate" into the secular life of the nation.[4]

Omar: Balance between Desire and Discernment

Omar Nahas immigrated to the Netherlands from Syria when he was twenty-five and pursued his higher education at Dutch universities. He is a scholar, writer, and media activist who founded the Yoesuf Foundation.[5] The foundation is an education center about Islam and social issues with a program in the field of "Islam and Sexuality Diversity."[6] In addition to this field, it administers programs in "Islam and the Position of Women" and "Islam and Youth." To promote public dialogue in these three fields, the foundation leads workshops, organizes conferences, and publishes books and pamphlets throughout the Benelux region (Belgium, the Netherlands, and Luxemburg). The Yoesuf Foundation intended to spread information about Islam and spark discussion through publishing and consciousness-raising workshops. Omar has published three books (first in Arabic and subsequently in Dutch) based upon the Islamic research of the foundation. The best way to introduce Omar is to document his involvement in the "El-Moumni Affair" of 2003, a political drama that tossed Muslims, secularists, and gay rights activists into a confusing debate.

To understand the importance of the "El-Moumni Affair" we can return to the verses of Raymtzer. The Moroccan rapper, as well as the younger generation for whom he speaks, is increasingly aware that he is seen not just as "Moroccan" but as Muslim, especially since the September 11, 2001 assault and the similar attacks across Europe. The markers of religious identity have begun to overwhelm those of ethnicity and regional belonging. In the song quoted above, Raymtzer demonstrates this dynamic in lines that come before the refrain quoted above:

> God knows who I am—shit, just a man
> I'm just as Dutch as I am Moroccan . . .
> I sell that stuff till I can get a little money
> Man, my words hit harder than el-Moumni
> You pick out just the negative lines I sing
> Scared to look for the more profound thing
> For then, the stereotypes seem not right
> But you prefer that I simply emigrate!

The rapper compares his hard-hitting lyrics to the voice of Imam el-Moumni, a Moroccan immigrant leader of a mosque in Rotterdam. Imam el-Moumni stirred a controversy by making statements against homosexuals in the name of Islam.

A Dutch journalist interviewed Imam el-Moumni as representative of the immigrant Moroccan community that makes up the largest group within the Muslim minority of the Netherlands. In the interview on May 3, 2001, Imam el-Moumni was asked about Islam's position on homosexuality. He replied, "God refers to the experience of the Tribe of Lot in many chapters of the Qur'an as a warning to Muslims to take precaution against that dangerous phenomenon [homosexuality]. . . . Islam commands that this phenomenon be obliterated for all time. For this reason, we were recently surprised by an announcement of a decision that homosexuality is officially legal. . . . Democracy does not mean that everything is possible, that you can do just what you want. Freedom does not want to say that you do as you please, even what is forbidden. Your freedom ends at the place where you infringe on the freedom of others. [If] homosexuality is not restricted then those with this sickness cause it to spread to others. . . . If it remains in one group, we can treat them and train them so that they can return to the correct path. In this way, we can bring an end to this deviation that is contrary to nature. It is against human nature, for God has not created us like that."[7] He pronounced that homosexuality is forbidden in the Qur'an, represents a deviation from the human nature which God created, and should be treated as a contagious sickness. This statement raised a storm of protest in the Netherlands.

Many Dutch heard this as "hate speech" against homosexual citizens who are protected by law and social consensus. They saw it as justifying violent attacks against homosexuals which had been on the rise in recent years and were often blamed on "young Moroccan men" on the street.[8] Young Muslims in the Netherlands supported Imam el-Moumni, hearing him defend them against entrenched racism against immigrants and Islamophobia. Many Muslims insist they can integrate into a democratic Netherlands without giving up their religious convictions or customs. However, many Dutch are fearful that Islam itself is homophobic and misogynistic and that it prevents Muslims—even those born in the Netherlands—from integrating into a liberal democracy.

In this polarized environment, the voices of gay, lesbian, and transgender Muslims from the minority population were drowned out, but Omar Nahas entered the controversy. In the Netherlands, rightist politicians articulate a strong form of secularism, calling upon members of the Muslim minority to "secularize" in the name of promoting and protecting human rights, by self-consciously giving up those parts of their religious tradition, in principle and in practice, which conflict with Dutch national political culture. Many see the rights of women and homosexuals as the "litmus test" defining the criterion of acceptability for integration into Dutch and wider European citizenship. They object to Muslims running their own communities by their own customs, since that custom is informed and shaped by the Islamic *shari'a* or moral law. The rights of women and homosexuals (whether women or men) are seen as the fault line which divides those whose loyalty is to the Dutch nation and those whose loyalty is to Islam.

As Dutch politics drifted to the right in the 1990s, Muslim beliefs and behaviors became a subject of scrutiny and political debate. In 2001 the El-Moumni Affair was the first tremor warning of future rifts.[9] Imam el-Moumni apologized because his comments sparked a nationwide debate about Islam's compatibility with the laws and social values of the Netherlands. He issued his apology in a statement with sixteen mosque committees, which sought to minimize the damage. Yet Imam el-Moumni upheld his representation of Islam as forbidding homosexuality. Dutch observers were incensed that Imam el-Moumni judged that homosexuality damages the Netherlands even though he cannot speak or read Dutch to fully understand the nation's laws or customs. In the interview, a journalist asked the imam, "Can Islam adjust to the mentality of the Netherlands?" The imam answered: "Islam orders us to integrate in every society, as long as it is not contrary to our religious duty, culture, and morality. I think that integration is going well in regards to science, education, and work, to do good deeds and oppose evil in the society. Homosexuality is harmful for society in general. . . . If this phenomenon spreads among the youth, among boys as well as girls, then it will lead to extinction. . . . How will there be any more children if men are marrying other men and women marrying other women? Therefore, the Dutch parliament has ordained the death of the Netherlands."[10] Such an exaggerated description of the consequences of accepting homosexuals as citizens—that everyone would become homosexual and the human race would be extinguished due to lack of reproductive heterosexual sex—struck most listeners as uninformed and paranoid. Further, many thought it constituted hate speech which is criminalized under Dutch law.

Imam el-Moumni was charged with discrimination and hate speech, despite his having said in the same interview that Muslims are not allowed to be violent against homosexuals. He said, "Islam forbids aggression against anyone, regardless of his circumstances and the sickness that he might have. Islam obliges us to protect people against dangers: like those presently posed by homosexuality, adultery, alcoholism, and drug addiction. We are not allowed to kill such people. It is not up to any individual to give punishment. It is up to the judge to put law into effect in accordance with the Qur'an. Islam does not accept any anarchy in the establishment of rule of law. If anyone is suffering from a sickness, such as we can call the deviance, then Islam commands that we lead him to a cure and save him from it. . . . If there is something good, we all benefit from it. If there is something bad, it harms us as well. We do not wish any harm to come to the Netherlands." Most Dutch listeners did not accept the imam's contention that he had the best interest of the Netherlands at heart. Charges were pressed against him. Imam el-Moumni was acquitted on the grounds that freedom of speech, especially in the field of religious convictions, prevented his pronouncement from being criminal. In the trial, many experts were called to answer whether the imam's words were an accurate representation of

Islamic texts and beliefs or whether they were his own opinion based on homophobia. The judge ruled that the imam's opinions reflected the Islamic tradition's basic beliefs. This exonerated him from the charge of hate speech.

Drawn into the el-Moumni controversy were gay, lesbian, and transgender Muslim support groups in the Netherlands. Journalists, followed by the court itself, turned to them for expert testimony on whether Imam el-Moumni's opinions accurately represented Islam. The Yoesuf Foundation was dragged into the controversy and Omar Nahas found himself in an uncomfortable position. As a gay activist he had argued that the conventional homophobic interpretation of Islam was only one interpretation that did not live up to the highest ethical ideals of Islam. However, as a Muslim living in the Netherlands, he was wary of the Islamophobia running deep in politics and wanted to protect Imam el-Moumni from being made a scapegoat by the media. Omar decided that taking neither side was the only ethical alternative. His difficult position in the El-Moumni Affair illustrates the dangers faced by gay, lesbian, and transgender Muslim support groups, as they represent minorities-within-minorities in a polarized social conflict. They have to use secular politics to solve the problems of their minority defined by sexual orientation and gender identity, but they have to adjust secular politics to the needs of their minority defined by religious belief.

Omar's careful attention to scriptural mandate and Arabic linguistics is clearly evident in his response to Imam el-Moumni. When questioned about his involvement, Omar replied, "There were quite a lot of gay organizations that wanted to sue him [Imam el-Moumni], but the Yoesuf Foundation said publicly that we are not going to sue him. What we did was to analyze exactly what he said. He said [in Arabic], 'Al-liwat marad,' meaning that homosexuality is a disease. He used two terms beside each other. The first is *liwat* [meaning sodomy], which was translated as homosexuality. So here comes our work [to differentiate between sodomy and homosexuality]. But I really think he [el-Moumni] meant homosexuality and not *liwat* [sodomy] because from his perception it is the same. He does not make a distinction—the projection of the Tribe of Lot upon homosexuals is a common fault with quite a lot of people. The second term is *marad*, meaning disease. He used the word *marad* but not the word *da'*. If you analyze the word *marad* according to the Qur'an, it comes in the verse . . . that says *In their hearts is an ailment* (Q 2:10). If you look in the books of *tafsir* [Qur'an interpretation], it can mean that in their heart is a kind of weakness, rather than a kind of illness or sickness. Anyway, I did not want to defend him [Imam el-Moumni] at all. . . . If we had moved to sue him, we would have cut the dialogue."[11]As Omar explains, the purpose of the Yoesuf Foundation is to promote dialogue, drawing both the Muslim community and Dutch society into a more informed, sensitive, and ethical discussion about homosexuality in Islam. If he had defended Imam el-Moumni or joined the attack against him, Omar would have jeopardized the dialogue he had tried for years to promote.

Omar's primary message to fellow Muslims is that there is a difference between sodomy and homosexuality, despite the traditional interpretations of Islam that conflate the two. In his view, Islam condemns sodomy but leaves room for accepting homosexual believers who live up to ethical principles. His message for Dutch citizens is that they need to educate themselves about Islam to engage in meaningful dialogue with Muslims, whom they should see as neighbors and citizens rather than as foreign "guest workers" with no status or stake in the country.

Omar came to such a nuanced position through his deep study of Islam combined with his ability to adjust theological issues to a secular human rights framework. Omar grew up in Damascus with an education in Arabic literature and Islamic theology. He came to understand he was gay in Syria, long before emigrating to the Netherlands at the age of twenty-five. He holds his personal development as evidence that homosexual orientation is innate from early childhood and is beyond an individual's choice—and that adoption of a homosexual identity is an internal reaction to this psychological orientation rather than an imposition of cultural conditioning. He wrote about this in Arabic in his first book, entitled *Sexual Orientation: Toward a Systematic Analysis of Homosexuality*. He coined a new term, *al-junusiyya*, to encapsulate the idea of sexual orientation as part of one's personal identity, as distinct from sexual acts.

In Arabic, *jins* means sex with all the ambivalence of the English term. Sex originally meant "kind of person," as in the old-fashioned phrase that labels women "the fairer sex"; it later came to refer to sexual acts, replacing the more old-fashioned and condemnatory "carnal acts." Similarly in Arabic, *jins* originally meant "kind of being" and may originally be derived from the Greek term *genus*. In the modern period, *jins* came to refer to sex acts. Later, as modern medical and psychological discourse took shape in Arabic, *jins* gave rise to a new term, *jinsiyya*, meaning sexuality. From this was created the translation of homosexuality as *al-jinsiyya al-mithliyya* (literally, "the sexuality of sameness") that is current in journalism and psychiatry. Omar observed that this term is too general since it refers to same-gender attraction and sex acts but not necessarily to identity. So he coined a new term, *junusiyya*, to refer to homosexual identity. Reflecting on his own biography, Omar writes: "I believe that my consciousness of homosexuality as personal sexual identity developed from a very early age, meaning before I reached the stage of receiving education in high school, and certainly before I ever became acquainted with any other homosexual persons."[12]

In this first book, Omar argues against the idea that homosexuality is a "Western" problem, an assumption common in Arab regions. Many believe that homosexuality was "imported" into Arab or Islamic communities through Western cultural influence.[13] According to Omar, this argument totally fails in the light of his own experience and that of other Arab homosexuals. "I once met in Damascus a man who came from a remote little village. . . . The time I met him, according to his account, was the first time he had left his village to come to the city. Yet he spoke about homosexuality and about sexual identity as if he were an educated teacher who was deeply experienced and rhetorically astute. Of course, he did not use the technical term 'homosexuality' (*junusiyya*) or the word 'identity.' Rather, he used words drawn from his local social context to express his own understanding of homosexuality and his sexual identity." Omar adds that this was "exactly as I did during the initial period of formation of my awareness of sexual identity."[14]

Omar contends that homosexuality is present within every society as an inherent psychological character of a minority, even in the absence of any organized homosexual subculture and despite religious condemnation of it. This is true even when there is no technical vocabulary to describe the phenomenon. Homosexuality is a phenomenon deeper than the social system that either accepts or rejects it, and deeper even than language, which may provide more or less nuanced means to express it.

Omar's analysis of linguistic terms has direct impact upon the issue of interpretation of the Qur'an. This analysis, published in 1997, predated the El-Moumni Affair by four years, yet illustrates exactly the conflation of terms which the imam pronounced in that controversial interview. Omar writes, "Many words are used to express sexual relationships that take place between man-and-man or between woman-and-woman. . . . Whether in modern standard Arabic or local dialects, there are terms like sexual deviance (al-shudhudh al-jinsiyya) and sodomy (al-liwat) and also homosexuality (al-junusiyya). . . . The problem is that most people use these different terms as synonyms, creating a situation of naming experiences with names that do not really fit, thereby generating misunderstanding and confusion about the topic of sexual orientation. . . . I see the critical importance of writing about homosexuality as the attempt to remove these confusing mix-ups of terms and issues."[15] In this crucial passage, Omar explains that his project is to differentiate between homosexuality and sodomy. In his understanding, the Qur'an condemns sodomy as the act of anal penetration rather than homosexuality as sexual orientation, while the Islamic legal tradition mistakenly conflates the two.[16]

The distinction between homosexuality and sodomy makes sense if one asserts that there is a psychological reality called sexual orientation, which is separate from and prior to any sexual act. He writes, "Sex is a phenomenon that happens by way of the body, whereas sexuality is a matter existing at the level of psyche and personality."[17] In his analysis, only a person with a psychological identity of constant and exclusive same-sex desire should be called "homosexual" (junusi in his terminology, or mithli jinsiyya in the Arabic terminology of other contemporary writers). The person who performs same-sex acts without doing so within the framework of exclusively homosexual orientation can be described as sodomite (luti). It is this behavior that characterizes the Tribe of Lot, who wanted to perform same-sex acts for reasons other than as a genuine expression of their sexual identity and psychological persona.[18] Omar's analysis challenges classical Islamic law. Jurists instituted practical norms forbidding same-sex acts such as sodomy (liwat), with the assumption that those performing them were, in their inmost character, actually heterosexual (or at least functionally bisexual).

Omar encourages his audience to rethink the applicability of the Islamic legal system, the shari'a, in the context of modern societies which make a conceptual distinction between sexual orientation and sex acts. The crucial point in debating Islamic legal norms is whether a person's acts reflect a certain intention (*niyya*). Therefore, before applying moral censure or enacting legal punishment, it is crucial for Muslims to assess in what ways homosexuality is a psychological component of a person's inner sense of identity. He writes that, "Performance of same-sex acts (*al-liwatiyya*) is governed by sexual orientation, because it is generated by behavior. In contrast, homosexuality is a sexual identity, because its existence is not conditioned by behavior."[19] Omar sets the terms for a constructive debate with Islamic scholars and mosque leaders through his careful logic and linguistic definition of terms. By drawing a clear distinction between sodomy (*liwat*) and homosexuality (*junusiyya*), he gives Muslims a way to understand homosexuals in their community and restore their human dignity. "The oppression which homosexuals suffer is caused by many factors. The most important of these causes is the lack of public understanding of homosexuality and homosexuals as people. Removing this oppression will come by giving the public clear information about the meaning of homosexuality. This will never be realized, in my opinion, until homosexuals get the opportunity to express themselves for themselves."[20]

Omar offers his own life story as an example of an Arab and Muslim homosexual taking "the opportunity to express themselves for themselves." The example of his book in Arabic has led other lesbian and gay Muslims in the Netherlands and neighboring Belgium to write their own accounts in Dutch. Such accounts were collected in *Mijn geloof en mijn geluk* (My Faith and My Fate) in 2002 by two journalists in the Netherlands of Palestinian and Turkish origin.[21] However, when Omar began writing, such a wealth of personal narratives did not exist, and he charts his own search for an authority figure (medical or religious) who could tell him how to react to his own self-knowledge of being gay.

Omar began writing an account of his life after visiting psychiatrists in Syria.[22] One Syrian psychiatrist told him that the cure was injection with male hormones; another suggested that he just try having sex with women. A third psychiatrist asked him to write a short summary of his life, which he did. He never returned to the psychiatrist but instead sent his brief life story to an Islamic scholar who taught in the *Kulliyat al-Shariʿa* (College of Islamic Law). The scholar wrote back explaining that his homosexuality was a psychic state and should not be expected to change easily, if at all; nevertheless he suggested that his behavior be modified to conform to heterosexual expectations, and that Omar marry a woman.[23] The scholar acknowledged the distinction between psychological identity and sexual acts, an insight Omar would develop in his own self-understanding, arriving at conclusions far from the strategic engagement with a woman that the scholar suggested. However, in Omar's conscience, marrying a woman would be torture toward himself, hypocrisy toward God, and deceit toward the woman.

Omar's search for knowledge took him to Damascus University and later, after immigrating to the Netherlands, led him to earn a master's degree in Middle Eastern Languages and Cultures at the University of Nijmegen. He earned his master's degree in cooperation with the University of Amsterdam's course in Homosexuality Studies. Moving to the Netherlands allowed him to pursue higher education in an open environment in which he could write about homosexuality and Islam, and also let him see how his childhood environment in Syria had been largely determined by Arab culture rather than Islam.[24] Seeing the difference between Arab culture and Islam was crucial for Omar to discover how Muslims conventionally view homosexuality through a prejudiced lens. In Omar's view, such prejudice is not inherent in the essence of Islam, but is ingrained deeply in Arab culture (as in many other patriarchal cultures).

A good example of the Arab and Islamic prejudice that Omar critiques is the El-Moumni Affair. The Moroccan imam in the Netherlands, el-Moumni thought that he was simply expressing what the *shariʿa* rules about homosexuality. But the imam did not admit the complexity of the *shariʿa* and the difficulty of applying it in situations where Muslims live as minority citizens of a nation-state. In addition, the imam did not discern that sexual orientation is different from sexual acts, an important insight which is part of the social consensus of the Netherlands and is the basis of its laws. According to Omar, the affair displayed the imam's shallow understanding, the Dutch media's racist antagonism, and the Muslim community's lack of foresight. In speaking of the El-Moumni Affair, Omar recalls that it was destructive: "[The Muslims] were totally separated from each other and they [the Dutch gay and lesbian critics] referred more to his religious ideas in general than to what he actually said. The whole country was against him. There was a media offensive against him." Omar was faced with the challenge of addressing the secular media, political parties, and court system in order to try to explain Islamic concepts and Muslim community dynamics.

Omar felt that the news media were wrong to focus solely upon Imam el-Moumni to the exclusion of other voices, especially as the imam was not a scholar in Islamic jurisprudence and had no training in secular knowledge. "According to my view, he is a conservative 'alim who knows only the basic things, who doesn't have the level of knowledge to give a *fatwa* (legal decision) at all. . . . It was a statement only. I was interviewed in the same program as him, and they [the news media] cut me [out] totally. I see *Nova*—the program that interviewed him—as the guilty party who should have been sued for the whole trouble! They focused only on negative things and put only that on television. . . . After that, they came to me many times and said they wanted to interview me, and I said no. So this brings me to my confrontation with the media . . . and modern journalistic methods in northwest Europe. They depend on an opinion and contradictory opinion." Omar explains that he created the Yoesuf Foundation not to fight but to promote dialogue through education and consciousness-raising. The foundation's methods were community building rather than conflict, favoring the *ijtihad* of thinking through issues carefully over the *jihad* of partisan conflict. "My strategy in the Yoesuf Foundation is only to build up without criticizing others. . . . It is my duty to build up something positive, but the media always wanted to hear that I am against this or against that." Omar's goal is to build understanding in both the Muslim minority and also in the Dutch majority that frames them as a nation. His foundation seeks to adjust secular political tools—like legal rights and media attention—to the needs of the Muslim minority community to help protect its most vulnerable members.

Rasheed: Solidarity with the Underdog

As the interview with Omar illustrates, the Yoesuf Foundation focuses on high-level dialogue with mainstream Muslim organizations and the secular government through media publicity. The foundation has been criticized for not working directly with the core constituency whose concerns it tries to communicate—that is, with actual gay, lesbian, and transgender Muslims. There is room in the field, even in a small nation like the Netherlands, for multiple organizations taking different approaches to the same issue. Accordingly, gay and lesbian Arabs in Amsterdam established a different sort of organization, called Stichting Habibi Ana ("My Beloved" Society). It began as a café run by and for gay and lesbian Arabs who felt alienated from mainstream Dutch homosexual venues, either because of racist attitudes encountered there or just because they missed Arab dance music. Habibi Ana provided an alternative social space, where Arabs called the shots in the ethnic mix of clientele, the languages of banter, and the music. The café became a unique space that brought together Middle Easterners (who might be Arab, Kurdish, Turkish, or Iranian) and North Africans (who might be Arab or Berber). These are communities which rarely come together in mosques or ethnic-based community centers. The convivial informality gave rise to discussions on social issues, religious topics, or political events that the clientele did not find elsewhere in the cultural capital of Amsterdam. The café's owner and others decided to establish a social support group that would promote these discussions in a more formal way, also called Habibi Ana. Their mandate was to serve as a social support network for gay, lesbian, and transgender people from immigrant backgrounds in Africa, Asia, and the Middle East—regardless of ethnicity or religion. Yet, because of the background of those who attend, there is a constant focus on Islam.[25]

One evening each week, the café turns into a meeting room for a dialogue with a set topic or guest speaker. This gives gay and lesbian members of minority communities a chance to share experiences, articulate their concerns, and access new information that might not be available through their family or community networks. As the society grew, it registered with the city government as a charitable organization, was granted financial support for outreach work, and opened an office. From there, volunteers run a telephone help line to serve members of minority communities who are in crisis or need information. The help line can refer people to health clinics, legal services, or shelters.[26] The organization also works with these service providers to educate them on the special needs of Arab and Middle Eastern minorities whose family structure, community pressure, and religious worldview may be confusing to mainstream Dutch professionals or social workers.

The Habibi Ana Society is run by volunteer labor. One volunteer, Rasheed, served as coordinator for its outreach projects. Rasheed is a law student at the University of Amsterdam in his mid-twenties, whose focus is on criminal defense law: "I would be a defender—I'm for the underdog." Rasheed grew up in the Netherlands in a family that immigrated from the Rif region of Morocco. He belongs to the second-generation Dutch Moroccan youth who form the largest component of the Muslim community and search for ways to be both Muslim and Dutch citizens at the same time. Like many in his generation, Rasheed is determined to succeed in education and professional life, against the stereotype of Moroccan youth who drop out to join gangs or commit petty crime. He finds great support for this mission in his family and ethnic community. But he feels cognitive dissonance when confronting religious loyalty and national belonging. He was raised in a practicing Islamic household yet attended Catholic school in a decidedly secular political environment; he has "come out" as gay to all his seven siblings who accept him, yet he hides the issue from his mother.

Rasheed's family moved from an Amazigh (or "Berber") region of Morocco to the Netherlands when he was four. "My father was working in a factory plant—he was not highly educated, and my mother cannot read or write, which says nothing about her intelligence, because I consider her a very intelligent person! She managed to raise us and she managed to survive." He described his parents as both "very religious" and he attended Islamic school on weekends. As a child, Rasheed prayed with his parents daily but they did not have complicated discussions about religion; for them, Islam was about solidarity with family and community in contradistinction to the society around them. Catholic school, however, gave Rasheed a critical perspective on his family's religiosity. "The Moroccans, gay and straight, have a very so-called Roman Catholic way of having their religion. The Roman Catholics are Christians but they don't read the Bible. Just like that, the Moroccans—especially the Moroccans in Holland, because they are Amazigh and they don't understand Arabic—don't know what is in the Qur'an. They only know a few verses so they can complete their prayers."

Rasheed received sex education in elementary school so he had some basic information when, as a teenager, he began to realize that he was gay. That was "when my body started to change and I became sexually [mature]. I guess that was around fourteen or fifteen years old. . . . I understood I was gay but in the beginning I denied it and it was very difficult to accept. I did not want to be gay, that is why I starting praying to God to make me straight. But it didn't change. . . . I didn't have the urge to have a coming out until I was sixteen, then I felt that I wanted to meet other gay people. . . . For a couple of years I was praying to God to make me straight, such that when I had an orgasm I felt disgusted with myself." In school, his sex education curriculum dealt with homosexuality as a natural human variation, but at home it was a matter of stigma and silence. "Islam says, *la haya fi'l-din*, meaning, 'No shame in religion.' You should be able to talk about everything, but we don't live up to this. There is a lot of shame." The difference between attitudes in the wider society and attitudes in his religious community created a grave conflict for Rasheed. "Actually, I gave up Islam for a period. . . . Muslims say that Islam says homosexuality is a sin and that you will go to hell if you are gay, and I thought, 'Well, if I can't be myself then I don't need such a religion any more." For a short while, he adopted a secularist solution. But Rasheed's atheism was not so much a rejection of God as it was a rejection of how Muslims in his community represented God. "In the eyes of many Moroccans I am an *afvallige*, an apostate, but I don't care about what they think. But later . . . I saw the beauty of Islam, then I did not hate it any more." Seeing the beauty of Islam came from meeting others from Muslim families who had managed to reconcile their sexuality and gender identity with their religion.

At the café of Habibi Ana, Rasheed began to meet Muslims who had an education in Islamic Studies. He moved to Amsterdam to start his university training in law and was able to live apart from his family. Secularism did not support his sense of self with its ethnic, religious, and even spiritual dimensions. "I started feeling very shallow inside. When I started to go to Habibi Ana, I met some gay Muslims who were so happy with themselves. They were gay and Muslim and they were not down—they were proud of themselves and still proud of Islam. But I was not proud of Islam any more! I was jealous of them, because they were so proud and had balance in their lives . . . Then I thought, maybe I had rushed a little bit too fast in rejecting my religion." These social connections changed Rasheed's perspective and he viewed his own family from a wider perspective, reclaiming Islam on his own terms.

"The Dutch gay establishment simply insists that you get 'emancipated' the way they did it. But I'm not a Dutchman. I have a Moroccan background that I'm proud of, and I'm going to do my struggle in my own way and not their way. Now this is a very bizarre thing, but through gay life I came closer to Islam. The Muslim gays that I knew taught me so much about Islam. . . . They have really changed my life. . . . Gay life has brought me closer to Islam! . . . I will always be grateful to Habibi Ana for that." Coming close to Islam means, for Rasheed, seeing "the beauty and the grace and the divine quality of Islam," and not just focusing on controversies or clashes with the secular system in the Netherlands.

As he grew in self-awareness and confidence, Rasheed learned to deal with the Dutch gay establishment on his own terms. He worked at the COC (Center for Culture and Leisure), the national homosexual rights organization whose goal is cultural, political, and legal "emancipation" of gay, lesbian, bisexual, and transgender people in the Netherlands.[27] The liberal laws and social tolerance of the Netherlands is largely due to the efforts of the COC.[28] It is, however, a largely "white" organization. Rasheed expresses frustration at the narrow-minded approach to "emancipation" that ignores cultural differences between white Dutch citizens and members of minority populations. He resents their overemphasis on individualistic values and chafes at their secular ideology, which limits their insight into the situation of Muslim youth from Moroccan or other ethnic backgrounds. Rasheed insists that their emphasis on coming out is not healthy for members of his own community. "Coming out is a way toward emancipation, not a goal in itself. A lot of Dutch people think that coming out is a goal, but it is not a goal—it is a method. It is one way to emancipation." The narrowly secular mission of the COC did not satisfy Rasheed, who does not see it as a useful strategy for reaching out to other Muslim homosexuals. Its secular norms and political vision needed to be adjusted to the cultural and religious reality of Muslim youth in the Netherlands. For Rasheed, being Muslim and Moroccan is an integral part of his identity—he cannot just abandon it in favor of secular emancipation. The most important thing about himself, Rasheed insists, is that he refuses to let his identity be fractured or let his life be compartmentalized.

As Rasheed says, "The healing effect of a discussion group is that, when your homosexuality is a secret, the discussion group just allows you to talk—the talking itself is the remedy. To hear the stories of other people is very good; it was very good for me. I think that other Moroccan gays should do this, but they don't go to discussion groups. . . . Some of them are married, or others are still living with their parents and pretending to be heterosexual, but even while going to discos, having a lover or a secret friend, they can keep their lives carefully arranged. They can have this part—having sex with a guy—very separate from that part—keeping loyal to the Moroccan community. They set up a double life. . . . If you go to a discussion, then you are not secret any more; you bring that part of yourself into the public meeting. . . . They can't handle that. . . . That is why they don't come to a discussion about homosexuality in general, or homosexuality in relation to Islam." This double life, observes Rasheed, gives them a sense of safety; their emotional and personal life stays insulated from their family and community life.

Rasheed rejected that form of safety which he calls "the double-bind." He tried to find a different, more integrated sense of balancing the many elements of his identity. "I didn't have the double-bind, or at least not so strongly as other people do. But what makes me a little different is that I made some choices. . . . I choose to have just one identity. . . . I am a human being in the broadest sense of the word! I am a student, also Berber, also Dutch, and also homosexual. I didn't want to have those separated. I wanted to have one identity, to find balance and harmony and a little serenity—and perhaps also a little happiness, with some luck. I thought, in order to have that, I had to make choices. I have chosen not to marry a woman. . . . When I made that decision I wanted to find out information about Islam. . . . And you know, once you have gone to a meeting or dialogue or discussion, it is easier to go to others. But it is difficult to go to the first one. It is my goal as a member of Habibi Ana Society, to find a way to reach those Moroccan gays who have not taken that first step."

Rasheed sees the need for organizations to be creative, to reach out to gay Moroccans in the Netherlands through their own cultural patterns, through symbols and activities which are distinctly theirs. "I see it as my golden goal to do something to reach those people. . . . I have to do something interesting for them, like a night with Dutch or Moroccan hip-hop." Rasheed wants to make the Habibi Ana Society more responsive to the needs and tastes of the Moroccans who make up such a large and vibrant segment of the urban population but who are so poorly served by its institutions. It is not surprising that Rasheed would turn to hip-hop music to design outreach programs that might attract Moroccan youth. Like them, Rasheed loves the Dutch rap scene. He hears rappers voice his own protests against racism and express solidarity with the underprivileged. But he admits, "The problem with Dutch underground hip-hop—which is produced incidentally mostly by Moroccans—is that the rap has lots of antigay sentiments."[29] Hip-hop artists are role models for Moroccan youth. They are culturally acclaimed by youth of all ethnicities, setting trends for social attitudes, political positions, and even religious loyalties. The music is commercially successful but still comes up from below, from garage bands and improvised studios in the ethnic neighborhoods. "Most of this is underground—you can only download it and you can't buy it, except for Ali B, of course. Ali B is not underground any more. No, Ali B is quite gay-friendly, and Raymzter too" (whose song against Dutch racism was cited at the beginning of this chapter). Rasheed observes that those hip-hop artists who gain commercial fame begin to promote the value of integration with Dutch society and soften the antigay sentiment, which makes them potential leaders of a new generation.

Even as Dutch Moroccan rappers like Ali B or Raymtzer hold up Imam el-Moumni as an example of an underdog speaking truth to power, they hold very different ideas about how Muslims should relate to homosexuality. Rasheed sees this music as one way to invite Moroccan youth, both homosexual and heterosexual, into the public dialogue. As Rasheed observes, "The Dutch hip-hop made by Moroccans is great. They are very dynamic and powerful. Their anger they put into the music, and sometimes it is even political. . . . Now about the antigay sentiments . . . to be very honest, I'm not offended by it. I'm not angered by it. . . . In Holland they have a saying that 'calling names doesn't hurt'—*schelden doet geen pijn*. Of course, it hurts—it hurts in the heart. But maybe because of solidarity I know we are both underdogs from minorities." This sense of solidarity allows Rasheed to brush off antigay remarks or sentiment from within his own community. For him, racism and Islamophobia from the white majority are more troublesome than homophobia from his own Moroccan or Muslim community.

Rasheed is one of a pioneering new generation of Muslim students who is getting through the higher education system and into professional life. "When I go to sit for an exam and I look around to see a bunch of other Moroccans sitting for the same exam, it fills my heart with joy. I think it is some kind of solidarity. Even though they dislike me for being gay, I'm still happy for them that they are also doing the exam and are succeeding in law school." His sense of solidarity is cultural and political and religious. Rasheed reflects on what it meant to grow up in a Moroccan family. "It is an 'us community.' Everything is 'we.' [The bad side of that is] the gossiping, but the good thing about the 'us community' is its solidarity. The Moroccans have solidarity with each other, but the gays don't have solidarity—they have lost it. . . . When gays are threatened in their homes, they have nobody to turn to, because their gay life is very hedonistic. . . . Solidarity is the opposite of hedonism. It means that . . . if someone is threatened by his neighbors then you will support him. But the Dutch gays don't have that kind of solidarity and support any more." This intense focus on solidarity was instilled in Rasheed from his childhood. It fuels his desire to reach out and help his fellow Moroccans who may be struggling with their homosexuality in silence, who have no positive role models for a strong and healthy identity; it also urges him to reach out to the wider Moroccan community who are presumed to be straight. Their antigay sentiments (often felt in silence and sometimes, as in the el-Moumni incident or in some underground hip-hop lyrics, spoken about openly) are bad for the health of their communities. It keeps them from integrating fully into Dutch society, and allows the media to project damaging stereotypes on them. At the furthest extreme, it leads some to say things that can be construed as hate speech and discrimination, bringing legal prosecution that is damaging for the community as a whole.

For this reason, Rasheed volunteered for an outreach project organized by COC Amsterdam and Cultinet. He hosted a dialogue at a gathering of Moroccan and Turkish students (of eighteen- to twenty-year-olds in Alkmaar near Amsterdam). There he shared his experience of growing up Moroccan, Muslim, Dutch, and gay. "It was the first time that the room was full of Turkish and Moroccan students. That is the dialogue that I want—that is what I hope to do with Habibi Ana Society. The topic was Homophobia versus Islamophobia. . . . I had a lovely feeling afterward because they respected me and asked me questions in a respectful way." Rasheed's honest answers to their questions demonstrated his sincerity to them, and they responded with respect. To hear such sentiments from a Moroccan youth who grew up in the Netherlands has great impact on these students, for they can identity with his family life and experiences growing up. "I would love to do this again with other groups and have the chance to inform them of my homosexual identity, and having peace with it, and not being afraid of God. I saw them observing me and not hating me or being disgusted with me. They had love in their eyes, both the girls and the boys. . . . It is good to inform others of how I feel my identity, how for me it is completely equal to heterosexual love, and it is given by God. . . . I don't care what other people think—it is between me and God."

In such dialogues with other Muslim students, Rasheed is sometimes asked about the tensions between Dutch laws about homosexuality and what Muslims see as God's law in the *shari'a*. Rasheed answers, "I can be very clear about that." He gives a very nuanced answer about the legal obligations of Muslims living as minority citizens of a democratic state, an answer that is in accord with the view of moderate Muslim scholars, like Tariq Ramadan.[30] Rasheed states, "The Qur'an says that you have to respect the government of the state that you are living in—the laws and rules of the state in the country where you are living. If there is friction or distance in ideas between Islam and the Dutch laws, the Qur'an says to us that we have to respect the laws of the country in which we reside." In Rasheed's view, his rights as a homosexual are legal rights, and all citizens, whether they are Muslim, Christian, Jewish, or atheist, must respect them because of the social contract inherent in citizenship. However, Muslims are new to this social contract and must be brought fully into the orbit of its norms and responsibilities with gradual education that affirms their dignity. Such integration will come about through dialogue and cannot be forced on them through legal action or political pressure.

The effects of such organizing may ultimately be stronger and more deeply rooted than legislation or court rulings. Adjusting the resources of secular politics and civic rights to the needs of the Muslim community in the Netherlands is a delicate balance. Rasheed volunteered at the office for Habibi Ana Society's "Information and Support Point." When it opened, the official at the ceremony, Ahmed Aboutaleb, was a politician of Moroccan descent who was prominent in city government (he was the Alderman for Social Affairs). His supportive speech, coming from one of the most visible members of the Moroccan community, was seen as a source of great encouragement to the fledgling project. Also at the opening was Rasheed's colleague, Osama, one of the driving forces behind the creation of the Habibi Ana Society and the administration of its office. His story sheds more light on the activist mode of adjusting secular politics to the needs of religious minorities.

Osama: Belonging despite Double Discrimination

When Habibi Ana Foundation's "Information and Support Point" opened, Osama was in his late twenties and was training to be a social worker. He had arrived only seven years before as a Palestinian refugee in the Netherlands, having fled Israel due to discrimination from his own family and immediate Palestinian community. Osama can identify with the Moroccan and Turkish youth who grew up in the Netherlands who come to the "Information and Support Point," even though his own background is so different from theirs. He sees in his own experience an analogous feeling of struggling against multiple layers of discrimination. "I am a Palestinian and a homosexual living in Israel. First, I was doubly discriminated against, like homosexual immigrants now in the Netherlands. The Jewish Israelis will never accept you. If they see you as Arab, they will never want to have anything to do with you. But if you play by their rules then maybe, just maybe, you can get inside. That is how I did it, unconsciously, in order to belong somewhere."[31] Osama knows that the legal protection of a state that claims to respect human rights does not effectively enable homosexual members of ethnic and religious minorities to negotiate with their families and secure a place in their communities. He sees the work of Habibi Ana Society and the Yoesuf Foundation as a way for homosexual Muslims from immigrant backgrounds in the Netherlands to "get inside" and claim their rights to legal protection, religious dignity, and privacy against the demands of their family and community; but at the same time, these support groups help them to assert their prerogative as citizens who are not from the white majority population, against the cultural expectations of Dutch institutions.

Osama grew up in a town of Christian and Muslim Palestinian Arabs that absorbed an ever-increasing influx of Jewish residents. His grandmother raised Osama upstairs while downstairs lived his mother, father, and ten siblings. His grandmother and her husband came from a Bedouin family who had been displaced by the war in 1948. She was a strong woman, having been expelled from her own family for supporting her husband's youthful participation in the Arab resistance movement, one of the longest-lived secular movements for political resistance in the past century. His grandmother was the primary influence upon him, but despite her inner strength she suffered from war trauma, flashbacks, and hallucinations. Her husband, Osama's paternal grandfather, lived with them but could not care for her, so it was left to Osama to comfort her during episodes of psychosis.

His grandmother had to explain to Osama that he needed to call the woman who lived downstairs "mother." His mother was from an urban Palestinian family, and brought a more adventurous attitude and secular education to her marriage with Osama's father, who still clung to his notion of Bedouin tradition, even forcing his sons to herd sheep. "I learned how to sing out there, as I would do my homework amid the sheep." Osama grew up between two worlds: "My father is a Bedouin but my mother was a city girl. . . . I grew up in the middle, seeing different sides of life and I was not convinced that what I see is all that there is." He was part of a bustling family but was raised separately from his brothers and sisters. He excelled in school but herded sheep in between an active town life and Bedouin memories of a nomadic past. He was a Palestinian Muslim but immersed in the wider potential of Israeli society.

School was a refuge for Osama and he knew it was the only means for him to gain independence from his family and society. He strove to finish high school early—at the age of seventeen—in order to get out faster and to pursue his dream of studying psychology, sociology, and social work. He was the only boy from his Arab neighborhood to go to university. He was trapped in the cultural predicament of an oppressed minority. Osama had to work harder in education to prove himself, being an Arab living in Israel with only limited prospects in civic and professional life; at the same time he was constantly being pulled back and undermined by his own community's sense of group loyalty and mistrust of the surrounding society.

Osama continually challenged his family's boundaries with his curiosity and adventurous spirit. He insisted on inviting Arab Christian friends home to visit. "This is taboo. You don't do that. I'm the first one, and still one of the only members of my family, to bring friends home who were Christians. . . . They said, 'Well, Osama is always strange and has some strange friends.' But then we talked and they said, 'OK, they are Christian but so what?' It is interesting how a black sheep of the family can start to become the moral authority!" He was the black sheep of the Bedouin family not because he was disobedient but because his aspirations were too wide. "I was always looking out of the circle, out beyond the bounds of their life. I always wanted to go out there, to go and to go. To check out what is going on, and find out what is that church and to get to know who this man [a Christian priest or monk] is who is always wearing black on the street. I was really curious. I don't think it has to do with my homosexuality. It was really long before that that I was interested in so many things."

Osama attended an Islamic school after secular school hours and on weekends. He was originally sent there by this father but soon adopted it as his own. "I felt that if I can get the love of my father and protection under his authority, I would be safe. . . . I thought maybe I should be more religious and get his respect." Between his twelfth and fifteenth years, Osama plunged into religion. This school was run in a mosque, which was a local center for the group called *Rijal al-Da'wa*, which is the Arabic name for the *Tablighi Jama'at* (the international Sunni missionary movement centered in South Asia). "They would stay in a mosque and walk around the neighborhood and call people to join them for a whole religious program in the mosque. . . . At twelve I started to attend classes at their school and by fourteen I was walking with them on their trips, wearing a turban, and carrying prayer beads." Osama's youthful involvement in the *Tablighi Jama'at*, a mild form of the Islamist movement, could be compared with activists who joined religious politics, like Fatima interviewed in the previous chapter.

However, Osama's involvement with religious politics was short-lived; his life path better illustrates a commitment to adjusting secular politics to the needs of his religious community. He joined the Islamist movement as a teenager primarily to win the love of his father. "My father tried very hard to get the *Rijal al-Da'wa* into our house. He was always saying [to the main teacher], 'If you are in the neighborhood, please, come on that day to our house and I'll make all my sons sit and listen to you.' Then he would call for all the sons to come home. . . . None of them were religious—I was the only one. It is interesting because when I got religious it was probably to earn the approval of my father and find a way to integrate into this family." Osama observed that his father was very attached to Islam, but as a means of exerting social control over his family rather than for spiritual or pious reasons. "When he wanted to do something, then he would use religion or his authority as a religious man to get it done within the family." His father was proud of him for being so devoted to Islam, but for Osama, going to this Islamic school and participating in its missionary trips was a way for him to reach out, socially and intellectually and spiritually, beyond the confines of the family that his father's religion enforced.

In the Islamic school he attended, Osama met two beloved teachers. One seemed to combine the attributes of his father and his grandmother into a single ideal personality. The other seemed to embody the qualities of motherly care but in a male authority figure. "When my father sent us to Islamic school, I had a teacher [named] Shaykh Qasim. He was a beautiful storyteller who could recite and explain things so wonderfully to us. He really showed me the beautiful side of my religion. . . . We studied mainly Qur'an and *hadith*." This model of Islamic piety was, in a way, a replacement for the father whom Osama was trying so hard to impress with his religious devotion, but whom he knew deep down would never accept him. Another beloved teacher was Shaykh Ameen, who Osama says "was gay, I'm sure of it. He was so soft, so caring. You could sense the motherhood role in his personality. But I think he did what Islam asked of him, which is not to practice sex and not to have any love or sexual life." Osama knew this because, during the years he participated in Islamic mission work, he was reaching sexual maturity and was increasingly aware of being homosexual in orientation. "At this time, when I was fourteen or fifteen, I started to ask questions of Shaykh Qasim about a lot of things. He would say to me sometimes, 'Osama, just leave it—that is not to be discussed.' . . . But after the lesson, Shaykh Ameen called me over . . . and we sat outside and had a very long conversation. I asked him a lot of things and I could really talk to him. This is what I found so beautiful about these two people, how they could explain things to children in a way that was fascinating and lovely. . . . [I had questions] about my homosexuality—I had trouble with that."

The recognition of his homosexuality began at around puberty when he realized he was different from other boys and began to experiment with sex. "[I and the neighborhood boys] played a lot of sexual games, and I liked it a lot. I remember that I had sex also with older guys, maybe four or five years older [than me]." Sexual play is fairly normal for boys his age, but Osama had a sense of growing disquiet, because he seemed to enjoy it more or differently than many others.[32] His sense of disquiet took the form of asking difficult questions of his Islamic mentors. For Osama at that age, prayer was not only about being in the presence of God, but also about being close to men. It was both sensual and holy, in a way that was intensely disturbing but also strangely comforting. "I spent so many hours praying and reading, in *khushu'* and asking God all the questions and asking God to help me, saying 'God, what is happening to me?' I knew already at age fourteen that there is something happening to me, and I didn't understand this. This is probably another reason that I went to the religion, to search for answers because there was nobody I could talk to about this. . . . Before you talk about it you have to figure out a certain phase by yourself, and ask, 'What is going on with me? . . . All night I was crying and crying and crying, then I would wake up and wait for the men to come in . . . everyone just out of bed, fresh. . . . You could go and then stand next to him, if you liked somebody, to pray next to him, standing and touching each other. But at night, again, I would be crying and asking these questions—'Please God, why am I doing this? What is this?'"

Despite his confusion, Osama understood clearly that he was not attracted to women sexually. "I knew that I was supposed to be attracted to women, but all the time when I did something with it [had a sexual experience] I thought about men." Osama discovered that some boys simply liked sex with other boys because there were no girls available, while others liked sex with other boys and saw sex as part of an affectionate and emotional attachment, while still others liked sex with other boys because they were male. Osama began to understand that he was in the latter category of those who were attracted to other males because of his inward disposition or sexual orientation, and that this made him unusual. "I still didn't give it a definition—of homosexual-ity—not yet. . . . I didn't think out it [clearly]. . . . In school, we didn't talk about gays—there were no gays. There were just men who like to do something with men. . . . With some of them I can tell you he is gay, and with others I can tell you he is not—that he just wanted to play. There were others who really admired you and touched you in a way that showed he really liked the male body."

In the absence of words or concepts, there was still an economy of sexual pleasure. There was still unspoken communication between young men about desire and its fulfillment. There were still roles to play—sexual roles often related to gender norms but sometimes to their transgression—and clues about what was demanded. "It is not allowed, though it is tolerated. . . . [With homosexuality in his Arab commu-nity] you know that it is happening but you don't talk about it, and at a certain age you have to stop. . . . It has to do with the lack of *seksuele vorlichting*—education about sexuality and sexual orientation."

Increasingly lonely, Osama studied more intensely at school and worked harder at his job to earn money to attend university. He knew that he was looking for more than boyish sex play in the neighbor-hood but also faced serious disadvantages to searching outside the neighborhood for an emotional gay relationship, as he was underage and Arab in an national environment made hostile by religious prej-udices, national law, and the Intifada. Despite these obstacles, Osama found his first boyfriend in a Russian Jew who was serving as a nurse in the Israeli military. Osama was fifteen and his boyfriend was twenty-one, and they took great risks in crossing the barriers of age, race, and religion. "We stayed together almost two years. . . . Of course, in the beginning it was really strange. I thought, 'What is this, what do I have with this guy?' The sex started to take longer and longer. We started to play around after sex. It was not just sex and getting dressed and run-ning off. . . . Yes, it was through flirting with each other, through miss-ing each other." Osama was both fascinated and alarmed by this grow-ing emotional attachment that was far deeper than just the sex play to which he was accustomed. "Sometimes I pushed him away, saying, 'No, I don't want contact with you, I don't want to know these things.' But he always reached out to me because he loved me. He just fought with me all the time. He was always coming back, always wanting to go on with the relationship. . . . I thought, 'No, it is not possible that I'm doing all this just for sex. There must be something else.' Then I realized that I loved him. I got scared. I went to look for help." Looking for help meant turning to a group that gave professional help on issues of gender and sexuality. They referred Osama to an Arab social worker—"a lovely lady, but she didn't know what to do with me." She treated him as she would treat someone for addiction and he was completely dissatisfied.

Osama asked to be transferred to a male social worker, and was treated by an Israeli psychologist who recognized homosexual orientation as an integral part of Osama's character. He saw Osama's ongoing relationship as a positive step in his personal development and guided him through the process of contacting other homosexual men in Israel. He eventually contacted an advocacy group supporting individual rights that had a youth project for people between sixteen and twenty-seven in which some gay men participated. Osama recalls, "Then my 'gay life' started." At seventeen he graduated from high school and got accepted to university in a different city where he joined a gay men's network. This university network progressed to formally establishing the Jerusalem Open House, a human rights organization for issues around gender and sexuality. He was one of the only Arabs involved (though presently the Open House sponsors a Palestinian Outreach Project which includes both Christian and Muslim Palestinians from within Israel proper and also the West Bank territories occupied by Israel).

At that time, though, Osama felt the need to reach out and find other Arab homosexuals. He met many young men from the West Bank who had run away from home and were living on the street, sometimes working as male prostitutes. They were often fleeing abusive families—sometimes the abuse was specifically account of their homosexuality and sometimes it was just due to general pressures and masculine violence. Seeing the desperation of his fellow Arabs who were struggling with the same issues but without the resources he had, Osama vowed to build a support network for gay Palestinians.

As a high school student, Osama had been involved in the Arab Youth Movement to empower young Palestinians growing up in Israel (whom the media now call "Israeli Arabs") to assert themselves through education and civic activism. During this first year in university, he deepened his interest in politics and social change by joining the movement to support a "two-state solution" with peace programs and dialogue between Jews and Arabs. He did a year of conflict resolution training at a village project called The Oasis of Peace and worked as an instructor for Israeli and Palestinian youth in a camp for nonviolent reconciliation. Through this work, he met other progressive Israelis with whom he could be "out" as a gay Arab. Some of them encouraged Osama to speak on national television about being gay and Arab. He assumed that the TV program would obscure his face and conceal his identity in order to protect his safety, so he agreed and became the first Arab in Israel to speak about his experiences as a homosexual. He spoke for ten minutes on a program in Arabic.

What Osama said on the program may have helped countless people but it sparked a family disaster for him. "My mother later said to me that she recognized me instantly just by the shape of my head! They [the TV journalists] didn't really obscure my features well at all. . . . [My parents] got a call from [relatives in] the south of the country saying, 'Turn on the TV right away and look at what your son is doing!'" The six months that followed were a severe test of Osama's strength as his family members closed ranks against him and also suffered a loss of pride in their close-knit community. The older males in his family pressured the TV program to make a public announcement that the family which had been disturbed by the program was not the one whose son had been featured, in an attempt to deflect neighborhood pressure against his father and brothers. His pregnant sister was verbally attacked by her husband's family, and instead of defending her the husband beat her and she lost her child; the incident was blamed on Osama and his homosexuality. Osama's mother and father began to hold each other responsible for warping their son's behavior, blaming on Osama difficulties in their relationship that had been manifesting themselves for several years. His father did not leave the house even to pray in the local mosque, afraid of the comments he might receive to wound his pride or shame him.

Osama was virtually imprisoned in his parental house. Finally, an uncle intervened with his father, saying "'Your son is sick . . . and he needs you.' He pictured the situation as a disease, as a mental disease. Actually that is what rescued me." When his sister began to insult him about his homosexuality, his mother reacted with anger, saying, "'How dare you talk to your brother like this? You are not going to humiliate him with his sickness!' This is the term through which she could understand it, and through it she was trying to protect me." Being seen as sick was actually a step toward positive relations.

At first, his family saw his homosexuality as sin and worse, as a betrayal of their honor. Osama reflects that their negative reaction was not based on religion but rather on an Arab culture of family pride and shame. "They knew that it is not allowed in Islam—that it is *haram* and all that. But the issue for them was social control. They really had a lot of problems dealing with the neighborhood. My brother once said to me, 'You don't know what you have done to us! We can't look people in the eye. We lost our authority and our honor. Anybody can say whatever they want to us, because if we object they will say, 'Go first to your gay brother,' and we will just shut our mouths and walk away like dogs with our tails between our legs.' They were humiliated." After seeing his homosexuality as a betrayal, they then saw it as a contagious disease, and finally as a mental illness. It was seeing it as a mental illness that allowed them to treat him relatively more humanely and seek positive ways to deal with their situation.

As someone suffering from a mental illness (*marad nafsani*), his family decided to have him cured by a psychiatrist. "They kept me at home for one month. Then I said, 'I know of a psychiatrist,' and this guy works for the support group [where I went to university].' So they let me call him up and I told him I needed a session with him. . . . They would take me out to [that city] to meet the psychiatrist for each session, and the psychiatrist told me to just agree with them and tell them whatever they needed to know. . . . He would tell them it was temporary—'He needs to come here to see me a few times. We can cure the problem.' This is what they needed to hear." However, his hometown had become dangerous for Osama. Men in his neighborhood attacked him and neither family nor police could protect him—"They felt it was natural that I should be attacked." When his family made indirect inquiries about the assault through neighbors, it was justified by rumors that Osama had been recently seen having sex with men in public. His family believed the rumors rather than their son's denials, and it became increasingly clear that Osama could not live in his own town.

Eventually, they allowed him to move back to the city where he attended university in order to be nearer the psychiatrist who was "curing" him. "Things became a little easier for me, and for them [the family] too. Nobody had to see me or deal with the facts. But then there were rumors. . . . Somebody said to my family that my name was on a list, as somebody who has to be killed. . . . There is some group that was . . . as they put it, 'trying to clean up the neighborhood.' I don't know if that was true. They were young macho people who had some guns and they wanted the honor of 'cleaning up the neighborhood.'" To avoid the potential threat of an "honor killing," Osama stayed in the city where he attended university for two months, hoping the crisis would blow over.

After a few months, he got a job in Tel Aviv. Osama tried to deflect the crisis by earning money and sending it back to his parents. This helped to convince them that he was fulfilling the role of a son and quieted complaints. However, after a few months, Osama was called to a family meeting. His family announced to Osama that he was getting married in a week. "They said to me, 'On Wednesday we can go to the family living in the West Bank where you can get a bride.' I said to my father, 'How? I don't even know her!' He said, 'Just be happy that somebody is agreeing to get married to you.' . . . Then he placed the ultimatum on me that 'If you don't want it, then we have to do it—we have to get it done.' This meant that they would have me killed, because they just could not take it any more from the people. If somebody would 'do it,' they would get their honor back in the eyes of the neighborhood. . . . First my father said to me, 'I can do it right now, right here, if I want—but first I want to give you this chance [to get married]. . . . My uncle said, 'Then I'll do it. I'll drive my taxi over him and we'll say it was an accident.' I was right there. So I said, 'OK, I'm getting married next week.'"

After Osama agreed to this plan, his friends bought him an airline ticket and arranged for a friend in the Netherlands to take him in. Osama was nineteen when he began this new phase of his life. It began with trauma and grief because he had lost his parents. "I told them that I had left the country and that there was no need to look for me. . . . They didn't believe it. They thought I was lying. . . . Then he [Osama's father] got really crazy. He went to the Jerusalem Open House and to the institution where I had worked [for Arab-Jewish Coexistence] and he started screaming and breaking things—'You knew and you helped him!' . . . My father was destroyed. His authority was totally gone. I broke his authority. I didn't listen to him. I just went. I didn't ask his permission to leave. Nothing. I actually gave him the message that he was nothing to me any more."

In the Netherlands, Osama applied for asylum on the grounds that he faced dangerous discrimination based on his sexual orientation back in his home country. The government denied him asylum because he had traveled on an Israeli passport and the laws in Israel were not deemed discriminatory, but Osama secured a student visa that gave him legal residency in the Netherlands. He completed his degree in social work—the field of studies that he had begun in Israel before it was interrupted by crisis. The framework for his social work is entirely secular. In his personal life, Osama has given up, at least for the present, practicing Islamic rituals. "I believe but I'm not religious—not now. I believe in a certain power—call it God. . . . As for religion, I was born a Muslim. I am a Muslim. I think I have the freedom in Islam to have my own religion, though some people will disagree with me. But one of the biggest examples is Muhammad himself—he had his own way of being religious. . . . He told people how to believe in things, and gave them the freedom, too, to believe in their own way. *Hij was en spiegel*—he was a mirror for others. Actually, he asked others to try to find their own way in religion."

Osama still struggles to heal the pain of his break with his parents. That affects how he sees religion. "I think that Islam . . . has changed from a religion to a way of keeping people under control." Osama is reflecting on both his experience with his family's coercive use of religion and also on the ascendancy of religious rhetoric in Arab politics and Islamic extremism internationally. "I have come to the conclusion that it [Islam] is a *grondwet*—a constitution—that had to be written by God or Muhammad or some great philosopher in order to keep law and order at that time. . . . This is the definition of religion for me. . . . I think Islam gave a lot of rest and peace of mind to people at that time." Osama observes that religion in earlier times provided a framework for political and social life, for peace and security; but those goals are today fulfilled by the secular state. In Osama's view, the way many Muslims interpret Islam as a ritual orthodoxy and a code of conduct is misleading. The *shari'a*, in his view, should not be an excuse for setting up a priestly caste of jurists and scholars and divines. "Muhammad never set up these men at al-Azhar [the *shari'a* academy in Egypt]. He never instituted this tradition. . . . For me, those people do not have absolute authority." Osama rejects these upholders of tradition because their decisions are informed by a defensive fear of secular laws and national systems which provide greater security and rights. He feels that these spokesmen for tradition are moved by political expediency and desire to preserve their own power rather than by a sincere spiritual quest for religious truth.

In contrast, Osama admires the Prophet Muhammad for having encouraged people to find their own way to God. For Osama, "finding one's own way" in religion means creating a harmonious balance in one's relationships with others in order to restore wholeness to oneself and preserve the dignity of others. This is the principle that leads him to become an activist, a principle that has deep roots in Islam. "Before I want people to see me as a homosexual, I want them to see me as a person. . . . Maybe this is why I am an activist. Most activists are not naïve, but they desire to create a certain harmonious balance. They desire a certain justice, a kind of equality and freedom of choice. I don't think I will, with my work with Habibi Ana or my work now in Rotterdam, create a miracle or change people's mentality. I don't want this to be attributed to me! No, people must change their attitudes by themselves, but sometimes you say things that may help them to think about certain issues. So in my activist work I encourage people to search for their own answers."

With professional training in social work and government support for his initiatives, Osama is able to pursue the activist work on behalf of homosexual Arabs and Muslims that he had dreamed of in Israel but that had been cut short by social violence. "At Habibi Ana, I also saw how people were treating each other and how they talk about relationships. I saw how people in my own circle were living with this identity conflict for so long, that some people were getting really psychotic from all these questions." Osama proposed a project to do outreach with homosexuals from immigrant communities (mainly Arab, Berber, Turkish, Kurdish, and Iranian minorities) and design a program for sexual health education and HIV prevention for them. "I went to the

Schorer Foundation [for sexual health education] and they agreed that by working with them, I could develop a project outside their foundation and they would give me guidance in that project. . . . The Habibi Ana Society will work on setting up meetings and self-help by sharing experiences, helping each other, developing certain themes. This is why the Information and Support Point is working now." The support center began as a volunteer effort funded by a national foundation for sexual health and well-being, but it grew under the guidance of Osama and other volunteers. "We began as just two people . . . [but now] we have the 'Information and Support Point' in an office where three nights a week we have hours where people can call or drop in to talk with volunteers who are also gays from other cultures. . . . They ask about sexual health, sexual orientation. I do the intakes. . . . I kept the cases that needed professional social work." Other volunteers give informal counseling while Osama handles cases that require a trained social worker.

The Habibi Ana Society's project was designed to address the needs of all ethnic minorities (*allochtoonen*, as they are known in Dutch political discourse) but specified that it would begin by focusing on groups from the Middle East and North Africa. It was essential to begin there because that is where the most acute social need was. "The contact and attention for this group was just not there. Now there is a lot of attention. . . . This has to do, really, with the revolution of Habibi Ana against the institutions that were claiming to work with homosexuals. We said [to Dutch government institutions and the COC], 'You're not doing anything about this, so now we are going to do it ourselves.'" In this way, Osama is trying to carve out a safe space which offers a sense of belonging to others at the same time as he does so for himself. He is discovering a sense of belonging in the Netherlands after suffering displacement upon displacement as a Palestinian homosexual in Israel.

Although the context of his life in Europe differs greatly from that of his youth in a Palestinian family, Osama applies the lessons learned in Israel about politics, religion, and psychology to try to get minority communities to engage in a dialogue about sexuality and gender. "This what I'm trying to address in my own work here in the Netherlands. Emancipation has to come from the people themselves. . . . It is the immigrant and minority organizations that have to talk together about how they think about the subject and what they want to do about it. If you come and say, 'Now you have to accept this—this is homosexuality,' they will answer, 'Well, that is nice for you, but you Dutch are still the rulers.' They never see it as a human rights issue but rather as an issue of those in charge coming to tell us what to do. So [they react by saying,] 'We are not going to take it up!' This was also the case in Israel."

Whether in Israel or in the Netherlands, Muslim minority communities resist discussing the issue not only or even primarily because of their religion or culture. Rather, the very fact of being a minority which perceives itself to be marginalized or oppressed generates the reaction that to discuss homosexuality openly is to abandon their values and religion. For this reason, it is not enough to have secular laws that decriminalize homosexual acts, protect against discrimination based on sexual orientation, or recognize same-sex partnerships and marriage. Rather, the process of social change involves the social forces of family and religious community which are resistant to legislated change. Secular political strategies must be adapted to the lived reality of diverse communities within the nation-state. Their goals must be restated in terms that make sense to communities whose terms of belonging are ethnic or religious. The activist initiatives of Osama and other volunteers in Habibi Ana try to fill this mediating role between secular norms and religious community.

This role can only be taken up by insiders who have grown up within these communities and know their idioms and ideals. The stark reality is that neither in the Netherlands nor in Israel do secular laws effectively protect homosexuals within minority communities. However, establishing a national law which recognizes homosexuals as citizens with equal rights does create a cultural climate which provokes change through education, active intervention, or in extreme cases, legal coercion.

Conclusion

Each year on May 4, citizens of the Netherlands hold a day of commemoration for martyrs of World War II. The trauma of Nazi occupation involved institutional racism and discrimination against ethnic, religious, and sexuality minorities in the Netherlands. For this reason, a memorial service is also held on this day at the Homo Monument in

Amsterdam.[33] There, the legal protection of homosexual and transgender people is displayed with the quiet dignity of a state ceremony. Representatives of the national government, the armed forces, the police and fire brigade, as well as the COC lay wreaths of flowers to honor the memory of those who suffered persecution and execution.

In 2006, I attended the ceremonies at the Homo Monument. Along with the audience I witnessed something unprecedented: wreaths were laid by a founding member of Habibi Ana Society and a Moroccan volunteer at COC Amsterdam, both gay men from Arab communities. Their presence was highly symbolic, showing that minority communities who are mainly Muslim (whether Arab, Berber, Turkish, or Iranian in ethnicity) are part of the ongoing movement to secure human rights in the field of sexual orientation for all citizens of the Netherlands. Their participation in this state ceremony is a vivid example of "adjusting secular politics." They took part in a secular state ceremony but suffused it with the presence of their ethnic group and religious community, significantly enlarging the symbolic value of the ceremony.

Adjusting secular politics is a strategy used by those interviewed in this chapter, who are all gay men living in the Netherlands. There, the strength of secular institutions encourages lesbian, transgender, and gay Muslim activists to use this mode of activism. Adjusting secular politics means altering the secular political process to the needs of a minority community which is, in the case of Muslims in the Netherlands, defined by religion as well as ethnicity. Through this strategy gay, lesbian, and transgender Muslim activists bring the resources of the state, political parties, and civic organizations to bear on their religious-ethnic minority. But to do this effectively, they must adjust the secular apparatus to the needs and sensitivities of their community. Great care is required so that secular pressure is not seen to threaten the religious community. They hope to alleviate the perception among many Muslims living as minorities that their religious values are threatened by the secular state and non-Muslims who wield power through it.

The activist strategy of "adjusting secular politics" helps to dissolve the apparent conflict between a secular state and religious communities among its citizens and residents. The Netherlands is a vivid arena for this mode of activism because of the strength of the secular state and the very recent appearance of a Muslim minority with it. Even as Muslim immigrants prosper by living and working in the Netherlands, many of them are reluctant to reexamine their allegiance to *sharīʿa* and Islamic customs. Few Muslims in immigrant communities advocate continuing the classical-era Islamic project to continuously reform the *sharīʿa*'s legal guidance. While Muslim minority communities in most places are reluctant to do this, in the Netherlands the situation is extreme. The Muslim migrants who settled there were primarily laborers from underdeveloped regions of Morocco and Turkey who lacked access to both secular education and Islamic intellectual traditions. The mosque leaders they brought over to service their communities came from the same background and are ill-equipped to adjust to secular politics and the demands for religious reform. For this reason, many young Muslims in the Netherlands strive for university education and professional training, as displayed in the interviews with Omar, Rasheed, and Osama.

Along with adopting secular education, these activists adjust secular political strategies to their goal of securing rights and welfare for those in the Muslim minority community who are lesbian, transgender, and gay. Of those activists interviewed in this chapter, Rasheed and Osama took to secular education exclusively. Rasheed's knowledge of Islam came mainly from his family while Osama attended mosque education run by an Islamist organization; yet both aspire to secular education and professional training. Through this secular work, they strive to actualize Islamic values—like protecting the vulnerable or promoting the welfare of others—without an overt appeal to the Islamic roots of those values. In contrast, the interview with Omar shows how he aspired to combine secular and religious education to revive the classic Islamic intellectual tradition. While Omar participates in Islamic discourse and scholarship, he works for a secular institution that cooperates with government, media, and community welfare organizations. Omar adjusts secular politics to the needs of his religious minority community, while at the same time engaging his religious tradition; it must be emphasized again that engaging in one mode of activism does not preclude simultaneously engaging in others.

Many in Muslim minority communities do not recognize the homophobic elements of their religious tradition that require reform to meet the basic requirements of citizenship under Dutch law. Muslims' prejudices against homosexuality can lead their community into danger. The activists interviewed in this chapter strive to point out this danger to their coreligionists. They argue that by clinging to outmoded customs or reifying the *shari'a*, Muslims in constitutional democracies actually impede the success of Islam and damage the long-term viability of a Muslim community in this space. This is amply demonstrated by the controversy over public statements by Imam el-Moumni, a Muslim leader in the Netherlands. Many of the activists interviewed in this chapter were involved in the el-Moumni case or used it as a touchstone for their own activist work. For this reason, it is instructive to follow how the el-Moumni controversy was resolved.

The el-Moumni case hardened Dutch public opinion against Muslims in the Netherlands, in ways that threaten the viability of Muslim communities in the nation. Imam el-Moumni made statements to the national news media that expressed his rejection of homosexuality based upon what he asserted were basic Islamic teachings. The imam was charged with hate speech, a criminal offense. But he was exonerated because of a Dutch legal conundrum that pits two cherished secular ideals against each other: freedom of religious belief and practice versus the legal rights of citizens with minority expression of sexual orientation or gender identity.[34]

After Imam el-Moumni was exonerated, there were calls for him to be expelled from the country, as he held Moroccan citizenship and was alleged to not uphold Dutch values or owe primary allegiance to the constitution. Such extreme reactions were not acted upon, partly because el-Moumni upheld the value of democracy and argued that Muslims must not use violence against lesbians and gays. However, el-Moumni's trial emboldened more extremist views. While he was still in court (in November 2001), another imam in the Netherlands pronounced that "public homosexuality deserved the death penalty," despite the fact that Dutch law explicitly forbids the death penalty for any crime and does not look upon homosexuality or same-sex sexual activities as a crime.[35] This imam provocatively confused rules encoded in the *shari'a* with the legal obligation of Muslims living in the Netherlands—a very dangerous move for this fledgling Muslim community which is in an increasingly fragile relationship with the majority of its fellow citizens. Many white Dutch citizens in the gay community feel threatened by the new visibility and assertiveness of Muslims and suspect that their religious beliefs are more inherently homophobic than those of other Christian or Jewish groups who have long since found a quiet place in Dutch society. Still more alarming, some in the white majority join right-wing parties and now use the issue of gay acceptance or lack thereof to further marginalize Muslims as a racial and religious minority that is changing the complexion of Dutch society.

These public debates highlight the urgent need for Muslims to reassess the *shari'a*, the legal code through which their values are translated from the private realm of belief into the public realm of social order. Having pledged allegiance to a secular nation-state, Muslims in the Netherlands—as in other secular democracies—can no longer uphold the *shari'a* in its classical form. Yet Muslims are very hesitant to face this challenge forthrightly, especially as it deals with the presence of transgender, lesbian, and gay Muslims in their community who are granted inalienable rights and legal protections under a secular constitution. Gay, lesbian, and transgender Muslim activists are often on the vanguard of alerting their religious community to the dangers of reifying the *shari'a*. Their strategy of adjusting secular politics is a way of showing their community's creative and effective alternatives. Secular politics are not anti-Islamic just because they are secular. Secular political parties, state bureaucracies, and civic organizations may uphold norms that are identical (or correlate) with Islamic values and norms. Further, secular politics may place much-needed pressure on the Islamic tradition to adjust and evolve, as it had in the classical period.

The interviews from the Netherlands presented in this chapter illustrate the activist mode of "adjusting secular politics" to the needs of a religious minority living in a constitutional democracy. This strategy is especially appealing in a country where democratic institutions are nourished in a strongly secular environment, in which religious beliefs are kept out of the public realm. But not all democracies are like this. In situations where legal rights are not so firmly guaranteed or where religion plays a role in public debates, activists may turn to other strategies. In such situations, an appealing strategy is the forging of minority alliances. Alliances between minority communities can help a group gain support in the absence of firm legal protections. This is a mode of activism which will be explored in the next chapter through interviews in the United States, Canada, and the United Kingdom.

5

Forging Minority Alliances

When the mountain of injustice will topple
When under our feet—we who suffer—the earth quakes
Over their heads—those who wield power—the bolts flare
We, too, shall see that day
When only the name of God will remain
That is absent yet present, seeing yet also seen
The cry of "I am truth" will rise, that is me and also is you[1]
The people of God alone will rule, that is me and also is you!
We, too, shall see that day

~Faiz, Hum Dekhenge

These fiery words belong to the Urdu poet and literary hero of Pakistan, Faiz Ahmad Faiz (died 1984). He protested against the injustices of British colonial rule, and after independence he railed against the corruption of the Pakistani government, especially its autocratic military rulers. When this poem, "We, too, shall see that day," was sung in Lahore by the *ghazal* artiste, Iqbal Bano (died 2009), her voice and his words tapped the long-suppressed hopes of 50,000 Pakistani listeners who erupted into sustained cheers of *Inqilab Zindabad!*—"Long Live the Revolution!"

Even though Faiz was in prison at that time, his voice reached the people and spoke in an incandescent fusion of messianic hope and secular protest to assert that Islam promises justice for all. He draws out images from the Qur'an that evoke "the last day" when God will judge those who have been unjust, and invokes Sufi images about the impoverished who live with nothing but love and speak truth to power. For Faiz, neither faith nor mystical love could bring about the radical justice he sought; rather, secular politics would return power to the ordinary citizen and allow each to speak for her- or himself. For Faiz, romantic love and revolutionary love were united—one called out for the other. He denounced authoritarian rule in Pakistan that increasingly turned to Islamic fundamentalism to bolster its power. Not surprisingly, he was jailed, persecuted, and driven into exile.

Muslim migrants from Pakistan and wider South Asia brought Islam and also their love for Urdu poetry to the United States, United Kingdom, and Canada, and with it they also brought their adoration for Faiz. Having risen up against Western imperial rule, Muslims in South Asia found that the promises of national independence rang increasingly hollow. Many left poverty and authoritarian rule to find new opportunities for prosperity and education in the West. Yet they found that real life in the West was characterized also by the disparity of wealth and racism. So they carried Faiz with them on paper and in song. His voice sustained them in their struggles to make a new home. Among these migrants and their children are lesbian, gay, and transgender Muslim activists. Some of them still find inspiration in Faiz and, like him, combine religious idealism with progressive politics.

Had Faiz lived to meet the gay and lesbian Muslims who establish support groups, he may not have found in them immediate allies, driven as he was by the vision of class struggle and the quest for economic justice. But hearing their words, he would empathize with their experiences of marginalization and oppression. As a political ally, Faiz would have understood the burning need for justice and yearning for self-actualization that drives them.

Gay, lesbian, and transgender Muslims must build bridges in their quest for justice. They are a minority within a minority within a minority: they are a few in terms of sexuality or gender identity from a non-Christian religion, and also part of the nonwhite ethnic group who live in a predominantly white, Christian, heterosexual population. In this situation, lesbian, gay, and transgender Muslims cannot rely on demographics to press for rights. In constitutional democracies, often their voices are ignored by the wider society that is more concerned to assuage the larger Muslim community or ethnic communities under which they are subsumed. For example, leaders in the United States make a show of respecting African American church leaders in order to prove that they are not racist, and conveniently ignore how some church leaders uphold bigoted stereotypes or religious hatred for gay, lesbian, and transgender members of their own African American community. In a similar way, some politicians and Christian leaders make a display of their respect for Muslim community leaders without holding them accountable for how Muslim communities treat vulnerable members within their own groups, like women and youth along with transgender, gay, and lesbian members.

For this reason, some activists from among gay, lesbian, and transgender Muslims focus on building bridges. Their strategy for social change depends upon cultivating allies in various minority groups far from their own communities. To do this, they advocate the politics of empathy. They urge others who may not be homosexual or transgender—or who may not be Muslim—to understand their plight through empathy. They ask their allies to see oneself in the other, witness their common humanity despite social differences, and to uphold the rights of others just as they would like their own rights upheld. Across the boundaries of ethnic group, sexuality, gender, and religion, these activists strive to build bridges and strengthen relationships of alliance and mutual understanding. We can call this mode of activism "forging minority alliances."

Faisal: Opener of Possibilities

In the Faiz poem quoted above, the poet sings, "The people of God alone will rule, that is me and also is you! We, too, shall see that day." The people of God who rule are known as *khalifa*, literally one who follows in the footsteps of the Prophet Muhammad who ruled. In Islamic history, the *khalifa* was an individual ruler who was first among equals. But as Islamic history quickly betrayed Islamic teachings, the *khalifa* became an autocratic king. Faiz's poem holds out the hope that history's perversion can yet be rectified—we can still recognize that the people of God who rule include both you and me.

This is a reformist notion of what it means to be a *khalifa*, a notion that is advocated by Muslim champions of democracy (like Abdullahi an-Naim) and Muslim feminists (like Amina Wadud). Both these Muslim thinkers in the United States espouse the idea that the *khalifa* is not a ruler but is rather any and every responsible and ethical person.

If there is one central principle of the Qur'anic message, it is for each believer to become the *khalifa* or vice-regent of God on earth. This means to strive to gain authentic knowledge of one's own nature, stay aware always of God's presence, and guard the rights of others even if it means sacrificing oneself.

For one young Muslim in the United States, Faisal Alam, this call to take responsibility for himself and others led him to take great risks. There is no one person responsible for establishing the international network of support groups for lesbian, gay, and transgender Muslims, for that is a collective effort of many. However, if there is one person who has been persistently responsible for goading informal groups to organize into formal organizations, it is Faisal. He founded Al-Fatiha Foundation in the United States in 1997, and he guided the establishment of other groups in Canada and the United Kingdom based on its model. One incident will serve as an example of his charismatic persona and his powerful Islamic message of taking personal responsibility, which serves to bind people together from very different backgrounds and communities. His story illustrates the activist mode of forging minority alliances.

As night settled over Washington, D.C., in May 2002, the fountain plaza at Dupont Square was unusually crowded. This central meeting place usually offers a leisurely cross section of the city's urban mix, where Americans who identify as black, white, Latino, or Asian cross paths, where straight and gay rub shoulders, where the affluent and the homeless share a bench, if only for a moment. But this night, a single candle flame pierced the dark, then spread to another candle, to two more, and then a multitude as the park around the fountain crowded with new faces, each glowing in the evocative light of a candle which wavered in the wind but refused to disappear. The park was crowded with a rally of lesbian, gay, and transgender Muslims with their supporters who had come to recite a *janaza* or funeral prayer.

They were praying to commemorate the deaths of members of their community who had been persecuted in the name of their religion— Islam. Gay, lesbian, and transgender Muslims gathered at the protest, along with their straight Muslim allies and non-Muslim supporters. They recited the prayer for those who had been judged without a hearing, whom preachers had chased out of mosques, or pressured into a debilitating silence. Those who gathered stood in neat rows to recite the *takbir*—"God is greater"—to dignify the memory of those who had been killed, persecuted, forced into inauthentic lives of lies, or driven to suicide.

The rally was organized by Al-Fatiha Foundation during its national conference for lesbian, gay, bisexual, transgender, queer, and questioning Muslims. Faisal Alam, who initiated the support group, spearheaded the prayer ritual. The public prayer for the dead highlighted how Muslim leaders, by condemning homosexual and transgender persons in their communities, inflict both real and symbolic violence on fellow believers, perhaps without realizing the consequences of their words. As Faisal explained, "When I have dialogues with imams I say—If you continue doing what you are doing, on the day of judgment is Allah going to say to me, 'Faisal, why, when this person came to Al-Fatiha, did you teach them how to pray?' or is Allah going to say to you, 'Imam, why did you say what you said in that Friday prayer [sermon] which caused this person to leave your mosque and never come back again?'"[2] In this rhetorical exchange, Faisal evokes a *hadith* that the Prophet reportedly said, "This religion is firm, so go with it gently. . . . Don't make the servants of God shun the worship of God."[3]

Faisal established Al-Fatiha Foundation in order to give Muslims who had been driven from mosques, communities, and families a place to seek refuge, solidarity, and healing in the face of enforced silence and persecution. Faisal and others led the funeral prayer so as to speak out against this marginalization, by means of symbol and ritual from within the Islamic tradition. In a speech before the prayer, Faisal quoted a *hadith* attributed to the Prophet Muhammad: If one witnesses injustice one should try to stop it with one's hand, and if one is not able, then one must change it by speaking out, and if one is not able, then one must change it in the heart, for that is the least form of faith. The funeral prayer was an effective way of lodging the protest of one's heart, when words have been ignored and actions resisted. The prayer was also nonviolent and confronted others only by wresting symbols of moral worth back from those who would use them as tools of oppression. Another important aspect of the protest was its location: Dupont Circle. This urban park is a social center of Washington, D.C., where people from all backgrounds converge and meet. By bringing the concerns of lesbian, transgender, and gay Muslims into a public center—one normally associated with secular values and socializing—the protest that Faisal organized was a bid to win allies from all quarters.

Faisal's life history is typical for the son of the latest generation of professional Muslim immigrants into the United States. It is bewilderingly international. Faisal was born in Germany where his Pakistani parents were working, then moved to Jedda (the cosmopolitan port city of Saudi Arabia) before his family returned to Karachi for a few years during his childhood. When he was ten and his younger brother five, the family moved to a small town near the prosperous New England city of Hartford. Faisal grew up as the only Muslim in school, and one of few students of nonwhite ethnic background. With school friends he and his brother spoke English and were under great pressure to act "American," but with their parents they spoke only Urdu, for English was banned in the home. Having a slightly "split personality" was simply a strategy to negotiate the cultural terrain, and is very typical for the families of South Asian immigrants to the United States in the 1960s and 1970s who settled in towns and suburbs, rather than in urban centers.

In Pakistan, his parents had been secular in lifestyle, but they became more religious while living in the United States, isolated from others in their Muslim community. Faisal and his brother attended weekend classes in Qur'an and Islamic knowledge at the nearest mosque. At age fifteen, Faisal started to really embrace religion; he let his new beard grow and wore a skullcap to school. He strove to be the model Muslim teen in his local mosque and won preaching awards in Islamic youth camps. He achieved some unique acceptance in high school as a boy who stood out and defended Islam publicly, but his father disapproved of his new religiosity. It looked "extremist" in his middle-class Pakistani eyes, and his father saw such overt religiosity as a sign of a low-class mentality and a precursor to giving up higher education and professional life. He thought it was the first step to dropping out to become a *mulla* or Muslim preacher. In this sense, Faisal's story is similar to that of many Muslim teenagers in the United States for whom a return to Islam—often in very ideologically conservative ways—is part of their youthful rebellion against parents who are often quite secular.[4]

Faisal bypassed his father's disapproval and gained recognition in the Muslim youth wings of ISNA (Islamic Society of North America) and ICNA (Islamic Council of North America), becoming a state and then a regional representative for New England. He helped to organize summer camps for Muslim youth and in general became an Islamic social activist. In the course of these activities he met a Muslim girl, also an activist in the same organizations, and their friendship grew. Under pressure of rumors that their friendship was an illicit romance, he proposed to marry her after he graduated from high school when we was eighteen and she was one year younger. His mother urged him to delay a year, keeping his plan from his father until he successfully completed his first year of university in the regional urban center, Boston. In agreement, he went off to university, where he was active in the MSA (Muslim Students Association, a loosely national network of university campus associations). With his strong speaking skills, keen sense of justice, and strong Islamic identity, he became secretary to his local campus chapter and was active regionally as well.

All this while, Faisal had an increasing awareness that he was gay. As a teen, he had experienced sexual attraction to other males which was very disturbing to him. He turned to the Qur'an for guidance and looked up homosexuality in the index, only to find no mention of it. Turning to other translations, he found reference to the verses about Lot, but was bewildered by differing translations of key phrases. In his mosque he met a white American convert to Islam in his mid-twenties, who was knowledgeable about religion and taught youth classes at the mosque but did not seem to be caught up in the "cultural baggage" of having grown up in a Pakistani Muslim family. To Faisal's surprise, he didn't show the usual signs of overt masculine assertiveness. Faisal turned to him increasingly for friendship and guidance, and they eventually entered an emotional relationship, which in time became sexually intimate. Faisal found him at ease with his sexuality, having already accepted himself as gay before converting to Islam and not seeing any incompatibility. But Faisal was not at ease, and would often be confused and guilt-ridden. Faisal would call him to tell him that what they were doing was wrong, that "Allah hates what we're doing," and would read the passages about the Tribe of Lot out loud to him over the phone. Their relationship did not last long, as Faisal could not integrate a homosexual relationship into his life at that point.

At university, Faisal was drawn toward political science and threw himself into MSA activities. The faculty member who was advisor to the MSA and many other student minority groups was rumored to be gay. Even though he was very helpful to the MSA, Faisal argued that their group should reject him as advisor because of his sexual orientation, that "it would taint the reputation of our MSA." Yet during the second semester of his first year at university, Faisal had befriended this advisor and asked him, "Have you ever felt something so deep in your heart that you know is right, but that everyone around in society insists vehemently is wrong?" The advisor answered, "Yes I have, and I know exactly what you are talking about." Faisal then admitted to being gay to this advisor, befriended other gay men on campus, and began exploring gay life off campus. He lived a self-confessedly "double life"—being a Muslim youth activist and MSA executive during the day and going out every night as a gay man.

After six months of this double life, Faisal experienced a nervous breakdown. As he recovered over two weeks in hospital, he vowed to God three things. First, that he would integrate as fully as possible these two parts of his personality, being Muslim and being gay. Second, that he would search for and contact other gay Muslims wherever he could find them. And third, that he would never let what he had suffered through happen to other young gay Muslims. He turned to a new tool, the Internet, to research if there were other self-consciously gay Muslims around. He discovered no positive outlook about homosexuality and Islam, but rather found a lot of very negative static on Islamic websites. He found ethnicity-based gay and lesbian support groups, but they avoided discussion of religion in general. So in 1997 he decided to fill the void by making his own Internet discussion group for gays and lesbians whose identification was with Islam first and with their ethnicity or region identity second.

He had already, as an MSA member, signed up to many e-mail discussion lists, which was a regular practice to share ideas and information and coordinate between different campus groups in a region. Faisal signed up to every MSA discussion group or list-serve in the United States and Canada, and others that he found in Britain and Japan. Then he wrote an e-mail to them all that alerted them, in a shocked tone, "that someone has dared to create an e-mail discussion group for gay Muslims!" He was shocked that within minutes, people were signing up to his new Internet forum—including some people who were to become central to the creation and support of Al-Fatiha Foundation in later years. Yet for six months, nobody wrote a word on the discussion group, except Faisal, who wrote whatever came to his mind about Islam, possible references to homosexuality in the Qur'an, about relationships and family. He later reflected that it was a sign of the "depth of internalized homophobia" in North American Muslim communities that everyone was petrified to even write over an anonymous medium like e-mail, for to write was to think explicitly and to think explicitly meant to confront internal fears and contradictions. It turned out that some members of the MSA group had joined the "gay Muslim listserve" to eavesdrop, and sniffed Faisal out. He was asked to resign from his offices in the MSA and the youth wing of ISNA, which he did. "I lost many friends and many people I loved" by being excluded from those groups and the activism which had sustained him in his teens and early adulthood.

To compensate, Faisal suggested that members of the Internet discussion group should meet face to face. Four courageous members turned out for an excursion to Washington, D.C., in the spring of 1998, consisting of Faisal, another male student who was president of the MSA at a major Southern university, and two female-to-male transgender Muslims. That meeting and the friendships that blossomed as a result of it emboldened them to call a larger gathering, an international spiritual retreat in October 1998. Forty people met for a weekend retreat at the campus of Faisal's university in Boston. About a fourth of the participants were women, and the group included individuals from Canada, the United Kingdom, the Netherlands, and South Africa (all the nations covered in this study). They called the spiritual retreat "Al-Fatiha—the Opening." They wanted this title to convey the sense of a breakthrough event (*fath*), the opening event of more to come—for the same reason that the opening chapter of the Qur'an is called *al-Fatiha*—and in the sense of a spiritual disclosure of truth (*futuh*). At the retreat they shared stories, voiced concerns, filled chalkboards with their observations, and compared translations of the Qur'an on key verses to argue the range of possible meanings.

That first spiritual retreat involved Faisal, Daayiee, and an Arab lesbian human rights activist from Amnesty International—along with many others from different backgrounds, diverse sectarian and devotional orientations, and with various professional expertise. They realized that their intimations of a truth they knew but could barely express had tapped into deep and profound issues that could not be exhausted in a single retreat. They vowed to form a group, a support group to carry on this work in an ongoing way, through Internet discussion, face-to-face local meetings, spiritual retreats, and international conferences. That organization took the name of the first retreat, Al-Fatiha or "The Opening."

Participants returned to their local cities to found regional chapters, at first in Washington, D.C., Atlanta, San Francisco, and New York, and later in other cities. They resolved to do grassroots outreach at the local level, build up a support community, and get back together in a national conference each year. By 1999, Al-Fatiha Foundation registered formally as an official tax-exempt, nonprofit, religious organization, launched a membership drive to generate ongoing revenue, and established a board of directors. Faisal served initially on the board of directors, then stepped down to allow new members to serve. At the time of this interview, Faisal was working as Program Assistant in the Minority Health Professions Foundation, as he has professional experience with designing and administering sexual health programs for minority populations, especially among Asians and Pacific Islanders in the United States.

Those who had come from other countries returned to establish chapters in their countries of origin, under the name Al-Fatiha or other names that were affiliated in a global network. In this way, the Canadian organization began as al-Fatiha in Toronto, but subsequently chose to operate autonomously and changed its name to Salaam Queer Community in 2001. Similarly, on a trip to London Faisal helped to organize the group that became Al-Fatiha UK, which subsequently changed its name to Imaan. The incentive to run these as autonomous national groups reflected a wide range of issues. Most important was the issue of applying in each nation for official government recognition as a nonprofit organization. But other factors also played a role, such as national pride, a sense that Muslims in each country faced different challenges and needed their own strategies, increasing frustration about the U.S. role in the "War on Terror," and discomfort with the name al-Fatiha which many felt to be too closely linked to the opening chapter of the Qur'an called *Surat al-Fatiha*.

Al-Fatiha has been effective in generating media coverage. Interfacing with the news media is activism through image and information, and through the media activists build bridges with other communities and parties to foster alliances. Lesbian and gay newspapers were the first to write about Al-Fatiha, but Faisal carefully crafted his message to appeal to anyone sensitive to human rights issues and minority struggles. He points out that the struggle of gay, lesbian, and transgender Muslims for recognition and rights involves the same principles as the struggle of African Americans against racial prejudice and women's struggle for feminist dignity. During public speeches, members of the audience sometimes express their dissatisfaction with a gay Muslim of Pakistani ancestry citing the ideals of these great civic rights movements that have changed U.S. society; some African Americans (especially conservative church leaders) accuse him of appropriating their movement. But Faisal lives in Atlanta, where the legacy of Martin Luther King is particularly vivid and he knows its nuances well. Martin Luther King also moved further in this direction as he matured, as when he said, "Injustice anywhere is a threat to justice everywhere." Before his assassination in 1968, Dr. King began to agitate against poverty whether it affected black or white Americans; he also began to protest against U.S. involvement in the Vietnam War. Some African American Christian leaders cover up these developments of Dr. King when his vision of liberation from oppression moved beyond the confines of racial discrimination; they refuse to see that Dr. King's legacy flows over into issues of class, sexism, or homophobia. However, there are others in the African American community who speak out against conservative religious forces and recognize the relevance of the civil rights struggle for lesbian and gay citizens who are also marginalized.[5]

In arguing that injustice toward some means no justice for any, Faisal conveys the message that the rights of gay, lesbian, and transgender Muslims are simply human rights. As he often says, this is a matter of a life, not a lifestyle. His message is effective and his organization has also been featured in mainstream publications including the *New York Times* and the *Washington Post*, among other U.S. newspapers. In August 1999, Al-Fatiha was featured in the *Akutel* magazine of Turkey (a mainstream "lifestyle" publication), and it has received coverage in Bangladesh, India, South Africa, and the Middle East. Members of Al-Fatiha have been featured on radio and TV programs including *BBC Radio* and *BBC World Television*. Perhaps because it is based in the United States, it receives more attention from the international media than other similar organizations in the United Kingdom, South Africa, or Europe.

Al-Fatiha Foundation tries to build alliances with others who are not Muslim or who are not homosexual or transgender. But it also strives to build bridges within the community of nonheterosexual Muslims who are themselves extremely diverse, with conflicting opinions and agendas. Therefore, Faisal designed Al-Fatiha Foundation to be an "ideologically open" organization without a manifesto. It has only a few principles. The first is that Muslims who are gay, lesbian, bisexual, transgender, or questioning are still Muslims and deserve dignified and humane treatment in their Islamic communities and families. The second principle is that they are also fully citizens of their nations and deserve full human rights and legal protections under national constitutions. The third principle is that open discussion of homosexuality and Islam is healthy for all, even if participants in the discussion come to different conclusions.

Faisal explains that Al-Fatiha Foundation does not have an official position on Islam's position vis-a-vis homosexuality, contrary to popular belief in the wider Muslim community that criticize the group for promoting homosexuality. "That is because we are the only place right now where all four or five different viewpoints can come together around a table and express their views and have a legitimate viable space to do that without being shut down or argued out . . . [so] it is more useful to create those forums and dialogues, to have people come together and meet other like-minded people, and to develop support networks." The group does not claim that there is a single way of life that can fully reconcile Islam and homosexuality, though it does argue that the search for one is valuable and that Muslims should be secure enough within themselves to engage in that search.

Faisal explains how necessary this ideologically open position is for the organization: "One thing that is unique about the queer [nonheterosexual] Muslim community is that we come from such different backgrounds and ideologies. . . . I don't think that as a community we are all on the same wavelength ideologically about Islam and its relationship to our sexuality. For example, there are still people in our community—a significant percentage actually, I would argue—who feel it is wrong to actually even engage in sexual relationships [with a person of the same gender] regardless of whether it is a committed relationship or not." The support group itself is an alliance of people who have many differing opinions on social issues and religious values, even though they are all nonheterosexual Muslims. Holding them together in one organization is a difficult feat.

For Al-Fatiha Foundation to have been ideologically open was not only beneficial for its members, but also essential for the functioning of the group. There are many lesbian, gay, and transgender Muslims who are confused, ambivalent, or conflicted when seeking to reconcile their sexuality and gender with their religious tradition, and the foundation sought to embrace them without judging where they are in their common search for dignity. "So I think that is the first struggle: there is a significant majority of people who do not believe that [a same-sex act or relationship] is acceptable in any fashion whatsoever. . . . One could argue that [same-sex] marriage is a way to get around that, to create these bonds that emphasize love and emotion more than sexual pleasure, but I feel that we are still far away from that ideal." Despite these reservations, Faisal thinks that as a support group, Al-Fatiha Foundation should advocate for Islamic same-sex marriage as an option for those who feel they need and want it. It should be an option, though never a dogma.

In a way, Faisal feels that the discussion of same-sex marriage in Islam is premature, at least in the United States. Homophobia and the antigay attitude of many government institutions and many Christian authorities—despite President Obama's personal affirmation of gay rights and same-sex marriage in 2013—reinforces the idea among the Muslim minority that it is completely forbidden. Though a few couples may benefit from same-sex marriages that would push their families and communities to recognize their homosexual relationships, most are involved in a very different struggle for basic self-acceptance. Most lesbian and gay Muslims are not even involved in Al-Fatiha Foundation or other support groups like it. Many are so conflicted that to even think of coming to a support group meeting is highly threatening.

Faisal observed that most people who come to Al-Fatiha Foundation have already undergone a long process of painful self-reflection, brought about by the experience of alienation and isolation in their families or communities. Many have rejected Islam completely, at least for a while, in order to embrace their sexual orientation; only then can they come to Al-Fatiha as a way to rediscover their religious heritage and try to integrate faith back into their lives. "Unfortunately, they have to go through abuse and rejection by their communities and faith, and suffer that for a long time, before they can come to Al-Fatiha. . . . We are so spiritually wounded as a community, especially in this country where we have this very strict orthodox majority opinion in Islam that is very much against homosexuality. We are so spiritually wounded that we need to learn how to start bringing faith back into our lives."

Faisal argues that support groups need to address the simplest practical issues as well as the most complex theological ones. He observes that Al-Fatiha's conferences need workshops on Qur'anic methodology and *hadith* and other theological topics, but at the same time its constituents also need workshops on how to pray in Islam. Many who attend do not know the basic ritual of prayer because they have forgotten or repressed the knowledge, or because they were never welcome in mosques or other ritual spaces. For many, praying *salat* brings up painful memories of family rejection or community suppression. But for some, coming back to prayer and standing shoulder-to-shoulder with other gay and lesbian Muslims is a hugely cathartic experience.

One of the great challenges for Faisal was to set up an organization that answers the needs of people who are incredibly diverse: to forge a support group that can be a bridge between many different points of view. The organization must be social, spiritual, and political all at once. Many are still scarred by rejection of family and community and are repelled by overtly Islamic rituals, but still see themselves as Muslim by cultural influence or ethnic heritage and seek fellowship on that level. Others are strongly devotional and crave an Islamic environment where they can still be themselves in terms of gender and sexuality. Still others are searching for more accurate information on Islamic perspectives on homosexuality and value an open discussion of the issues. Some are simply searching for friendship in a world where neither Muslim community nor Western gay community offers much compassion.

Faisal has been present at the initiation of almost every groundbreaking event for gay, lesbian, and transgender Muslims. "I attended the first [same-sex marriage] that Daayiee ever did. . . . It was a *nikah*, not a civil partnership. It was unique. It was . . . between two people who had been together for a long time . . . for many years before getting married. . . . For people who value that, it is definitely crucial and amazing, so there is definitely value in it, there is no arguing with that. . . . For many the religious element is more personal. They don't need to have a ritual or ceremony that legitimizes their relationship in the eyes of God. I think that is why a lot of people want this concept of a gay Islamic marriage, to legitimize in their eyes or in the eyes of their family, that their relationship is as valid as those of others [heterosexual couples]." Faisal observes that in his own national context—in the United States— there is less need to have same-sex *nikah* because same-sex marriage is not legal under federal law. But in other nations where Muslims have access to legal same-sex marriage, there is extra motivation to devise an Islamic ritual dimension to the marriage, to make it not merely the signing of a contract and a community ceremony. "[In the United Kingdom now] and in South Africa as well, I think we are going to see, as queer [nonheterosexual] Muslim communities grow, an increasing need for people like Daayiee [to conduct same-sex Islamic partnerships and marriages], because people in those countries are going to want to Islamicize some of these rights that they are getting."

While same-sex marriages are not legal under U.S. federal law, there is a slow accumulation of individual states that are legalizing such marriages or civil unions. The message of Al-Fatiha Foundation is having a similarly slow but steady effect upon these debates. Its message is that Muslims do not automatically oppose same-sex marriage, civic unions, or other legal rights. It invites Muslims among mainstream members of the religious minority to reconsider their opinions in the light of justice for all. And its invitation appears to be bearing some fruit. For example, when Washington State leaned toward legalizing same-sex marriage, conservatives proposed amending the state constitution to define marriage as only between a woman and a man. But some progressive religious leaders opposed this proposed amendment. In addition to Christian and Jewish leaders who publicly supported the right of homosexuals to marry, there was a Muslim chaplain, Nayer Taheri, who challenged traditional religious authorities who have "closed their eyes to the beauty of all people," including gays, lesbians, bisexuals, and transgender people.[6] Similarly, in Canada where same-sex marriage is legal, some Muslim authorities seek to undermine it by urging the prime minister to use the "Notwithstanding Clause." However, a small minority of Canadian Muslims have spoken out in support of same-sex marriage, arguing that if they do not support the human rights of a homosexual minority then other minorities such as Muslims might also be targeted for exclusion. Accordingly, a Muslim barrister in Canada who represents the Muslim Canadian Congress pronounced, "I urge Canada's Muslim community and other minority communities to show solidarity with Canada's gays and lesbians even if they have reservations about homosexuality. We don't have to agree with each other to stand up for the human rights of those with whom we disagree."[7] A few Muslim leaders may step out of the mainstream to question traditional values and interpretations, but nobody involved thinks the task is easy. Al-Fatiha Foundation and other support groups like it encourage such leaders to take the risk of speaking out against commonly held prejudices.

Still, Faisal admits that it will be a long struggle before same-sex marriage is legal in U.S. federal law. But until then, homosexual commitments are being made, whether legal or not, whether accepted or not. Faisal accepts the variety of forms that such relationships can take. Surveying the membership of Al-Fatiha Foundation, one sees a whole spectrum of relationships. Some people are in years-long committed same-sex partnerships (despite the lack of legal recognition under secular law) and think in terms of marriage. Some are in stable and emotionally profound relationships, but do not feel the need to formalize them in terms of witness and contracts and family recognition. Some enjoy same-sex relationships without demanding of them any Islamic legitimacy or expecting from them any longevity; they take from their relationships or give to them as the quotidian requirements of love demand. Some are contentedly celibate, perhaps because they feel Islam forbids them from same-sex intercourse. Others are single but searching because it is hard to find a homosexual partner who is on the same wavelength. For everyone, Al-Fatiha Foundation could be a refuge, Faisal hopes; each can find in it a home. He sees it as his responsibility to simply bring them together in an alliance, like a family. Together, they may find an opening to a new and deeper commitment to life. One of the members of this found family is Rashida, one of the first women to attend an Al-Fatiha Foundation meeting in the United Kingdom. Although she worked in a very different context than Faisal—as a lesbian woman in a very closely connected Muslim minority population in London—her work to build a support group that cultivated minority alliances was in parallel with Faisal's efforts.

Rashida: A Better Muslim for Being Gay

Rashida went to the first meeting of Al-Fatiha in London despite gut feelings of fear. Rashida, like many others, suffered from the terror of being "found out." So when a newspaper advertised a meeting of lesbian and gay Muslims in London, she was both drawn toward it and repelled by fear. She suspected that the announcement might be a trap by family or self-appointed Islamic morality police. Yet still she went, and the friends she found there at the Al-Fatiha meeting changed her life and gave rise to the support group Imaan.

Rashida is a university-educated and professional woman from a Pakistani British family. In her early thirties, she has a degree in Middle Eastern Studies and has learned Arabic, both for devotional purposes and professional interests. She works in media with sustained contact with Middle Eastern and Arabic news agencies. Growing up in Britain gave Rashida access to modern university education, secular professional training, and a very modern outlook on life; yet being a lesbian in a Pakistani family in a very tight-knit community raised serious obstacles for her. It took all her creativity and courage to overcome these obstacles. Despite her many successes, she is still struggling with them.

Rashida was one of the founding members of the United Kingdom's first support group for gay, lesbian, and transgender Muslims. It began as Al-Fatiha UK but later changed its name to Imaan. She recalls how the group got started in a typical mix of informal networking, sharing of experiences and common problems, and a determination to address one's own difficulties by reaching out to help others. In her mid-twenties, Rashida was experiencing an acute inner crisis: she was sure from within that she was a lesbian but was equally convinced that she would marry a man due to family pressure and religious duty. In her youth,

she had experienced lesbian relationships, but they were very temporary affairs; she found herself unable to sustain them for she was convinced that her family and her religion required her to marry a man.
Expectation and conviction conflicted with desire and self-recognition,
leading to a nervous breakdown that almost ruined her.

At that time in 1998, Rashida discovered an advertisement in a gay
and lesbian newspaper, *The Pink Paper*, announcing a meeting in London of a group called Al-Fatiha. The U.S. group's founder, Faisal Alam,
had placed the advertisement because he was going to be in London
and wanted to see if there was interest in starting a parallel group in the
United Kingdom. The advertisement offered Rashida an opportunity
to meet other lesbian and gay Muslims in London. Sharing her experiences with them might ease her burden. Yet like many, she did not trust
the advertisement and harbored fears about attending the announced
meeting.

She turned to the Internet, where Al-Fatiha Foundation had begun
as a discussion group in 1997. The Internet buffers one from the danger of meeting others face-to-face in a local community, and through it
Rashida corresponded with a gay Muslim doctor with Pakistani roots
who had been one of the founding members of Al-Fatiha in the United
States. He encouraged her to attend the meeting. Rashida recalls the
deep effect of those anonymous words, sent electronically from across
the ocean: he spoke to her of God's entrusting deep problems only to
those God trusts, and that "gave me some kind of peace of mind. . . . I've
always felt very close to religion, though I wasn't practicing at that time,
so that gave me a lot of comfort. Then I decided to go down to the meeting and meet all the others."[8]

The others turned out to be a group of thirty people many of who
were, like Rashida, from Pakistani British families struggling with similar issues. About one-third of those attending were women, which also
gave her confidence. Sparks flew at that meeting in September 1998,
generating a crackling energy from the group's common experiences
and shared fears. She recalls that moment: "We had this big discussion . . . [and] there was a lot of excitement. A lot of people said they
wanted to get involved and to help out. So we decided to meet again
a few days later at another café in Soho. We met and we decided to
write down concretely what we planned to do and who was going to

be involved, who was going to be in charge, and who was going to help out." The informal collection of people decided to form a formal group, called Al-Fatiha UK. They vowed to organize a conference in London six months later in the summer of 1999. Rashida volunteered to be the deputy director. Others at that first meeting became core members of the group and are still active in it, years later. Many of them became Rashida's close friends and acted like a surrogate family.

For Rashida, this support group came together at a crucial moment. She was in a lesbian relationship that was becoming serious, causing her to rethink her commitment to parental expectations and also making her seriously question her faith in Islam. She began to consider whether the faith taught by family and community was the only possible way to be a Muslim, or whether there were alternatives. "I had just started to go out with my first serious girlfriend at that point. . . . I didn't know that many gay people generally—I wasn't active in any lesbian group or women's advocacy group then." With the start of Al-Fatiha UK, she vaulted from being uninvolved in activism to being one of the leaders of the country's only gay and lesbian Muslim advocacy group at that time.

Al-Fatiha UK organized a conference in London for Muslims who are lesbian, gay, bisexual, transgender along with those questioning their sexuality or gender. In 1999, it was the first of its kind in the United Kingdom, generating much excitement but also raising many fears. At that time, London was a center for Islamic fundamentalism in Europe. In the prevailing climate of "multiculturalism," the government and police hesitated to interfere in "the internal affairs" of religious and ethnic minorities. Firebrand preachers were relatively free to make speeches calling for violence against those they perceived as enemies of Islam. In particular, the fundamentalist movement calling itself *Jama'at al-Muhajirun* [Those Who Leave Corrupt Society] was growing in popularity.[9] It called for Muslims in European countries to reject secular government, enforce the *shari'a*, and ultimately spark an Islamic revolution in Europe. *Jama'at al-Muhajirun* had offices in the United Kingdom, France, Germany, the United States, and Pakistan, and acted as a front organization for *Hizb al-Tahrir* (The Islamic Liberation Party, an international Islamist movement which grew out of the Islamic Brotherhood or *al-Ikhwan al-Muslimun*). It also claimed to be in alliance with the International Islamic Front for Jihad against Jews and Crusaders (formal title for the al-Qaʻida organization).

In this environment, the nascent support group had great fears for its security, and Rashida took up the task of organizing security for the planned conference. She recalls, "I got in touch with the police . . . to put forty riot police outside the venue of our conference, and they did eventually do it. . . . Apparently someone had leaked some information or found out that this conference was going ahead and . . . a notice that went out by a group called *al-Muhajirun*, said they were going to march and find out our venue and throw bricks through the window. So we had an almost comical situation where delegates were happily tucking into tea and biscuits and enjoying the conference, while the two of us [organizers] stood obscuring the view from the window of a small army down below."[10] Despite the threat, no fundamentalist march disrupted the conference. However, *Jamaʻat al-Muhajirun* continued to harass Al-Fatiha UK and issued a *fatwa* saying that any member of the support group was branded a non-Muslim and was liable to be killed as an apostate (*murtadd*). Undeterred by the *fatwa*, Al-Fatiha UK persisted under a new name, Imaan, in 2001 to show that they were independent from Al-Fatiha Foundation in the United States.

Rashida helped forge an alliance with the London police which endured; later Pakistani British police officers were sent to Imaan events, not to protect its members but to learn from them and sensitize themselves as professionals to the social issues its members faced. As Imaan, the group organized further conferences in 2002 and 2005, each time attracting a larger spectrum of the community. Each participant takes from the conference a sense of consolation knowing that there are others who share the same burden even if not all their questions are answered and all their issues resolved. In coming together they no longer have to suffer as victims in silence. Remembering her reaction to the first conference, Rashida says, "What the first conference gave me was real peace of mind. I felt really comfortable with being gay and Muslim and not having any problems in my mind. That whole issue, when I was having the 'nervous breakdown'—as I call it—had disappeared . . . just by meeting other people and hearing other people's stories—and hearing other stories harder than my own! I've had it quite easy, I think, compared to some other people. . . . I've not gotten married and had kids out of pressure from my family." The diversity and variety of people who attend makes it possible for everyone, like Rashida, to feel that she or he is not alone and has not suffered the most.

Rashida does not think herself very important and does not tout the label "activist" very assertively. She calls her activism "involvement," emphasizing her togetherness with other like-minded people rather than her boldness in being part of a vanguard. Through organizing and attending conferences "I got a real identity, a real sense of purpose and a goal. So that's why I stayed involved . . . with the goal of being with a small group of people and realizing that it was a very important issue and that we needed to do something about it, and through reaching out to other people. That's why we all stayed involved." She does not see herself as a crusader. Instead, she sees herself very humbly as part of a greater whole, as someone who brings disparate people together and reveals to them their intrinsic connection. "I just feel part of nature, really. I feel part of a big plan—that I have a small part in this big plan, and that everything is connected to it in some way." Yet she has not only helped organize the day-to-day affairs of the support group and organized three national conferences, but also given media interviews to BBC World radio, Channel 4 television, and has written a chapter reflecting on her life experiences for a recent book entitled *The Way We Are Now*. What kind of person would take up the challenges that she did when she was only twenty-five years old?

Rashida's parents immigrated from Pakistan to London's East End in the mid-1960s, joining a large but insular South Asian community. "Like thousands of others they flocked to areas where Asian families were already established. Safety in numbers was part of it but there was also a need to preserve the culture, which was then, as it is now, enmeshed in a rather narrow interpretation of religion. It was an interpretation that did not question or challenge religious orthodoxy, for this would be deemed at best unnecessary and at worst blasphemous. . . . Our parents were busy establishing themselves economically and socially in a country that was far from hospitable to immigrants from the former colonies. Education was a luxury they could not afford—for themselves at least."[11]

However, her parents pushed their children to get an education, both secular and religious, even if this opened contradictions between a controlling community and a permissive society. "I came from a very traditional Pakistani family. My mom is very religious—she prays five times a day, goes to mosque every Friday, and is very involved in the Muslim community in East London. . . . At the same time, we [her brothers and sisters] still had a relatively easy time compared to a lot of my school friends. We went to a school in East London that was predominantly Asian where there were a lot of Muslim girls, or rather Asian girls, who were under intense pressure to get married—and a lot of them did. But from my parents' [point of] view, they wanted us first to get an education. So we were able to find some freedom through getting our education, and after that through securing our jobs. So I think [my parents] were hoping very much that after we settled into our jobs we'd get married." Rashida attended a government school in East London that was largely Asian (meaning that Sikhs, Hindus, and Muslims made up about 70 percent of the school population, with some Afro-Caribbean and a few white British). East London was relatively impoverished with largely working-class Asian families just making ends meet and sticking very close to their own communities, partly because racism in the wider society limited their options.

There were few purpose-built mosques or schools for religious education, yet from the age of seven until fourteen Rashida and her siblings attended a makeshift Islamic school every day after secular school. Despite her lively interest in learning Arabic and the Qur'an, the method of education was stultifying. "I'm sure it was for only an hour, but it seemed like several hours! It was the same dumb thing every day . . . come home from school, have your tea, and head off to the mosque—awful. We were bored out of our minds." The teaching method was rote memorization of the Qur'an, with boys and girls separated. "Me and my sister were always bored and mucking about but obviously having to concentrate and learn Arabic to read the Qur'an. It was boring because nothing was really taught to us of what it all means and why were doing it. . . . [It consisted of] learning a page or two, reading through it, practicing it, and then reciting it back. . . . [There was] never a discussion of the meaning—never never never!"

In Rashida's understanding, this unsatisfying way of learning religion reflects a deeper problem. In her community, religion was totally intertwined with culture and habit, such that morality meant simply doing

what your family demanded without critical reflection or religious jus-
tification. In family discussions of religion, she recalls, "We were given
information about how you should live your life and what was expected
of you, but it all came from a cultural perspective. . . . The cultural and
religious got all mixed up together. So my mom would teach us that 'You
are supposed to do your prayers five times a day and you are supposed
to get married at some point and we'll find somebody for you.' So we all
knew from a very young age that we were supposed to have arranged
marriages. That was without a doubt. But we were never taught that the
reason you should get married is because of this . . . or that the Qur'an
says this about marriage . . . or that relationships should always be like
this." Discussions of morality did not go back to the Qur'an explicitly or
to arguments about the Prophet Muhammad's example, it was just that
culturally "that's what people do."

Rashida recalls a moment when she realized that the religion she was
being taught was less about Islam and more about obeying her mother:
"I remember at one point sitting at home reading with my mom. All of
us [were] sitting around the kitchen table and reading the Qur'an. . . . I
remember saying, 'I don't understand what it is about! I don't understand what I'm reading.' And then she hit us and she said, 'It means
God, it means God, it means God!' And that was the end of the explanation she could give us." Despite the beating, Rashida did not hold a
grudge against her mother for she realized that her mother, too, did not
understand the Arabic they were all reciting. Later, she and her mother
began reading the Qur'an in Urdu translation, and she saw her mother
begin to learn more about the scripture directly. "All the stuff I heard
from my parents and learned from my community never touched me
spiritually at all. . . . I remember doing *namaz* [prayer] together with
my mom, that was when I was eleven or twelve and I wanted to be like
my mom. . . . So I just did the actions: stand up, bow, put your hands to
your chest, kneel down. I would just copy her. She seemed to think that
was good enough, but . . . I was doing it just because I was copying my
mom and didn't even know what the prayers were!"

Despite this disappointment with family and community, Rashida
was still interested in spiritual questions and felt a strong devotion to
Islam. However, once she left home to attend university, she found a
way to learn more only through secular paths. From 1991 until 1994, she

attended Leeds University and hoped to become a psychologist. However, she was admitted to study her backup option, which she listed as Arabic. "I decided Arabic would be a good idea because I was interested in Islam. Also the course I studied would allow me to travel to the Middle East and study there. That gave me the sense that this was a legitimate way for me to leave home and experience something and be educated at the same time." Rashida attended Ayn Shams University in Cairo for one year, studying Islamic history, Arabic grammar, literature, culture, and poetry. Then she returned to Leeds to earn her degree in Modern Arabic Studies. Even as her friends and family questioned her choices, she was content—"I think it was my fate in life, and I thank God, actually! I had a vague feeling as I was applying for this course that it would always be useful to me even as people would say to me, 'What are you going to with an Arabic degree, for God's sake?' But I thought, it is always going to be relevant to me and I'm always going to be able to refer to it, because I'm always going to be a Muslim. I'm going to learn to read Arabic and it's always going to help me, I thought. I knew that I wouldn't regret it, and I was absolutely right."

At university, Rashida studied the Qur'an and *hadith* in her Arabic course, but focused more on modern Arabic literature and the language of contemporary media. Reading religious texts in a more engaged environment and with the language skills to actually understand and critique the sources "started to open my mind and started to make me feel very interested." Yet like many lesbian, gay, and transgender Muslims, she had been taught to fear the Qur'an. She admits that, "After I had gotten involved with Al-Fatiha, I decided—finally—that I'm going to confront the Qur'an and read it properly for the first time, with translations and with my Arabic. I'm going to see exactly what's there that I'm supposed to be so frightened of. When I started reading, and looking through the translations and the notes [commentaries] and understanding the historical context and everything, it was just amazing to me. And still now, when I read the Qur'an, it is amazing to me. I have no fear whatsoever. I have no apprehension and no worries about what I might find." Approaching the Qur'an from outside her family's habits, with linguistic tools that she earned herself, Rashida began to find fresh meaning in it.

With greater self-knowledge, she began to hear the Qur'an speak to her in more profound ways. "Yes, absolutely it addressed me . . . as a human being. . . . On the one hand, it talked about nature and the purpose of everything, about the greatness of God and how he creates everything, saying, 'Look around yourself, there are signs everywhere that God does exist.' . . . Everything in the world seemed so interconnected, so intricate, so well-thought-out, that to me it just did not seem like an accident. There must be some sort of a plan there. So the Qur'an confirmed that for me." Reading the Qur'an for herself was a revelation. She did not find in it confirmation of the gender roles imposed upon her by her Pakistani family, which they had always claimed were justified by Islam and the Qur'an. "I didn't read anything in the Qur'an that told me what my parents said about my role as a woman, as a female, as a wife."

With her education and exploration of the Qur'an, Rashida felt empowered to question the cultural assumptions of family and community. "The Qur'an seemed a lot kinder, or humane, more understanding [than what my family had taught me]. It was talking to my soul. It was not constrictive. The way I was brought up, Islam seemed to me to be a very constraining, constrictive, and harsh—an imprisoning kind of faith. That is not at all what I realized when I found the Qur'an and read it myself!" Reading the Qur'an for herself, Rashida could enter into debates about religion armed with her own understanding of the sources. "I can have these discussions now and nobody can tell me that I need to do this and that, have to dress like this, or have to talk to this person and can't talk to that one—you know, the kinds of rules and regulations that my parents imposed. . . . I made a really conscious decision when I was nineteen or twenty to separate my religion from my culture. And as soon as I did that, everything became a lot clearer."

Rashida's is an intimate rebellion. Though she rejects her family's expectations of her, she does not reject her family. "I don't have any fear of culture any more, fear that I'll be shoveled off into a false marriage and be made to do the cooking or to cook for my brothers, to serve them, to give them tea, or iron their clothes. You must be joking! I have no need to do that. I'm under no obligation to do that, and I won't!" She does not take personally the narrowness of the rules they impose in the name of Islam. She sees her family's expectations of her as an effect of culture, and this helps her not to take it too personally, not to reject the persons in her family even as she struggles against their ideas.

Rashida rejects what her family and community expect of her, but does so by embracing the essential text of the religion that they hold as dear as she does. This is a strategy called "the politics of counter-rejection" by the sociologist Andrew Yip, an astute observer of religious gays and lesbians in Britain, in both Christian and Muslim communities.[12] For Rashida, as a woman the largest issue is pressure to get married through a family arrangement, a pressure she shares with heterosexual women in her community (and many men as well). She understands that the Qur'an urges Muslim women and men to marry, yet claims an exception for herself because of her existential situation. "There is a *surat* that you sometimes see on wedding invitations . . . that God creates two souls to be together and to be kind to one another. It's the same two lines on every invitation: that two souls are meant to be together." Rashida refers to Qur'an 30:21 which says, *One of God's signs is that mates are created for you from yourselves that you may find rest in them, and God made between you love and compassion.* But she perceives that the Qur'an says "mates" (*azwaj*) in a much broader sense than conventional heterosexual interpretation. "I don't identify them as being male and female. I can't understand it that way—it doesn't make sense that you must meet a man, or a person of the opposite sex, to have that companionship. That's not how I understand it. That's coming from my heart. . . . When I read the Qur'an it touches me, and I read it as if it's talking to me directly. And if I read it like that, then how can it be saying, 'You must marry a man'? Because to me, the thought of marrying a man would be like being in prison . . . being forced to do something I really don't want to do. I could never do it, never do it."

She feels that God has created her for a purpose, but that purpose is not to marry a man and fulfill those roles through which a majority of heterosexual Muslims might find fulfillment. Rather, she asserts that she is a different part of God's diverse creation. "The thing that comes to me from the Qur'an is especially nature: living things, things created with a reason, that are supposed to interact with each other for a reason . . . the trees and the plants, with their colors and different kind of vegetation. It's all created for us for a purpose—and me, too, of course." With this insight, Rashida is echoing the Qur'an which says, *One of God's signs is the creation of the heavens and the earth and the diversity of your tongues and your colors, in which there are signs for those who know* (Q 30:22).[13] Our diversity as human beings goes much deeper than the color of our skins, but rather extends into the inner core of our personalities where language, concepts, beliefs, and experiences lie. The different colors of diverse creation might also, in Rashida's understanding, apply to people of different sexual orientations.

With her focus on the dynamic role of nature, Rashida draws from the images of the philosopher poet, Muhammad Iqbal. His ideals were a part of the culture that Pakistani migrants brought along with the poet Faiz. Iqbal's poetry combines an existentialist philosophy with Qur'anic dynamism to celebrate nature and encourage self-assertion. In Iqbal's view, each person must come to understand her- or himself through struggle not through slavish obedience, and only from that position can they know God with sincerity. He took the Sufi aphorism "Whoever knows the self knows the Lord," and recast it into a more modern and assertive mold. Like Muhammad Iqbal, Rashida asks, "What is my purpose?" She answers by suggesting that, "This comes back to the question of when Muslims argue about homosexuality and they say that it's a test from God and you must overcome this test and avoid sinful activity. . . . Well, my attitude is that [others] cannot tell me about my test in life. My test in life is between me and God. So I try to listen to my heart and try to avoid my more frivolous thoughts and try to be honest with myself and think, 'What is God trying to tell me?' . . . I think that my test is to overcome my problems with homosexuality and to educate other people, to help other people, to spread the word to people from Muslim backgrounds who have fled from Islam because they see the prejudice, and bring them back to Islam and say, 'You can be gay and you can be Muslim. . . . There is nobody who can tell you that you are not a Muslim. It depends on you, how you feel, and what you believe in your heart.'" By following the Qur'an's insistence that believers must be sincere and honest, Rashida asserts that gay and lesbian Muslims can be believers, even if they must contradict the religious customs of their family and community.

But for Rashida, that does not mean cutting her ties to her family. She remains close to her family, especially her heterosexual sister, who she fears is drifting away from Islam. Being a lesbian does not condemn her to hell, asserts Rashida, just as simply as being straight and getting married does not get one into heaven. "I know that there are things I do in my life that I should not be doing, but those things are not related to my sexuality. . . . My ideal lifestyle should be—and it should be what I'm striving to attain—that I should be in a monogamous relationship with somebody, I should pray, I should conform to the five pillars, read the Qur'an, be aware, do righteous deeds, remember God, and go on hajj. . . . It is not important for me to do what my parents say because the next-door neighbors are complaining or gossiping, or pretending that I'm one person when in reality I'm not."

However, concern for family and care for them cannot justify hypocrisy, in her view. She feels that people should be given the freedom to become Muslims in their own way, so as to find a path toward sincere honesty: "Hypocrisy I have no time for." This opinion was only strengthened by her involvement in Arab countries and companies, where she observed first-hand the kind of hypocrisy carried out by the so-called upholders of Islam. "I find a lot of so-called Islamic countries to be very un-Islamic. . . . Since I graduated from university, I've spent most of my working life in Middle Eastern environments while working in the news, particularly in Middle Eastern news. I see what goes on around the world and I'm sickened by what I see in places like Saudi Arabia." She feels that Muslims in the United Kingdom living under a secular regime are freer to live Islamically than those who are coerced by so-called Islamic countries that mix religion with the interests of the state. "From what I've seen of it and read of it and what I've seen in the Middle East, I don't think there is one Islamic country in this world. I disagree with the idea that Islam and politics should mix and I don't think there should be 'Islamic' governments. I do not trust anyone on this earth to interpret it in the way it was meant to be interpreted; I don't think humans are able to so. I don't think they should. People should be free to get involved with Islam and be Muslims in the way that they see fit."

Part of the reason that Rashida doesn't trust the upholders of the *shari'a* is because of their personal hypocrisy, but it is also partly because of the way the *shari'a* was built. As a system of rules and a code of behaviors, it was based upon the Qur'an and also, even in larger part, upon *hadith* reports that purport to say what the Prophet Muhammad said and did in particular situations. The more she studied *hadith* reports, the more she came to distrust them as accurate guides to the Prophet Muhammad's religion. She noted that each *hadith* report is prefaced by its chain of transmitters (*isnad*): "So-and-so reported that this person said this, and this is repeated many times before you get to the actual *hadith* report. So it occurred to me that that cannot be quite reliable. It's like Chinese whispers: if I tell it to you and you tell it to someone else who tells someone else and goes all the way about the room, the message that you get at the end of it you can't guarantee will be the same message that you originally said. If you think that a *hadith* report went through centuries and generations before being written down, how can you possible rely on it? . . . I realized that the Qur'an is supposed to be the final word of God, the final and complete word of God, so for me there is no reason to look to *hadith*." She notes that *hadith* reports were only written down in a systematic way about two centuries after the Prophet's death, so she concludes that the Qur'an alone provides sure guidance. "If there are issues that are ambiguous in the Qur'an, then I have to look within my heart and be really truthful with myself and very honest with myself, and do what I feel is right."

While most upholders of orthodoxy would argue that *hadith* reports are reliable, they often do so without detailed study of how these reports were transmitted and how transmission preserved contradictory reports. Some upholders of orthodoxy even charge that doubting the authenticity and reliability of *hadith* reports is a form of disrespect to the Prophet Muhammad, but Rashida fundamentally disagrees. "I absolutely have total respect, like every other Muslim, for Muhammad being the first Muslim and showing the ideal way to live your life. But I don't know exactly what he did because . . . [the *hadith* reports] are so unreliable. . . . I'm only a human being. I can't know everything—I can only know what's in front of me and use my own judgment." With this perspective, Rashida takes her part in the wider Progressive Muslims movement. This is a loose network of believers who share a critical perspective on how the Islamic tradition developed over time and the conviction that it needs to be renewed by both reaching into the tradition itself and reaching out to embrace the challenges of life in modern societies.

On issues like interpretation of the Qur'an and the reliability of *hadith* reports, Rashida parts company with conventional Islamic theology. But she still promotes alliance building and sustained dialogue with mainstream Muslim organizations, even if they do not show respect for Imaan or its members. Rashida insists on meeting with mainstream Muslim organizations and building partnerships with them on strategic issues that both sides value, because Muslims of all kinds face discrimination in the United Kingdom. The Muslim Council of Britain (MCB) is the formal body of Islamic scholars and imams which claims to represent the Muslim community to the British government and strives to regulate the Muslim community's internal affairs.[14] The MCB has shied away from discussion with the support group Imaan, while noting its existence in informal ways.

While the support group Imaan has not held any formal discussion with the MCB, its representatives meet in various fora to promote anti-discrimination in British society. Rashida reports that, "The metropolitan police ran a campaign on fighting discrimination recently in 2004; they invited to their campaign conference people facing discrimination, including both Muslims and also gay people, and including our then-chair person [a gay Muslim]. He came to the meeting and met some imams from the local area. They all met and greeted one another and shook hands, but that was about as far as it got—there were no real discussions." The MCB still looks upon gay, lesbian, and transgender Muslims as uneducated, ideologically misled, or obstinately sinful. Their view is based more on stereotypes and prejudice than on real experience, but it will take a long time to change.

While mainstream Muslim opinion will change only slowly, Rashida observes that government and civic organizations are changing their opinion much faster. The Imaan conference in 2005 was attended by Pakistani British members of the U.K. police force so that officers could learn from those attending about their experiences with family and community; the police deemed this necessary since officers are called into Muslim homes during family disputes that may involve issues of homosexuality. Rashida and other leaders of Imaan also cultivate other kinds of allies. Conference organizers invited the Muslim parents of gay or lesbian children to speak. They invited imams from mainstream mosques to attend the conference, to both listen to participants and to share their own opinion on the issues at hand; they offered imams anonymity so that their own mosque communities would not condemn them for attending. In the 2005 conference, one imam accepted this invitation and spoke at the conference; though he emphasized that the Qur'an explicitly forbids homosexual acts, he expressed his sincere belief that all Muslims should be treated with dignity by their families and communities. He hoped that a "dispassionate dialogue" might be held between lesbian and gay Muslims and authorities within the mosques. "Love is love," he shrugged at the end of his talk, "when it happens, what can you do?"

Everyone attending Imaan's conferences understands that such a dispassionate dialogue will take a long time to develop. Perhaps the catalyst for change will be informal meetings where both sides meet because they have common interests beyond their particular argument. If both sides can see the other as representatives of oppressed groups who suffer discrimination, perhaps they will come to some reconciliation. In this way, Rashida hopes to forge alliances between different groups within the Muslim community, and inviting imams into a dialogue is one facet of this effort. Despite their disagreements over homosexuality or gender identity, they are all members of a Muslim minority, a minority that is rarely accepted wholeheartedly in the United Kingdom or other Western countries. Overcoming internal disagreements is one way to strengthen the religious minority as a whole.

But Rashida insists that overcoming disagreements is not the same as denying real diversity within the Muslim community or suppressing divergence of opinion. Rather, divergence of opinion should be characterized by dignified disagreement. In the Islamic tradition this is known as *adab*—reserving the right to disagree while preserving the other's dignity. Until then, Rashida insists that "being gay has made me a better Muslim" because it has taught her to question, to search, and to struggle and not be content with easy answers or habitual formulas.

El-Farouk: Building Bridges

El-Farouk Khaki provides an excellent example of a mode of activism focusing on coalitions and political alliances. He is a Toronto lawyer in his early forties specializing in immigration. He is also a human rights activist who helped found Salaam Queer Community in 2001 together with a small group of like-minded activists. His family background is a confluence of different groups and places, which he is very quick to highlight as a positive aspect of his family and ancestry. El-Farouk was born in Dar es-Salaam, Tanzania, a territory that attracted Muslim populations from Gujarat and Yemen and other locales bordering the Indian Ocean. He is proud of his mixed ethnicity in which all these populations mingled, and resists identifying with any one group, whether Asian or Arab, whether Sunni or Isma'ili.

El-Farouk's family immigrated to Canada in the early 1970s, fleeing political pressure in Tanzania. He was ten when his family moved to Canada and he grew up in the Vancouver area. "I was in my mid-teens when I spoke to my parents for the first time about being gay. They were wonderful. They said it was a natural part of puberty to be questioning your sexuality and it was something I would grow out of."[15] But homosexuality was more than a passing phase for El-Farouk. While attending the University of British Columbia, he first began to struggle with being gay, but did not come out openly until several years later when he was in law school. "I think my coming out had a lot to do with the stress and pressures of law school. I really hated law school, as a bastion of social conservatism and elitism that was predominantly white, particularly in the mid-1980s."

After completing his law degree he moved to Ottawa and then to Toronto where he set up his legal practice. "When I came to Toronto, I started meeting people who were gay, lesbian, bisexual, transgender—and Muslim," and from those meetings was born Salaam Queer Community. The name was chosen to highlight the term "queer" which gay activists reappropriated from an insult that had been hurled at them. The term queer is now used as an umbrella term for a coalition of people who are not heterosexual, including lesbian, gay, and transgender persons in addition to bisexuals and those questioning their orientation and identity.

Salaam Queer Community was originally established as Al-Fatiha Toronto, but it changed its name in 2001 when it became an independent support group based in Canada. El-Farouk explains, "Salaam is a unique organization because we have a true diversity in gender as well as a diversity in [sexual] orientation. Our coordinators, as well as our membership, come from diverse racial backgrounds. We have Iranians, Indo-Pakistanis, Turks, Isma'ili, Shi'i, Sunni. We have people who are religious and people who are not, people who are believers and people who are not. We've also had non-Muslims or people who don't identify

as Muslim." The group was particularly careful to invite the active participation of friends, supporters, or spouses who were not Muslims.
El-Farouk's partner played a role in helping to organize events, though
he came from a French Canadian family from Quebec. El-Farouk's religious life was a part of their life together, although his partner was not
formally a Muslim. His partner used to accompany El-Farouk to the
mosque sometimes to pray, especially on Eid holidays. El-Farouk conceived of their relationship as a marriage without any legal formality
or ritual ceremony—it was just between them, their friends, and their
families. But it lasted for fifteen years until his partner passed away.

Perhaps because his partner came from a predominantly Catholic
region, El-Farouk realized early on that the struggle of Muslims with
their own tradition is not so very different from that of Christians,
Jews, or other religious believers. In parallel ways, each tradition asserts
patriarchal norms and condemns homosexuality. "One of the difficult
parts of coming out as a Muslim—or in any religious tradition—is the
religious condemnation and the religious interpretations of text which
demonize same-sex relationships. As a believer, that was a problem for
me." To deal with this condemnation, El-Farouk turned to study and
reflection, following the command of his favorite verses of the Qur'an—
*Read, by the name of your Lord who created, created the human being
from a blood clot! Read, for your Lord is full of honor, who taught to write
with the pen, who taught humankind what was never known before* (Q
96:1–5). As El-Farouk read and reread the story of Lot he found himself understanding it "as a condemnation of rape, not of homosexuals."[16] Though this gave him confidence to speak publicly and organize,
neither he nor the group feel the need to argue that there is only one
correct interpretation. "We're not interested in debating or challenging
or confronting the larger Muslim community—that's not our goal. Our
goal is to provide a sense of community and safety for people who come
to us. Bringing people together is the cornerstone of Salaam's work."

Contrary to the notion that homosexual and transgender people are
isolated because they are few in number and marginalized in society,
El-Farouk sees them as potentially a very strong catalyst in bringing
together different elements of society. This is because they have multiple dimensions to their identity and must cultivate this multidimen-
sionality in order to survive. Thus they can act as a bridge and play a

188 << FORGING MINORITY ALLIANCES

crucial role in progressive politics. This is all the more important since the September 11 attacks and the rise of violent extremism among some Muslims. "I think it is very important right now for Muslim organizations to be building bridges. We need to recognize that there is a fringe element at the present time within the Muslim community that resorts to violence. . . . We need to isolate this element and identify what leads to this sort of alienation and this psychology of violence." One of the most important events each year organized by Salaam is an *iftar* meal, which epitomizes how the organization plays a unique role in bringing together people who otherwise might never share stories over shared food. He explains, "Every Ramadan, we host a fast-breaking dinner called an *iftar* for about 150 people. It's an interesting event, because it is 50 percent Muslim and 50 percent non-Muslim, 50 percent queer and 50 percent not queer." Rather than allowing Ramadan to become a ritual event that separates Muslims who are fasting from others who are not, the group turns the fast-breaking meal into a time for sharing, so that a religious event blends seamlessly into progressive politics.

In recent years, Canada has passed increasingly progressive legislation to protect the rights of gay and lesbian citizens. In this sense, Canada resembles European nations rather than the United States. Antidiscrimination laws governing workplace policies, housing rentals, same-sex partnerships, and marriage are all a part of life in Canada now. El-Farouk notes that this legislation creates a new climate for social change in families and religious communities. "We are, overall, more accepted and more secure. That legitimacy makes it more difficult for people to hate us. As more queers come out publicly, it makes it much harder for people in the Muslim community to exclude or condemn us."

As he comes out publicly, El-Farouk is building bridges through progressive politics. He has served as the Secretary General of the Muslim Canadian Congress (MCC), an organization that defines itself as a grassroots organization that represents Muslims marginalized by other Islamic organizations that are authoritarian. In this way, he participates in wider community politics as an openly "out of the closet" gay Muslim. As a gay Muslim, he has participated in wider Muslim community issues and progressive movements. On June 4, 2006 Canadian authorities arrested seventeen Canadian Muslims in Ottawa in an alleged bomb plan; El-Farouk, in a press release on behalf of the MCC, blamed the

U.S.-led war on terror as the proximate cause. "Canadians need to wake up and realize the recipe offered by George Bush and Tony Blair, and now being adopted by Stephen Harper [the conservative Canadian Prime Minister], has only led to an increase of terrorism fueled by the invasion of Iraq and Afghanistan."[17] An Anglo-Canadian professor on governance at the University of Toronto disagreed and blamed the plot on Islamic extremism that, according to him, is hostile to Western values despite Canadian policies of open immigration policy, its liberal citizenship, and its public embrace of multiculturalism. But according to El-Farouk, the policy of multiculturalism is good for gays, lesbians, and transgender people, and i̇ also good for Muslims. But the interests of all can be kept in balance only if all support certain ethical principles, regardless of religious belief, sexual orientation, gender identity, or ethnic background. It is the challenge of a pluralistic and democratic society, he feels, to articulate those principles clearly and then build laws based upon them and allow all groups to flourish in such a way that each protects its interests by defending the interests of others.

In this way, the progressive vision articulated by El-Farouk and others in Salaam Queer Community is quite different from that propounded by Canada's more famous advocate for gay and lesbian rights, Irshad Manji. El-Farouk's vision is one of building coalitions by identifying with people from other minority communities through shared values. Manji's strategy is to stand alone in the full light of media exposure and appeal to powerful institutions. Manji had a successful career in television journalism based in Toronto, and then published her book *The Trouble with Islam Today,* which vaulted her to international fame. Hers was a highly personal call for reform among Muslims, but it was not articulated from within the Islamic tradition through emotional and devotional attachment to Islamic symbols and practices. Her portrait of growing up in Muslim minority communities in North America is very different from those given by the activists interviewed in this book.

Those active in Salaam Queer Community tend to downplay the importance of mavericks like Manji. They focus instead on the more quiet work of grassroots community development and social justice projects. As stigma increasingly falls away from lesbian, transgender, and gay Muslims in Canada, they are able to participate in protecting the rights of others and having others protect their rights. As a lawyer,

El-Farouk specializes in advocating on behalf of immigrants to Canada, especially those seeking asylum, whether due to their sexual orientation or due to political danger.[18] He and members of his community have joined protests against the Iraq war and for just resolution of the Palestine-Israel conflict. Other Muslims can see that their interest in justice in not limited to self-interest. El-Farouk points out that once the Salaam Queer community sponsored a discussion at Toronto's Gay and Lesbian Community Centre in which a heterosexual Muslim woman who wore a *hijab* took part. "That wouldn't have happened ten years ago. A religious straight woman would probably have not wanted to associate herself with us. Now it's less of a problem. . . . September 11 has forced progressive and moderate Muslims into the spotlight. . . . There was a blossoming of a global progressive Muslim movement and queer Muslims were a part of that."[19]

Conclusion

Gay, lesbian, and transgender Muslim activists appeal for support to others beyond their own community. Activists build bridges with other religious communities who are also minority populations. They also appeal to women's rights organizations to uphold the common struggle that feminists share with them against patriarchal norms which are enshrined in most religious traditions. This strategy engages with progressive politics in a direct way. It does not merely appeal to the state to protect its minority citizens. It appeals to the common humanity that all citizens share, a common humanity that is not just an abstract political concept but rather one practically forged through friendships and supporting others when they are in need.

Forging minority alliances is one mode of activism used by gay, lesbian, and transgender Muslims. The activities and outlook of those interviewed in this chapter illustrate this mode of forging minority alliances. In this mode, activists articulate common values and threats that unite their minority with other vulnerable groups, such that others advocate their rights as part of a common struggle for justice and well-being. Activists like Faisal, Rasheed, and El-Farouk who engage in this mode do not merely appeal to secular state norms but rather strive to build coalitions among parties and groups at the grassroots level. This strategy depends on personal contacts as well as formal organizational alliances. Its success depends upon the belief that groups with divergent conditions can nonetheless find common ground to support each other.

This strategy is most useful when secular political institutions are not strong or when secular legal rights are not extended to homosexual and transgender people. The interviews in this chapter reveal how this strategy has been used by activists in the United States, the United Kingdom, and Canada. Anglophone countries developed democratic traditions of "soft secularism" where public religiosity is on display in public debate and in election campaigns; this contrasts with the situation in the Netherlands, where democratic institutions are very strong, secularism is boldly assertive, and religious discourse is muted in public debate. In the Netherlands and comparable countries (the Netherlands model may apply as well to continental European countries that inherited Napoleonic traditions), the activist mode of "adjusting secular politics" promises to bear fruit. But in the United States and Canada, gay, lesbian, and transgender activists cannot place full faith in secular institutions to uphold their legal rights and secure their welfare. This is even truer for the Muslims among them, who often feel marginalized by the persistence of overtly Christian rhetoric in public debate. In democracies with soft secularism, activists turn to building alliances with other minority groups, to find support and protection in the absence of strong state secularism and legal rights.

The two modes of activism, forging minority alliances and adapting secular politics, both focus on political means toward achieving social acceptance. Whether activists opt for one mode or the other, they trust that political advances will get them social acceptance, that social acceptance will secure for them their rights, and that securing their rights is the key to living a happy life. Yet other lesbian, transgender, and gay Muslims doubt this equation. They do not see happiness coming from political rights or social acceptance. They believe instead that happiness comes from individual fulfillment. Individual fulfillment may not come from political and social advances, but it does depend on the development of individual identity. Such activists often see life as a spiritual or psychological journey toward individual fulfillment, and this mode of activism will be explored in the next chapter.

6

Journeying toward Individual Identity

My heart can take on many forms
For gazelles a meadow, a cloister for monks
For idols a sacred ground, Ka`ba for the pilgrims
Tables of the Torah, scrolls of the Qur'an
I profess the religion of love, wherever its caravan turns
Along the way, that is my belief, the faith I keep
                    ~Ibn Arabi, Tarjuman al-Ashwaq

With these simple but bold words, the Sufi thinker Ibn Arabi sets forth a
manifesto of mystical love. His religion is love and he accepts it in whatever form it may present itself, even if it is unconventional or seem-
ingly heretical. As a Sufi, Ibn Arabi (died 1240) argued that Islam is outwardly a religion of rituals and beliefs but is inwardly a religion of love.
This argument emerges in a most beautiful form in the few couplets
from his poetry collection, *Tarjuman al-Ashwaq* or Stations of Desire,
as ably translated by Michael Sells.[1] These verses form not just a manifesto but also a song, and many Sufi musicians have set these verses to
music.[2] Sufis like Ibn Arabi have interpreted Islam as a spiritual quest. It
is a quest to find ways of living in closer and closer intimacy with God's
presence in this world and the next. It is a quest that involves social
belonging in Sufi orders but also allows room for individual searching which might call into question socially accepted norms. Ibn Arabi
imagines this quest as a journey in the caravan of lovers: whichever way

the caravan train may twist and turn during the journey, he is confident that the ultimate goal is love. To this alone he is faithful. "I profess the religion of love, wherever its caravan turns along the way."

Muslim activists have much to learn from the Sufi movement. It offers many spiritual and ethical resources in the quest for greater personal integrity and spiritual depth even in the face of social ostracism. Some Sufis were unflinchingly bold in rejecting social conventions for the sake of love.[3] Some lesbian, transgender, and gay activists interviewed for this book were deeply influenced by the Sufi tradition, though few of them claimed actual membership in a Sufi order. Yet these activists often display a mode of activism that can be called "journeying toward individual identity." They engage this mode of activism when they hold that the individual journey toward greater self-awareness and personality integration is more important than fidelity to the religious norms of Islam or enacting social change through political means. Some of them explicitly invoke Sufi precedents in describing this spiritual journey while others refer to the language of counseling and self-help. Whether they articulate their goals in the language of medieval mysticism or modern psychiatry, these activists argue that the essence of Islam is for people to achieve self-knowledge and come to peace with themselves in such a way that they can worship God with integrity, out of love rather than out of fear.

Community organization is only one dimension of the effort of activists who volunteer to build a transnational network of support groups for gay, lesbian, and transgender Muslims. It is an outer dimension that is relatively easy to document. But just as important is the inner dimension of identity formation. It is more subtle and harder to analyze. This is why the interviews in this book focus on the protagonists' life story, family history, religious training, and spiritual experience rather than solely on their activist work, political positions, and theological views. If it were not for a process of identity formation, these individuals would never have come to play an activist role in such organizations. Further, such organizations function to provide a forum for others to continue the process of honing their personal identity by finding social networks of like-minded people, sharing experiences, overcoming alienation, and expressing solidarity. Identity formation is thus the cause of these support groups' existence and also their practical goal.

Activism in support for transgender, lesbian, and gay people is often dismissed as mere "identity politics." But this dismissal is too quick. Identity politics is the practical result of identity formation, a complex phenomenon that happens within individuals and between individuals who belong to a group. The introduction to this book provided a detailed discussion of how identity formation involves individual psychology, family relationships, community loyalty, and national belonging. Identity formation is not merely fuel for factionalism; rather it is a crucial element of social solidarity, devotional spirituality, and even the quest for wisdom. As Sufi thinkers like Ibn Arabi often say, "The one who knows the self knows the Lord." This wise maxim is so influential in Islamic discourses that it is often remembered as a *hadith* of the Prophet Muhammad or a saying of his intimate follower, Imam ʻAli. Regardless of the origin of this saying, it is perfectly compatible with Islamic teachings. Indeed it is the core of the Islamic search for wisdom (whether undertaken through Sufi mysticism, neoplatonic philosophy, or ascetic devotion). This saying reveals that identity formation is the key to worshiping God sincerely. One needs to know the self deeply in all its conditions, limitations, and transcendental potential before one can really know God; and conversely, the spiritual quest to know and worship God is the means to gain authentic knowledge of the self. The support groups for lesbian, gay, and transgender Muslims documented in this book aim to provide a secure space in which members can get to know their selves, gain confidence to be themselves, and learn to worship in sincerity.

Before delving into the spiritual meaning of identity formation, we need to comprehend it as a complex process. The activists interviewed here help us to appreciate the complexity of identity formation. Identities form over time on a number of different levels, from individual to family to community to nation. But one could argue that the basis for identity is the level of individual psyche; such as identity forms as one comes to understand the elements of one's own inner disposition, psychological potential, resources, and limitations. This is a process that many of the activists interviewed here speak about as coming to know one's "inner self," discovering one's "true self," or growing into one's "own soul." These images are often posed against a false self that is displayed to others and has been forced upon one by family and community, such that the inner self takes on actuality only in conflict with one's social circle and against pressure to conform to its expectations. For transgender, lesbian, and gay Muslims, this element of conflict may be more critical than for heterosexual Muslims. This is because crucial elements of their self—elements of sexual orientation or gender identity—are silenced or suppressed by family expectations and community norms, to the extent that discovering, exploring, and accepting these elements of one's personality into one's identity becomes fraught with danger.

The importance of the individual psyche in identity formation should not overshadow the factors of familial relations, religious community, and national belonging. Earlier chapters focused more intently on activist engagement with religion (chapters 1 and 3), family (chapter 2), national legal codes (chapter 4), and political alliances (chapter 5). In contrast, this chapter will focus on activists who display the strategy of "journeying toward individual identity." These activists tend to doubt the efficacy of brash political activism whether it is through secular norms or religious ideals. They also doubt whether it is worthwhile to compromise with social custom and family ties. If they engage in Islamic practices, it is not out of a sense of conformity with society or solidarity with family, but rather because they feel that Islamic rituals can further their individual journey toward greater spiritual or psychological strength. This chapter presents the voices of two activists who appeal to this strategy of focusing on a journey toward individual identity.

Aziz: Advocate for Actualization

Aziz is a core member of The Inner Circle in South Africa. He runs its psychological counseling service and is a professional psychiatrist with an advanced medical degree. He is an excellent example of a gay Muslim whose mode of activism focuses on a journey toward individual identity. He does not see himself as an activist but rather as a seeker, healer, and counselor. Yet these activities form an important component of the activism of support groups for transgender, lesbian, and gay Muslims.

Aziz grew up as a homosexual man in the "Indian Muslim" community in Johannesburg. Indian Muslims occupy a distinct place within the spectrum of race, ethnicity, and religion in South Africa, and youth from this community grow up in a deeply patriarchal community. Indian

Muslims import imams from Pakistan and India who have been buff-
ered from modernization rather than training South African Muslims
to run their religious institutions. The fundamentalist *Tablighi Jama'at*
movement is very influential in the Indian Muslim community in South
Africa and it aggressively reinforces patriarchal values. In addition, the
Indian Muslim community in South Africa excels in business while
being forced into an insular pocket of society by apartheid, so marriages
within the community are often arranged to enhance a family's business,
putting great pressure on the youth to repress their sexual identity and
romantic desires whether they are homosexual or heterosexual.

While growing up in a tight-knit Indian Muslim neighborhood in
Johannesburg, Aziz experienced these pressures while also benefiting
from the opportunities they afforded him. He is the son of a successful
businessman. He recalls, "My dad's idea was that 'You are the only son
in the family, so you will go and study medicine, become a doctor, and
make our family very proud.'" At university at age nineteen, he switched
his field to psychology. "This is hard to say, but I think I was trying to
search for answers for myself. . . . I wanted to understand myself better and understand my own identity better as well. It was something
that nobody in the Indian community ever entertained doing, so I
think I also wanted to be different! I also wanted to defy my father."
His intense focus on education helped Aziz to suppress any thought of
being gay, though he knew from a young age that he was different and
unusual. "I knew I didn't think like other children. I was quite a high
achiever in school, but I had no idea that I was gay at all. I think it
was not until I got into my honors course that I really grappled with
my identity. . . . All through my life I had a subconscious notion that I
might be, but I only really started to grapple with it when . . . we were
doing a course on counseling gay people." This course in psychotherapy
forced him to confront what he had for so long repressed. To his colleagues at university, he tried to prove that he was heterosexual by dating three different women during his student years before ever having
sexual or romantic contact with a man. Yet the topic came up in class
and he could not shy away from it. "I think that is when it really struck
me, when it really dawned upon me that 'this is potentially who I really
am.'" His education, through which Aziz had avoided confronting his
sexual orientation, led him to unexpectedly confront the issue head on.

Although these developments were playing out in the field of secular education, for Aziz they were intimately related to his religious tradition. Aziz's family life was deeply religious but insisted on both secular and Islamic education. "Having been brought up in a very conservative Muslim home, I went to the *madrasa* classes after school every day. . . . My father insisted that I read the Qur'an and learn it by heart to become a *hafiz*." Aziz took to basic religious education enthusiastically and as he was finishing high school, he faced a hard decision: whether to attend university to prepare for a secular career or to attend an institute of higher Islamic learning and become an imam, a *mufti*, or other religious specialist by attending a *Dar al-Ulum* academy. Aziz's father harbored unfulfilled urges to become an imam and thwarted desires to become a doctor, but was forced by apartheid policies to deal in business. So both of these goals were imposed upon Aziz as the only son: he was expected to both memorize the Qur'an by attending an Islamic academy and also become a medical doctor by studying at a secular university. "So my dad wanted the best of both worlds. I don't think those were my dreams—those were his dreams. Despite that, I did have a strong interest in religious instruction and did very well in *madrasa*. I enjoyed it thoroughly and I was always plagued by questions about religion." His father pushed him to attend university to become a doctor and to also memorize the entire Qur'an in preparation for religious leadership. It was too much pressure, and Aziz opted for university and eventually rejected his father's insistence that he become a medical doctor. Years later, Aziz was able to return to the study of religion through his clinical work in psychotherapy, and took on a leadership role in a religious community through his work with The Inner Circle, but through a path which his father could never accept.

Aziz's mother might have had more sympathy with the choices he made, if she had not passed away at a critical moment in his growth. In Aziz's life, his mother represented a kind of Islamic spirituality that had a deep understanding of human nature and allowed all dogmas to be questioned in a caring way. Losing her was therefore very difficult for him and caused a crisis of faith. "I had a much closer bond with my mom than with my dad. . . . I just think she would have accepted me and not had any issues about it, and that would have made my coming out much easier if she had been around." His mother passed away when

Aziz was twenty, and he began a long process of coming out, first to himself and then to his family. "Perhaps if my dad had my mom around [as I came out as gay] it would have made it easier for him to deal with the issue and not wait ten years to be able to accept the whole situation." Unlike the teachers at his *madrasa* and unlike his father, Aziz's mother was not troubled by difficult questions and she did not see them as challenging her authority. Her untimely death pushed Aziz to deepen his faith, speak more openly with his sole surviving parent, and take greater risks in life. "Having to deal with her death was very difficult. Coming to terms with it was tough, but that is one of the things that made me come out of my shell, made me realize that I must deal with it [homosexuality]. But at that time, I was very angry. I was very angry with God. . . . How could he do this to me? How could he just cut the umbilical cord short? How could he make me go through all this pain and trauma?" The pain and trauma, however, may have saved Aziz's sincerity from being forever submerged in hypocrisy.

His troubled reaction to his mother's death closed for him the possibility of attending a *Dar al-Ulum* academy for higher religious studies. "I think this is why I didn't pursue my Islamic studies [and decided to continue in secular university] because I was very angry with God." However, Aziz is very clear that refusing higher religious education was not turning away from God—far from it. "I think that if I had gone to the *Dar al-Ulum*, I would be a Tablighi [a follower of the *Tablighi Jama'at*] by now . . . in a sort of remote-control way where I didn't have to employ *ijtihad* or critical reasoning to Islamic jurisprudence." Several friends from Aziz's local community have gone down that path. Many young gay Muslims, before they fully come to grips with their situation, either choose to go to *Dar al-Ulum* or are forced to attend it by their families. Aziz reflects, "I think a lot of them [young gay Muslims who have not come out] had, in an attempt to understand themselves, found themselves in the *Dar al-Ulum* and you find a lot of this subtle sexual activity happening but it is never spoken about. . . . It bothers me that whatever might happen in the Indian community, people just don't want to talk about it. 'Do not question things! This is just the way it is!'" Had Aziz attended a *Dar al-Ulum* academy, he would have been under great pressure to adopt the *Tablighi Jama'at* line of thinking and suppress critical questioning. He observes that the *Jami'at al-'Ulama* (the Council of Muslim Theologians of Gauteng-Johannesburg that makes doctrinal decisions and encourages uniformity among Muslims in the area) is largely run by the *Tablighi Jama'at* and imposes patriarchal values in the name of Islam.

In this way, Aziz avoided using religion to obscure difficult issues. He did not let Islam become an excuse for not confronting his own personality. After his mother's death Aziz completed his degree and returned to Johannesburg for his master's degree in clinical psychology. He entered into a gay relationship, completed his studies, earned his doctorate, and started his clinical practice. But Aziz had great difficulty coming out to his father who resisted any attempt to discuss it. Religion offered him a surprising way to come out. When he was twenty-six, Aziz prepared to go on the hajj to Mecca with his gay partner, who was also a Muslim. Before going on hajj, Muslims prepare for death by repaying loans, clarifying issues of inheritance, and asking forgiveness for any trespasses. Aziz decided to invite everyone close to him, including family and friends, to his home for a farewell celebration. "I decided that I would invite all my family and also all my gay friends to come over and greet me the night before we were leaving. I got seventy people all in the same place, at the same time, under one roof. I didn't warn anybody about what was going to happen. I thought, 'You are all just going to have to deal with this!' I didn't tell my family that gay friends were coming, and I didn't tell gay friends that my whole family was coming over. Both sides were shell-shocked! I found all the gay guys running into the kitchen—I found them huddled in the pantry—saying, 'His family is here!' I thought that was the only way I could break this [deadlock]. . . . I needed to shock my family. I needed them to see that there are gay people out there, who exist in this world, because they are brought up in a totally shallow way. I thought, 'They can't kill me because I'm going on hajj and neither can they shout at me and scream at me, because I'm on the way to Mecca.'" Going on a real-life spiritual journey, a pilgrimage, offered Aziz a way to start his inward journey as a gay Muslim. After the initial shock, Aziz's family was forced to confront the issue. His three younger sisters have fully accepted him as a gay brother, but his elder sister refuses to speak with him. His father has not disowned him but is still reluctant to speak about the issue.

The spiritual journey of the hajj created an environment in which Aziz could come out to family without causing a conflagration, but it also revealed the limits of flexibility in his Muslim community. While on hajj, Aziz and his partner were part of a group led by a *mufti* from South Africa, who preached eloquently about forgiveness, humility, and tolerance. Aziz remembers that he used to preach to the pilgrims: "Go back and tell people about the hajj—don't judge people, you have to humble yourself for when you come back from hajj you are going to be a different person." In the context of the hajj, Aziz and his partner were simply believers. But later, when members of The Inner Circle gave radio and television interviews on the subject of Islam and homosexuality, the same *mufti* condemned them and declared them to be unbelievers and said that they should not have a Muslim burial when they die. Aziz was alarmed at what he perceived to be utter hypocrisy on the part of the Islamic cleric. "He didn't know at that point in time that we were gay, but the minute he found out [one of us] is gay, then he is branded out of the fold of Islam. I found that to be quite contradictory! . . . For me, it answered the question that was in my head all along: 'Will the imams and the *Jami'at al-'Ulama* ever understand the issue of homosexuality in Islam?' I don't think they are ready for it. I don't think the clergy are ready to enter into a debate on this issue. This is what is making it so difficult for most Muslim gay people, whether lesbian or [male] homosexual, to come to terms with their own identity."

When I interviewed Aziz, he was in the tenth year of his clinical practice in Johannesburg. Gay Muslim clients are referred to him by health care professionals who know his reputation or by members of the local Muslim community themselves, when ad hoc solutions to family crisis by Islamic authorities fail. Practices that Muslim authorities see as "spiritual healing" can leave deep scars and only intensify alienation. Aziz reflects that "You can't escape from the reality of the fact that religion shapes who you are—especially as a Muslim. It shapes who you are as a person. I think that it helps me in understanding gay patients . . . in the issues that they deal with. Some of the issues I deal with in therapy are issues of having to reconcile sexuality and religion, and that is the biggest dilemma. Most of my patients who come for therapy come for exactly this reason: [They say,] 'I cannot reconcile the two and therefore I want to commit suicide—I want to kill myself because I cannot reconcile my sexuality with my religion.'" He finds that discussing ideas from the Progressive Muslim movement can really help his patients, especially the idea that alternative or multiple interpretations of the Qur'an are valid, so that they do not have to fully accept the moral judgments that their families or communities impose in the name of religion.

In this light, Aziz's fusion of personal conviction and professional training is beneficial to many Muslims. He finds the two dimensions of his personality sometimes hard to reconcile, but ultimately each has a role to play in helping others. "As a psychotherapist I am very much a background kind of person: I do a lot of observation and introspection. Rather than being out there and outspoken, I'd be in the background observing interactions, patterns, ways of relating, noting the kinds of conversations that people are having, and the operational dynamics. I think that makes me take a back seat somewhat [by playing the role of] a researcher and academic. Rather than an activist I am more of an advocate. I see my role more as advocacy than activism." Independent of his professional activities, Aziz was an organizing member of the first support group to take shape in Johannesburg, the Gay Muslim Outreach. He was also instrumental in helping that group merge with the Cape Town–based support group, then called Al-Fitra. The resulting reorganization gave rise to The Inner Circle, and Aziz participates avidly in the Johannesburg branch and helps to run their *halaqa* sessions for theological reflection and discussion.

Many doctors in the field of psychotherapy have secular training that does not empower them to effectively treat clients for whom religious belief is an integral part of their personality (whether in terms of their own conviction or their family context). This is an especially acute problem for Muslims, who are a minority in South Africa (as in the other European and American sites surveyed in this study), where detailed information about Islamic beliefs and practices may not be widely known. In this environment, Aziz finds that he has a crucial role to play. As a secular professional he upholds medical standards and as a Muslim believer he knows intimately the worldview of religious clients and the concerns of their families. He has struggled himself with the questions that they face and can therefore effectively take up the role of guide if they seek him out.

Patients come to him of their own volition, often after having been treated by imams or spiritual healers who, without a psychological theory of sexual orientation, end up causing more damage than good. He notes with alarm that as professional standards change in the field of medicine and social work toward more "gay affirmative" approaches to therapy in South Africa, imams and other authorities in the Muslim community are outsourcing the cases they confront to spiritual healers from India or Pakistan. They thereby avoid having to confront South African law and modern medical standards. Aziz observes that most gay Muslims are treated by local imams with "the amulets and holy water, or going to a *hakim* . . . [who] would not be from Johannesburg, but rather from India and knows someone in Johannesburg who would invite him." The *hakim* is a practitioner of *unani* medicine, the traditional healing system of Islamic societies derived from the ancient Greek system of balancing the body's humors (analogous to homeopathic medicine in Europe and North America). In this system of *unani* cures, the physical and herbal treatment of disease blurs into *ruhani* cures of spiritual healing, involving prayers or incantations to remove malevolent spirits and the effect of the evil eye or other supernatural forces. "Imams would not refer people to the psychologist but rather to the *hakim*, saying, 'You need some traditional medicine to cure you and get this devil out of you, to remove this evil spirit that you have.'" Aziz observes that most of his clients have undergone such rituals before coming for clinical therapy. "When people finally get into therapy they say, 'I've been through this whole process—having to read the Qur'an, recite *namaz* five times a day, drink holy water, wear a *ta'wiz*, do whatever one is required to do by the imam and his *hakim*—but I'm still here and I'm still gay! I'm still attracted to men, so help me to deal with it.' . . . What I have helped people to do is to accept themselves—that is as far as I can go. I can walk that road with them only so far. But in terms of success, I'm still fighting a battle there."

Aziz is still fighting this battle, because it is not just a struggle of individual clients but rather a struggle against the prejudgments of a whole community based upon religious tradition. Yet Aziz avoids heated discussions with Islamic authorities to focus instead on his professional work in clinical counseling. He regularly counsels the sons and daughters of Muslim families who fail to deal constructively or humanely with social issues and conflicts. When families turn to imams and religious leaders of their communities to help, the issues are usually exacerbated rather than ameliorated. "I think that it does have to start at the level of community, family, and friends. [But they] come back to you and say . . . 'The imam says in the Qur'an it is not acceptable.' So people still place a lot of emphasis on what the imams say [and] they even control the minds and hearts of the families, of the mothers, brothers, and sisters, who are trying to accept the sexual identity of a person who is gay in the family." In the end, Aziz thought that gradual change in the perceptions of lesbian and gay members of the Muslim community will come by quiet persuasion, the pressure of demographic change, and the breakdown of previous isolation that was enforced by apartheid. It is common people, not religious authorities, who will begin to look at the issue in a more creative light. And it is his duty to help common people—gay Muslims and their family members—to navigate their own paths toward a more integrated personality and a more fulfilling life.

Ibrahim: Acceptance in God's Eyes

Ibrahim, a volunteer in the support group Imaan in London, also illustrates the activist mode of journeying toward individual identity. Like Aziz, Ibrahim conceives of his life as a spiritual journey. But while Aziz carries out his journey as a gay man, Ibrahim's personal journey calls into question what it means to be a man. Ibrahim has a vibrant personality and gives us insight into the ambiguities of gender.

Ibrahim was born male and socialized as a Muslim man in the United Kingdom. He does not identify as a transgender person but he also hesitates to identify as a man. His personality can teach us much about gender identity. His sense of gender ambiguity is heightened by his attachment to Islamic spirituality in a specifically Sufi form, which he sees as transcending the social categories of gender. Now in his late thirties, Ibrahim works in community health projects and devotes much of his time to activist work in HIV/AIDS prevention and education and also to community building through the support group Imaan in London. He advocates journeying toward individual identity, even when that journey is blocked by social conventions and religious dogma.

Ibrahim is quick to point out that he is not easy to classify. His family is South Asian, but he was born in East Africa and grew up in the United Kingdom. Thus he slips out of the contentious binary of "British or Asian?" which shapes so much of his political and ethnic environment in the United Kingdom. By speaking of himself as a Sufi, he also avoids the binary of "orthodox Muslim or irreligious?" that plagues many members of Imaan and the wider community of second-generation Muslims born in the United Kingdom from immigrant parents. Ibrahim's story reveals the limitations of thinking about gender as a binary "either/or" proposition. Though he admits that his sexual orientation is homosexual, he hesitates to identify simply as a gay man, because in his eyes this means capitulation to defining oneself only by sexual activity. This, he feels, falls right into the stereotype through which most Muslims view the issue, with their obsessive focus on illegal or immoral sexual intercourse. Rather, Ibrahim feels that if one defines one's difference in terms of gender, there is more open space for discussion and more creative potential for reconciliation. "If you ask everybody to put themselves in a box, then I would categorize myself as a third-gender person. In the eyes of people who look at the world in black and white, . . . [most see only] the male-to-male and female-to-female equation."[4]

Though we tend to think of gender as a binary opposition of female to male, it is not so simple. A binary pairing always generates two fields that are in tension, and the tension creates ambiguity. The ambiguity might be expressed in terms of some elements crossing over the boundary that separates the two fields, or it might be expressed by some elements exhibiting characteristics of both fields, with belonging determined by predominance rather than absolute distinction. Or even further, ambiguity might be expressed by elements that reside directly between the two fields, therefore belonging to neither one. Let us apply this abstract schema to real persons: a transsexual person is gender ambiguous in that she or he crosses over the boundary that routinely distinguishes males from females. A transgender person is ambiguous in that such a person displays elements of both genders—often suffering some feeling of disharmony with a subsequent yearning to find complete identification with one gender or the other. But there are also people who do not strongly identify as either female or male, who see themselves as somehow transcending gender categories altogether. If they feel uncomfortable with the social demands imposed by the gender binary, they don't resolve the discomfort by crossing over from ascribed gender to felt gender; rather they resolve it by denying the gender binary itself.

To give these categories a human face, we can summarize the interviews that have been presented before. The story of Fatima in chapter 3 shows the struggle of a Muslim female-to-male transsexual whose outer transformation began after a long process of inner development. Nafeesa's story in chapter 1 displays the life challenges of a male-to-female transgender person, who is more at peace having a male body while living out a female persona. In contrast, Ibrahim does not identify strongly as either male or female. Though he accepts that his body is male in terms of sex and that his desires are gay in terms of sexual orientation, he does not accept his socialization as a masculine person as defined against femininity. Rather he strives to accept within himself those personality traits that society defines as feminine as well as those defined as masculine.

For Ibrahim, the goal is to find balance between the masculine and feminine elements of his own persona, a goal expressed as spiritual growth rather than as alteration of the body's materiality. Though he identifies as a gay man, he claims not to act upon his sexual desires. Though he does not advocate celibacy for others and does not see it as the preferential way to resolve the conflicts between homosexuality and Islam, Ibrahim in general refuses to act upon his sexual urges and desires. He feels that restraining sexual desire makes him a stronger, purer, and more spiritually potent person. In this way, he admires the eunuchs, though he does not yearn for physical castration in any way. Ibrahim reflects, "I compared myself to the eunuchs at the Prophet's tomb, because that is the only time I've known from people that there are people like us, or should I say, people of the third gender. [That is when I found out that this phenomenon] exists and that it is accepted in Islam. . . . They were only people like me, they were given this responsibility and this task to look after the most sacred places." Eunuchs are people of ambiguous gender in Islamic societies of the past who are neither-men-nor-women. He does not call himself a eunuch because a eunuch is defined by physical castration. Rather he identifies with the eunuchs' subsequent gender neutrality and idealizes the spiritual potency and social status that Islamic societies traditionally granted to them.

A eunuch is a person born with male sex organs and raised as a boy until castrated. It is not clear whether eunuchs were castrated before the onset of puberty or after, but they were instantly removed from the classification of "male." Eunuchs did not become female, but rather inhabited an in-between position that was legally and socially of neither gender; in this way they occupied a useful and high status function as guards and servants for the women's quarters of aristocratic households, where sexually potent men were not allowed access. Eunuchs stood at the threshold in between two separate realms—they could move between them while belonging to neither realm, and therefore served as guards, wardens, and intimate protectors of sacred or inviolable spaces.

The Prophet Muhammad allowed a eunuch servant to live with his Egyptian wife, Marya the Copt.[5] In medieval Islamic empires, eunuchs often served as bodyguards for the sultan, acting as highly symbolic markers of an inviolable space around the ruler into which routine men could not enter. In such a court structure and aristocratic class, eunuchs could rise to positions of great power and authority, in compensation for their exposure to enslavement, violence, and mutilation as youths. Some Muslim eunuchs became highly successful courtiers or generals.[6] Eunuchs who served at royal courts "retired" to serve an even higher authority—the Prophet Muhammad himself. Until the recent past, elderly eunuchs guarded the Prophet's tomb in Medina, as noted by Ibrahim in his interview. It was their privilege to light the tomb's lamps and sweep its inner chamber. They intercede—as those who are neither-man-nor-woman—between a powerful male figure and common petitioners.

Ibrahim is unusual in being aware of this sacred role for eunuchs, for most Muslims are ignorant of this fact except those who have spent considerable time around the Prophet's tomb. Many who know it are bewildered when they visit the Prophet's tomb to pay their respects and keep silent about the strange figures who keep order at the shrine. But for Ibrahim, these eunuchs represent a ray of hope for gay, lesbian, and transgender Muslims.[7] Even though the tradition of eunuchs at the Prophet's tomb seems to be dying out, Muslims have accepted them and given them such a high status role at a sacred shrine; this means that other groups who are seen as marginal or strange—like lesbian and gay or transgender people—can also be granted a place in Islamic communities even if they are outside the norm.

Although Ibrahim does not consider himself a eunuch, he sees himself as analogous to one. He theorizes that gay men are like eunuchs

because both are outside the heterosexual norm of pairing for reproductive sex. Eunuchs are outside that norm by force of castration while
homosexual men are outside it as a result of sexual orientation. The two
are even closer in analogy if a gay man were to give up having sexual
intercourse, as Ibrahim has done for long stretches of his life. "If they
[the eunuchs] were that respected and that special to be allowed in [to
the Prophet's tomb] and to be allowed to look after it, then they could
not be bad people. Although there were in olden days eunuchs who
looked after the shrine, I don't really think in this day and age the people looking after the holy shrine are really castrated eunuchs. I think
they might be more like gay men. That is what I thought. . . . I've heard
about them from one of my aunts and from my sister. . . . She said these
very effeminate men come [to those lingering at the Prophet's tomb]
and say, 'Now get out out out!' So the thought comes up, '*Yeh kon hai,
bhai, mard hai ya awrat?* [Who is this, brother, a man or a woman?]'
But the most important thing is that they are accepted. That was, for
me, acceptance in God's eyes."

Ibrahim thinks in terms of social relationships rather than in
abstractions. Before he ever analyzed Islamic theology he was thinking
critically and creatively about the relationships he observed in Islamic
communities. The fact that eunuchs were present and granted high status was an indication for Ibrahim that gay men too might be able to
find a dignified place in Islamic communities. Knowing of eunuchs and
their sacred duties was his first glimpse into an optimistic future as a
gay Muslim. "Before that, I wasn't aware that there is no such word as
homosexuality in the Qur'an or even that the word sexuality was not in
the Qur'an. I knew only that the Prophet Lut is in there and what is said
about the Prophet and his people [the Tribe of Lot], but I didn't know
how to interpret that. All I remember is how they [other Muslims] say
what I'm doing is wrong and being me is wrong. I always knew that I
was created by Allah who loved me—no matter what. . . . So for me,
[seeing that eunuchs were serving at the Prophet's tomb] meant that
what I was doing was not wrong, as long as I was not abusing my body
and abusing the teachings and being a nasty human being and hating people, [as long as I] followed some basic principles and knew my
wrong and right. As long as my sense of wrong and right was strong, I
knew I would survive."

Despite this inner strength and confidence in the intuition that God loves every created being, Ibrahim had a difficult time reconciling being a gay man and also a believing Muslim. This was especially difficult because of his strong spiritual inclination, which did not allow him to discard Islamic practices or find fulfillment in living a secular lifestyle. But while remaining loyal to spiritual traditions in Islam, Ibrahim flatly rejects the need for conformity to Islamic social and legal norms. He strongly asserts the capacity for Islam to embrace a diverse array of people and accept their diversity. If Muslims don't live up to this spiritual mandate, then Ibrahim is willing to tell them that he does not belong to their categories, while still holding fast to his personal vision of Islamic spirituality and ethics. "In the eyes of society . . . especially the Muslim society at large, you are seen as somebody who is not accepted. So rather than [gay Muslims] saying, 'We're here and we're part of you,' I just say create a whole new identity and a whole new box. [We can] say, 'This is who we are—we don't belong to you—we don't belong to you and yet we are here.' . . . When I have to describe myself I feel that I am one of those special chosen people. Then when somebody wants to put me down, saying, 'Oh, you are gay—you're one of those people who takes it up the bum,' or 'You're a sinner and are going straight to hell,' then I turn around and say, 'Why? The people who look after the two holy shrines are like me, and they are going straight to heaven, because they've been given such a very special job. They look after holy shrines . . . yet you turn around and say that we are wrong, that we are going to hell?" Using the unique role of eunuchs as a point of argument, Ibrahim tries to appeal to some element within Islamic culture and history to transcend the conflict-ridden dichotomy of the two terms "gay" and "Muslim."

Though raised in the United Kingdom, Ibrahim sees himself as being rather out of step with contemporary trends in both the British Muslim community and the secular gay community. Rather, he sees himself in continuity with much older traditions reaching back many generations in his family. Part of his individual journey is keeping up his ancient family attachment to Sufism, even if that makes him seem quaint or eccentric to others. "I was born in East Africa, and came here [to the United Kingdom] at the age of thirteen and I ended up staying. I consider all of it to be my home. [We're] 'old Sunni' who believe in the Prophets and the saints. [We believe] in everything that a Wahhabi doesn't, which is what most of my family has become! My mother died ten years ago. She didn't become a Wahhabi—she believed in the old ways, so I'm like that. . . . But the others—my sisters and sisters' husbands and everybody from my generation—[they say,] 'No more *milad al-nabi* [celebration of the birth of Muhammad], no more *niyaz* [vows at saints' tombs], no more *dhikr* [meditation]!' . . . As far as I'm concerned, my mother did it and my *nana* [maternal grandmother] did it, so I'm going to do it. On the day of judgment if I find out that I'm wrong then at least I'll be in good company with my mother and *nana* there with me!" The biggest problem for Ibrahim is his family's drift into neotraditionalist Islamic movements (like the Wahhabis or the *Tablighi Jama'at*) with its overtly patriarchal and aggressive tone. He feels that his family members are losing their old Islamic grounding in spirituality that is largely informed by the Sufi tradition and shaped by the women in his family. He feels that if people stay close to the older Sunni tradition infused with Sufi spirituality, then they are more gentle, more flexible, and more accepting of people who don't conform to rigid gender or sexuality roles.

With this deep sense of maternal guidance and continuity with the Islam of his female ancestors, Ibrahim cites his mother as his greatest consolation. He was the youngest child. For this reason he enjoyed a special relationship with his mother and he had a unique role in the family. "I could live my own life and not worry about anyone else! . . . I think my mother knew what I was [gay]. . . . She did say one thing [as a testament before she died], 'What I ask you to do is just three things: never hurt anyone, be yourself and be happy, and never forget God.' She always used to tell me, . . . 'Be your own person and lead your own life and just remember to always remember Allah.' . . . Then after my mother had died, I was told, my aunts more than anybody else used to complain that she died without my being married, without having seen me settled down. But I know that she wasn't worried about me. Before she died she said that she was worried about me being alone, not having a partner, because of my being the closest to her. I know that she said, 'He will be the one who will miss me the most, and I certainly wish that he had somebody close to look after him.' In her way, I think she meant a male partner, somebody to whom I was close, who could look after me." In his mother's blessing, Ibrahim sees an Islamic basis for his journey toward individual identity and fulfillment, even if it means abandoning community norms.

Although Ibrahim never told his mother that he was gay, he is sure that she sensed and accepted it. He himself knew from childhood not only that he was "different" but that his difference had to do with gender roles. "I knew even from that very early age. . . . I didn't think I would grow up and this was all wrong. . . . Then at age ten . . . I would always think, 'I wonder if these people feel the same way as I do?' . . . There are things that upset others but don't upset me at all, and visa versa. There are things that others are not sensitive about that I'm very sensitive about. This is one of them—I never thought it was strange, but rather normal. For example, I've gone through this with my father—he said on a couple of occasions, 'I wish I had drowned you. I wish I had drowned you when you were born. If I had known you were going to grow up like this I would have killed you.' I've mentioned it to some people, even one who is a trained counselor, and they said, 'I want to discuss that more.' But I feel that there is nothing there to discuss. This person said to me, 'That is something that would really upset other people, but you are just smiling?' I thought, 'Well, yes, he just said that. But I'm here, I'm living—so tough, deal with it.'"

When asked how his father knew he was gay in order to express such severe disapproval, Ibrahim notes that it was just apparent from his own trespassing of gender norms. He simply never acted like a conventional boy or man. "I never told him [my father]. I never told anyone. He just knows. Even my mother knew. My mother and I had a beautiful relationship. We used to sit together, sing together, sew together, used to watch films together, and go shopping together. We used to do everything together. . . . I still do my nieces' eyebrows. . . . For the henna application a couple of nights before Eid, they ask, 'Can we book you for henna?' I know that is coming—so in that role, they all know who I am and what I am, but it's just not discussed." For the men in his family, Ibrahim's expertise in clothes and cosmetics is a matter of conflict, for it displays his failure to live up to heterosexual male roles. But for the women in his family, it is a subtler problem. They may not be able to accept his speaking openly about being gay, but they can enjoy his company and aesthetic taste just as they would enjoy that of a sister or aunt. In a way, they accept Ibrahim's gender identity even if they cannot accept any articulation of his sexual orientation. They enjoy his company as long as the issue of sex is suppressed and gender takes on a playful role in their relationships.

Ibrahim feels that his being not-a-real-man gives him insight into aesthetics and also into spirituality and healing. He feels that his having given up rigid gender roles allows him to see deeper into people's hearts. He feels that he is able to understand their soul's problems better than ordinary people who are stuck in the binary roles of gender. "I have a very strong spiritual side of me, and I feel that I'm moving towards spirituality and maybe things like healing. . . . Or maybe I have a slightly stronger connection [to God] than other people. . . . In their own way, maybe people recognize me as being different and as being somebody who is not following the norm. [They feel] it's ok for them to ridicule me when they feel like it, but then they will turn around and ask me for help when they are down and out, when they are not being listened to by God, like people who used to go to shrines and saints and to Ajmer Sharif [were asked to pray for the welfare of others]. So they look to you and ask you to pray for them. So this is also a belief that lots of people don't have any more [due to Wahhabi-style fundamentalism]." Ibrahim cites Ajmer, the town where Mu'in al-Din Chishti, a great Sufi leader of South Asia, lived and died. His tomb is a popular place of pilgrimage for those Muslims who still value Sufi teachings. By honoring the memory of a great saint and venerating his tomb, people seek his help in conveying their petitions and prayers to God. Of course, God is everywhere listening to people's petitions and prayers, but the problem is caused by people and not God. People often feel alienated from God, as if "they are not being listened to by God." As people ask another (whether living or dead) to pray for them, they seek refuge in humility in order to rekindle their awareness of God's closeness. Such Sufi practices at the tombs of great saints of the Islamic past are still current in South Asia, East Africa, and other places to which Ibrahim feels a great connection.

But these spiritual practices are under increasing attack by Wahhabi fundamentalists in the Arab world and the West. Ibrahim feels that there is great power in Sufi spiritual training and sees this tradition as the real heart of Islam, even as it is denounced as mere Muslim folk practice. Sufi training encourages one to meditate through *dhikr*, or repetition of the names of God in every breath. It forces one to be humble and refuse to judge others. Indeed *hijras* or third-gender persons in South Asia are welcome in the annual pilgrimage to the tomb of Mu'in al-Din Chishti at Ajmer, where their presence has for centuries been part of local tradition. The Sufi tradition invites one to love God by loving others and caring for their needs.[8]

When Ibrahim insists on remaining a Muslim even while he is gay, he means the "old Sunni" way of being Muslim and engaging in Sufi practices. For him, this means learning how to love. He struggled long with loneliness and found a way out of its dark corner through activist work to care for the health and well-being of others. "From age eighteen, I knew that there were gay clubs and pubs and stuff, but I was not comfortable going out in London. . . . I never felt comfortable—I really hated it. I wouldn't end up talking to anybody or feeling comfortable. . . . So all that became very nasty and I thought, 'If this is what gay life is about, then I don't want any part of it!' I withdrew into a shell and only kept in touch with [a couple of] friends and their long-term partners. So my whole time I spent just being alone. I felt alone and isolated and that there was nothing out there for me." Ten years of feeling alone went by as Ibrahim wondered how to find a loving partner as a gay Muslim man.

Activism helped to provide part of an answer. Ibrahim was encouraged to attend a community-building workshop for gay men of color. Someone he trusted told him, "'There's a friend of mine running a workshop at PACE (a counseling and support group for gay people in North London) called Asian Gay and Proud, and I want you to go to it.' . . . I asked 'Why?' He said, 'I just feel that you are holding yourself back for no reason and maybe it's time to explore what the issues are and maybe just have a little fun. I'm sorry to do this, but I'm placing an ultimatum on you. If you don't go, I'll never talk to you again.' I said, 'All right, I'll go,' just to show him. When I got to the weekend workshop . . . I was talking with people and interacting, and I thought maybe this is good closure for me. I had spent ten years praying that I would meet my man and wondering how I'm going to meet him, yet it hadn't happened. Maybe it wasn't going to happen and I was destined to be alone. So I thought, 'Now just use this to explore the issues, put a closure to this whole gay thing, and just go home.' . . . Maybe I thought that that weekend would just be the closure."

But it was not closure—it was an opening. One new friend he made at this community building session told Ibrahim about a support group, Al-Fatiha UK (later known as Imaan), which was a support group for lesbian, gay, bisexual, or transgender Muslims. This new friend invited Ibrahim to join the support group. "He said 'Just come to al-Fatiha and see what happens.' So I thought to myself, 'Well fine, I'll try it.' I met [the facilitator] and he said that they needed more people and asked if I would join them, saying, 'We feel that you are the kind of person we want on board.' I didn't know what they meant by that. I returned home and suddenly thought, 'Yes, I have been through ten years of hell. I have been to the point that I cry myself to sleep through most nights. I didn't have anyone to talk to. I knew more about loneliness and solitude and everything I had gone through. . . . I thought of all those who had helped me, and I didn't want anyone else to feel [what I had suffered]. . . . I didn't want anyone else to go through what I had gone through. I didn't want anyone else to feel lonely or that there was nobody there." Ibrahim got involved in social outreach and activist work through Imaan dealing with issues faced by Muslims as a religious minority.

His activist work gave Ibrahim a lease on life, a new vibrancy, and a new optimism. He found a way to overcome his loneliness by reaching out to others. He discovered that he had a flair for conversation, and that his gender ambiguity allowed people to open up to him easily. He made an ideal volunteer at various public health initiatives, which try to reach out to gay men from minorities to raise their awareness about sexual health and the dangers of HIV/AIDS infection. Whether the minority groups are ethnic or religious (or both in the case of South Asian Muslims like Ibrahim himself), they often face a compound alienation; as an antidote, many turn to self-destructive habits like alcoholism, drug abuse, or unsafe sexual practices. "I actually work part-time for the gay men's health project [doing] outreach work in my local boroughs. . . . We go to our local area's pubs and clubs, and because that is West London, there are lots more Asians there. So we go to places where minority crowds are—Latino, Afro-Caribbean, and South Asian. I have my leaflets with me for Imaan or [other support groups]. We normally go in early and set up a table with condoms, postcards, and leaflets. . . . They get free lube [water-based lubricant] and free condoms." For Ibrahim, this volunteer work is effective because it is non-judgmental. He may not like the atmosphere in clubs and pubs, but his presence in the midst of it helps gain the trust of people who learn by bitter experience not to trust others. His membership in various minority groups helps him get the message out to people to care for their own welfare, physically and mentally. He also urges them to care for others, whether they are sexual partners or friends. For Ibrahim, taking care of each other is intensely Islamic. It is the most profound kind of Islamic spirituality because it means manifesting God's quality of being *rahman*, the Compassionate One.

Ibrahim has found that it is difficult to talk about sexual health to men who would rather just have fun and avoid troubling realities. It is difficult to talk about spirituality with gay, lesbian, and transgender people, many of whom have had bitter experiences with religious authorities. Ibrahim finds that he still often feels alone, even with his extensive outreach work through activist projects and support groups. While this work has revived his optimism and allowed him to meet more like-minded people, he still has not found the life partner he has been looking for. In the end, Ibrahim is unsure whether his strong belief in spiritual growth actually helps or hurts in meeting the right romantic partner. "All I can say is that I believe in my spiritual side, which is much stronger in me than in other people. Yes, I have conflict sometimes, because I believe that every single breath we take is only with Allah's permission. Each breath has to ask permission before the next breath—each heartbeat has to ask permission before the next heartbeat. I think then that every single person you interact with, every person you meet, every person we deal with, is by the will of Allah. My big issue with Allah is my being single. Deep in my heart, that is my only issue with Allah. . . . I'd like to be married [to a male partner with] a *nikah* with the whole ceremony—why not?—with a *nikah-nama* [formal marriage contract]. I don't care about anybody else being there—family or anything—as long as it is me and him and our commitment to each other. [I'd like as witnesses] friends who would be happy for us. I don't think my family would come, even if they were invited. I probably wouldn't tell them. I'm more worried about what I'm going to wear and what he's going to wear and how we are going to do it and where we'll go on honeymoon. And where we are going to live. And whether he'll kick me out of bed for *fajr* [dawn prayer] and whether he'll force me to go to *jum'a* [Friday congregational prayer] with him."

While Ibrahim imagines living with a gay Muslim like himself, he is open to someone who is not a Muslim. But his partner would have to be spiritual, regardless of what religion he professed. "Whoever it is would probably have to enjoy similar things to me—that would be important. To me, going out is not as important as staying in. To me, more important is going for a walk on the beach holding hands, walking in the garden, going for a drive at night and sitting under the stars, watching movies or listening to music. Those are more important than meeting up with people to go to a club and dancing. . . . It is probably something that I thought would never happen, but the conference [of Imaan in 2005] has given me hope and I think now, maybe, there are people like that."

In the end, feeling "acceptance in God's eyes" does not make it easy to find acceptance in the eyes of another person. While the search for integrity in Islamic theology is long and hard, as is the search for acceptance in family, it is even harder to find simple love with some person and to give the same. Whether one defines one's struggle in terms of gender identity or sexual orientation (or some combination of the two), the search for love can take a lifetime. Ibrahim defines his activism as just one part of his search for love and acceptance. For Ibrahim, more important than changing laws, social conventions, or family expectations is the need to find love and fulfillment in his relations with others. For him, the most effective activist strategy is journeying toward individual identity and the sense that God accepts him, and the rest will come gradually from there.

Conclusion

Building a strong and healthy identity as individuals is a powerful mode of activism for transgender, lesbian, and gay Muslims. Those who engage in this mode of activism often portray life as a journey the goal of which is individual fulfillment. Religion, politics, family, and community are important resources for this journey, but they are not the ultimate goal. If these structures impede one's individual journey rather than provide resources for arriving at the goal, then they can be sidelined or even jettisoned. Individual fulfillment could be imagined as either happiness in this world or salvation in the next world (or both together, as in the oft-repeated prayer by the Prophet Muhammad— "Oh God, give us what is good in this world and what is good in the next world").

Activists who engage this strategy articulate individual identity in different ways. Aziz uses primarily psychological language to talk about the struggle to come to a healthy identity and overcome the trauma of being rejected or marginalized. Ibrahim uses more spiritual language to explain his journey toward finding acceptance in God's eyes, an acceptance that is reflected in caring relationships with other people around him. Despite these different idioms used to describe identity, those who engage this mode of activism often portray Islam as a spiritual tradition rather than as dogma or ideology; they highlight its mystical or devotional aspects and downplay its legal and social aspects.

In this way, both of the activists interviewed in this chapter show a strong affinity for the Sufi tradition within Islam. The Sufi tradition represents the mystical current which functions as an "inner dimension" to the Islamic tradition. This affinity for Sufism might also be heightened because both activists interviewed come from South Asian diaspora backgrounds and Sufism remains a strong and vibrant tradition in Islamic culture in this region. The activists interviewed are also males who feel that loyalty to this spiritual tradition comes from their strong attachment to their mothers; female members of their family serve as strong role models and sources of inspiration, encouragement, and blessing, even as they rebel against conformity to masculine stereotypes and male authority figures. Very often women in Muslim families retain an allegiance to Sufi spirituality even if males dismiss it, so the overlap between attraction to Sufi thought and intimacy with female role models is not accidental in the lives of these activists.

"Journeying toward individual identity" is a mode of activism that is often quiet or invisible. It is seldom documented by journalists or visible through the media. We tend to assume that activism is a loud and brash activity—after all, activists speak up, organize groups, denounce injustices, and clash with opposition. But those who see activism as a journey toward individual identity do not necessarily do these things (though they might do so by engaging other modes of activism at the same time). They make take up other roles in gay, lesbian, and transgender support groups, roles that are nurturing, supporting, caring, or therapeutic.

Of those interviewed in this chapter, Aziz voices concern that he is not really an activist because his mode of engagement is quieter and more linked to psychotherapy than to politics; his ultimate concern is not social change in itself but rather his ability (and that of his fellows) to live a fulfilling life in society. Ibrahim goes further in sidelining social change in favor of a journey toward individual identity. He openly questions society's gender norms and imagines himself to be on a spiritual journey in which society plays little role. His journey's twin goals are acceptance in God's eyes and marriage to a loving partner, while all else matters little. Still he volunteers his time and energy to outreach and organizing, but does this as an expression of care for his fellow travelers and hope for spreading love in all dark places.

Those who engage with this mode of activism assert their ability to forge ahead beyond the limits of family expectation or religious dogma to search for viable individual identities that will allow them to live fulfilling and creative lives. Islam urges them onward in this search, they argue, even if their fellow Muslims would rather hold them back. Religious solidarity can be compromised or rejected, they feel—especially if their coreligionists do not strive to sincerely understand them and their existential position with regard to sexual orientation and gender identity. In the end, they uphold the teaching that God judges each person as an individual according to his or her intention and action. As the Qur'an intones: *On that day [of judgment] people come forward, each differently, to witness their deeds. So whoever does an atom's weight of good sees its consequence. And whoever does an atom's weight of harm sees its consequence* (Q 99:6–8). Each one comes forward differently and individually, such that family standing and community solidarity mean nothing when facing God. Citing this message in the contemporary social struggle for acceptance and justice is a potent form of activism, one that authorizes an individual journey that disregards social conventions if they are deemed unjust or discriminatory.

Conclusion

In the body a small piece of flesh which, if it is wholesome
the whole body is wholesome and if it is does not work the
whole body fails to work; surely that is the heart.
~The Prophet Muhammad, in a *hadith* report[1]

In Islamic thought, the heart is the center of the human being rather than
just an organ of the body. It is not merely a muscle to pump blood to all
the body's tissues, but a moral center, the place that connects the spirit and
the body. In the heart, faith shines like a light and in the heart intention
is formed which guides a person's thoughts and actions. There are many
teachings of the Prophet Muhammad that convey this message, including
the *hadith* report quoted above and a report which tells that the Prophet
Muhammad used to pray to God to grant him "a heart that is wholesome."
In this prayer, Muhammad was meditating on the Qur'anic message that
*On the day of judgment one will not be aided by wealth or family, but only
by presenting to God a heart that is wholesome* (Q 26:88–89).

Just as the heart is the center of a healthy body, so a sound heart
is the basic foundation of family, community, and society. The Muslim

activists interviewed in this book reflect this teaching in their own ways, as they insist on holding onto their faith while finding ways to seek justice and welfare in society. Spirituality resides in the heart, giving rise to feelings of love and the intuition that the self is not complete without being part of a great wholeness. These feelings from the heart mingle with cognition from the mind, giving rise to identity formation, causing people to ask, "Who am I?" "Why am I here?" and "What must I do in this short life?" For some, these questions are not answered adequately by common perceptions of one's social place as the child of a family, member of an ethnic group, or fellow of a religious community. This is especially true if one's innermost feelings of identity and desire lead one to a kind of love which one's family and community deem immoral. This, as we have seen, is the case for gay, lesbian, and transgender people in Muslim communities. Their feelings of conflict with family, community, and religion lead to a long and complex process of identity formation.

For those strong enough to endure this process and achieve a viable identity as gay, lesbian, or transgender Muslims, the result can be motivation for creative action in society: activism. Activism does not consist merely of political maneuvers or media interventions. Activism, as this book has shown, is any self-conscious engagement with others in order to change the social order. The goal is make the social order more just, so that all can live in it with sincerity, integrity, and fulfillment. Activism happens when the distance between "what is" and "what ought to be"—the very breeding ground of alienation—is filled with creative and energetic action so that a person does not slip into despair, disillusion, and depression.

The activists we have met in this book have shared their life stories; they have explained how their religious beliefs have led them to volunteer in various support groups and how voluntary activity with such groups has led them to reformulate their understanding of their religious tradition. While they have come from very diverse backgrounds, they are unified in their shared struggle with identity formation and their collective investment in building support groups for lesbian, transgender, and gay Muslims like themselves.

Despite the diversity of their lives, common patterns emerge from these interviews. These activists chose not to relinquish Islam as their religion, even as their levels of ritual engagement with Islam range from intense to lax. They realize that holding onto Islam as a religion is a highly political act, leading them to confront the authoritative spokesmen of Islam in various ways ranging from open debate to subtle questioning. In holding onto Islam as a religious belief and communal framework, these activists find in Islam both resources and obstacles. The resources in Islam are spiritual teachings that give them hope, moral guidance that gives them inspiration, and ideal symbols that give them a means of communication with fellow believers. This means of communication may ultimately be persuasive even among those who are dismissive at first. The obstacles in Islam that they find are patriarchal values that have long been absorbed into the religion, entrenched interpretations that many refuse to question, and traditional norms that stem from medieval jurisprudence. The activists interviewed here, as a group, do not believe that these obstacles are inherent in the Islamic tradition.

The activists believe that the ideals of Islam can be distilled from the traditional forms of the religion and reworked into a new form that accepts more social pluralism and individual rights, including diversity in sexual orientation and gender identity. They may disagree about the details of how Islam can be reformed to achieve this goal, but they all agree that Islam should not be jettisoned. Continued belonging to their Muslim families and communities is a vital part of their personhood. They adopt different strategies or "modes of action" to achieve some kind of reform. Some focus on the Islamic tradition while others address their Muslim families and communities. Some engage national structures of politics and law, while others turn their attention to individual resources in psychology and spirituality. Most engage simultaneously in multiple modes of activism. But all come together through volunteer work in building support groups for themselves and others like them.

These support groups serve an important function in connecting like-minded individuals to form an "intentional community." This community building role is especially crucial because those who join have been marginalized and alienated from the communities in which they were born, such as family, ethnic group, neighborhood, and religious group. Many of those interviewed here were threatened or harmed by their close community—sometimes even by their family members. All of them lived in fear of such harm, whether it materialized or not. And all recognized that such harm is reinforced or justified by traditional Islamic interpretations. Yet their impulse has been to question the interpretation and critically examine its social origins rather than to blame the religion or abandon belief in it. The support groups that these activists have volunteered to build provide a safe space for lesbian, gay, and transgender Muslims to question their faith tradition, assess its traditional interpretations, and explore the possibility of alternatives.

The interviews presented in this book illustrate not only the lives of the activists but also the workings of the support groups that they helped establish and run. Their work has been shaped by the social and legal conditions of these countries with secular democratic constitutions, yet their work has had an international impact because of media and the Internet. The groups see themselves as part of a network of support groups, which often meet, exchange information and experiences, and build a wider international platform for the rights and welfare of sexuality and gender minorities among Muslims. Though the support groups operate in countries where Muslims are a minority, they impact public education and policy debate in countries where Muslims are a majority—in the so-called "Muslim world" of nations in Africa, the Middle East, and Asia.

This book represents only a modest beginning of research into this network of support groups for Muslim members of sexuality and gender minorities. There is much potential for future work, and it is hoped that this volume will encourage other researchers, and that the "oral history" that it presents will lay the groundwork for future study. The network of support groups has existed now for over a decade, dating from the late 1990s, and has increased in viability with new technology. While a group might be active for some years and then disband, the network of such groups continues to expand. When one group disbands, it appears that another group in the same region subsequently forms to address the same concerns and serve the same clientele.

As we have seen, transgender, lesbian, and gay Muslims are hemmed in by stigma and stereotype from many sides, a situation that complicates their formulation of action to demand justice and seek well-being. There is the general problem of being a social minority defined by sexuality or gender identity; even in so-called liberal societies in the West, lesbian, gay, and transgender people face significant stigma and persistent stereotypes that limit their welfare in legal, educational, professional, and social fields. While some legal protection is granted by constitutional systems, not all nations recognize discrimination based on sexual orientation and gender identity to the same extent.

The problem is even more acute for gay, lesbian, and transgender Muslims, who are also members of an ethnic or religious minority. They tend to face double discrimination. Mainstream "gay rights" groups which are predominantly white and Judeo-Christian may see them as "other" through the lens of race, ethnicity, and religion, while members of their religious or ethnic group may alienate them as "other" because of their sexual orientation and gender identity. Empathetic compassion and accurate information are often absent from both sides. Many people in so-called liberal societies bear pernicious prejudices against Muslims and think of Islam as fanatical or inherently violent. Often mainstream "gay rights" groups expect transgender, lesbian, or gay Muslims to reject their religion and reinforce a negative stereotype of Islam as a retrograde threat to modernity. Such mainstream groups may expect lesbian, gay, and transgender Muslims to see themselves as "victims" and to denounce their religious community. This dynamic sets up significant obstacles for gay, lesbian, and transgender Muslims in forming their identity and seeking ways to secure their rights. Moreover, members of Muslim communities may also push them to renounce Islam if they refuse to conform to patriarchal expectations, often by ostracizing them from Islamic rituals and spaces. Support groups such as those documented in this book thus fulfill a crucial function in creating safe spaces where gay, lesbian, and transgender Muslims can reclaim their religion on their own terms. Safe from the double pressure of denouncing Islam or renouncing Islam, in these support groups they can explore what aspects of Islam are compatible with their progressive and feminist projects of asserting the rights of sexuality and gender minorities.

Despite the persistence of stigma and stereotype, the national contexts for the gay, lesbian, and transgender Muslims interviewed in this book are largely optimistic. Most nations in which they live show a trend toward recognizing homosexual and transgender persons as full citizens, and in some nations there is a dramatic movement toward offering them civil rights and legal protection. But this progressive trend is not inevitable or guaranteed. Rather, it is the result of constant activist effort and consequent shifts in popular opinion in the national culture. There can be setbacks in the legal recognition of gay, lesbian, and transgender citizens, as illustrated by the state of affairs in the United States in comparison with the more progressive situation in Canada. And there is no guarantee that constitutional rights and legal protection are actually afforded to individuals, as illustrated by the situation in South Africa; there, Muslim citizens have extensive legal rights but most are embedded in families and communities that can seriously limit their expression of those rights or access to protections. For Muslims living in secular democratic states, things are never simple. They cannot simply trust in progressive legislation to grant them welfare.

Gay, lesbian, and transgender Muslims living in democratic countries must come to an understanding of their role as Muslims in an environment that is not simply "non-Islamic" but one that has a civic ethos of participatory democracy. In these national contexts, Muslim citizens are invited into the civic society as legal residents and citizens with a contractual system of rights and obligations under a constitution shared with their non-Muslim neighbors. They are encouraged to keep Islam as a religious practice, while finding ways to participate in civic society as citizens. This civic participation is based on shared values that are rooted in secular politics but may be compatible with Islam.

In other words, religion as a coercive system is increasingly breaking down among Muslims living as minorities in democratic nations. Religion's authoritarian spokesmen (mainly men) no longer have the last word. In this context, believers struggle to "re-create" their religion as an authoritative force rather than an authoritarian tradition. This situation creates a great challenge for Muslims, first in terms of identity formation and then in terms of a deep engagement with internal reform of their own religious tradition. Muslims in these minority contexts practice Islam conscientiously; they can critique Islamic customs for perceived injustices and reform Islamic discourse with regard to inadequacies or distortions that have accumulated over time. Groups which have been traditionally marginalized by Islamic authoritarian spokesmen—including women, youth, sectarian minorities, and skeptics—can now find their voices and speak as critically reformist Muslims in this new civic context. These marginalized groups are joined by gay, lesbian, and transgender persons from Muslim communities. Their voices are now heard above the silence that was formerly imposed upon them. The self-appointed guardians of authoritarian Islam may dismiss these voices, but they have a vital role to play in articulating an Islamic identity and practice that promotes the welfare of Muslims as citizens of democratic nations.

Democratic nations are increasingly abandoning patriarchy as the organizing system of their moral norms and legal rights. Patriarchy is a system of moral order and social control in which men are empowered to have authority over women, youth, and other disempowered men (whether they are slaves, nonhouseholders, workers, or eunuchs). Patriarchal values and power relationships have structured many premodern legal norms and most world religions, including Islam. One of the great moral challenges in modern democratic nations is how to change patriarchal values. In the past century, progress toward granting human dignity and legal rights to women has been slow but steady. In the wake of the feminist movement, youths too have asserted their rights against elders who had played an authoritarian role. Progress has been uneven and every advance has led to backlash from conservative elements, especially among neotraditionalist spokesmen for religious traditions.[2] Despite this, all the five nations covered in this study—the United States, Canada, the United Kingdom, the Netherlands, and the Republic of South Africa—have moved considerably in the direction of defining the legal rights of all citizens in ways that openly challenge patriarchal values. They have legalized measures such as allowing women to vote as equal citizens, granting women equal share in educational institutions, allowing women to hold political office, penalizing workplace discrimination on the basis of gender, encouraging women to exercise more control over their bodies in terms of reproductive health, and enforcing equitable treatment in cases of divorce.

Such measures have forced heterosexual couples to reconsider the meaning and function of partnership, love, marriage, and child rearing. Religious customs are being quietly analyzed and reformed to suit the new social context of emerging nonpatriarchal societies forged under democratic constitutions. Muslim citizens of these nations are taking part in this quiet reformation. It is increasingly common for Muslim women to appeal to secular law in order to promote gender equality in the home, just as it is common for Muslim women to pursue education and careers beyond the bounds of their religious community. Customs like unilateral divorce for Muslim men or male custody over children are challenged by legal norms within these nations. Though it is still controversial, an increasing number of Muslim women are asserting the right to marry a non-Muslim spouse just as Muslim men have long enjoyed the privilege of marrying women from another faith tradition. The definition of rights and obligations in Islamic marriages, which in the past had been decidedly unequal based on gender roles, is becoming more egalitarian for Muslims living in the West.

What is surprising is how quietly this revolution is happening. It is occurring piecemeal, as individuals and couples work out new arrangements and understandings between themselves and within their extended families. The changes they are making at home are gradually percolating up through Muslim communities, such that imams and religious leaders have to change the assumptions under which they give marital advice and communities have to change how they perceive divorce. This gradual shift in religious practice happens most slowly (or perhaps halts altogether) when it comes to highly symbolic events, like communal prayer. The push to have mosques accommodate both female and male believers in a single space or in an equitably divided space has been hotly contested in the last few years; a recent movement to establish communal prayer in which women can lead a mixed-gender congregation has stirred much controversy.[3] However, the debate about these highly symbolic events only underscores the range of issues that are barely discussed any more, in which Muslims have already changed their practice of religion to adapt to a less patriarchal environment. This adaptation is not simply practical—in order for Muslims to be accepted as fellow citizens—but it is also highly spiritual. Many Muslims in the West, both female and male, feel that the nonpatriarchal practice of their religion is truer to the ideals of Islam and has great spiritual potential to enact good and justice in the wider world and the world to come.

It is in this context that gay, lesbian, and transgender citizens—both Muslims and others—play an important social role. The still unfolding success of the feminist movement has created new possibilities for lesbian, transgender, and gay members of society to speak out and demand justice. Most proponents of the feminist movement in the West probably did not foresee this result, but that in no way diminishes the intimate link between them and activists for rights for minorities defined by sexual orientation and gender identity. Like feminists, proponents of lesbian, gay, and transgender rights push the debate about human nature and human rights toward more inclusive and universal principles. Like feminists, they deepen the discussion of which values are most essential to the pursuit of human flourishing.

The voice of gender and sexuality minorities has a powerful role to play for the majority of heterosexual members of society. Transgender, gay, and lesbian citizens call into question why marriage is instituted, what norms should guide it, and what ideals its social form expresses. But this questioning is constructive rather than destructive. If marriage is understood in nonpatriarchal terms as the partnership of two equal persons who strive for each other's welfare, intimate pleasure, and ultimate happiness while protecting any children born to them, then why can that social bond not be extended to same-sex partners who play the same role in their lives as a couple? The challenge to give equal rights to similar persons encourages the ethical search for underlying principles through which to regulate our human affairs. As homosexual and transgender persons find greater public voice and a protected space in society, they will contribute to these necessary debates. All citizens, regardless of their gender identity or sexual orientation, benefit from such debate and ethical scrutiny of our social institutions.

However, people are not merely citizens but also potentially religious believers. Many of them do not welcome such ethical scrutiny—especially not when it is prompted by people they see as strange, sinful, or even heretical. Muslims in the West appeal to constitutional norms and civic values to protect their minority community. Yet many Muslims denounce the application of these same norms and values to minorities defined by sexual orientation and gender identity, especially when this application is advocated by members of their own minority religious community. In the eyes of many conservatives, the fact that Muslims who are gay, lesbian, and transgender build alliances with non-Muslims of the same orientation makes them even more suspicious. This is true even if conservative Muslims find surprising allies among non-Muslims—primarily orthodox Jews, Evangelical Protestants, conservative Catholics, and Mormons—for their stand opposing the extension of rights and recognition to gay, lesbian, and transgender citizens. These cross-religious alliances tend to obscure the fact that issues of sexual orientation and gender identity are sparking an intense debate among Muslims themselves over the personality of God, the nature of God's creation, divine intent for human life, and the role of Islamic tradition in fulfilling that intent.

The interviews offered in this book reveal how deep that debate goes, and how urgent the stakes are for the welfare of vulnerable members of these minority communities. The debate is very complex; it involves not only questions of religious tradition and scriptural interpretation, but also scientific research into personality and political assertion of rights guaranteed by a constitution.

Ultimately, identity formation is about the heart. The heart is what motivates action in the body's limbs that can be assessed in the field of legal obligation and has effect in the field of political action. When we fall in love, the experience challenges our routine ways of being, of conceiving of the self, and of displaying the self to others in society. When gay, lesbian, and transgender Muslims "come out," they make known publicly their identity formation and its consequences; they form a subculture for themselves and launch a demand for recognition and accommodation by others in the dominant society. They do this because they fall in love and they want their love to be connected to the wider aspirations of the good life—to love one's family, to support one's community, and to contribute to the welfare of one's nation.

We all fall in love. Lesbian, gay, and transgender Muslims are unusual in that they fall in love in a slightly different pattern than most of their fellow believers. Yet love is still love, and it is this simple fact that allows them to appeal for understanding and sympathy from those around them who might otherwise feel alienated from their identity or behavior. For gay, lesbian, and transgender Muslims, falling in love is both a self-transforming event to celebrate and a potential disaster to fear, especially if one has not formed a strong enough identity to face its challenges. The activists we have met in these pages strive to form an identity that can withstand the potential disaster of loving and learning to live through that love. Their transnational network of support groups reaches out to others to promote the formation and strengthening of such identities.

One cannot love another sincerely unless one can find the means to love oneself for who one really is. Love overflows the boundaries of eros and sexuality, spilling over into love of family, loyalty to friends, self-sacrifice for strangers, and ethical care for all humanity; for many, love is ultimately refined into devotion for God. In medieval times, Muslims wrote extraordinary narratives on erotic love between human beings that led them to love for God. Many Muslim authorities, especially those with Sufi insight, have written similar expositions on the value of love in prose and poetry. Yet contemporary Muslims often neglect or reject this part of their religious heritage. The presence of lesbian, transgender, and gay Muslims encourages their religious community to remember this integral part of its spiritual legacy. All Muslims together—whatever their sexual orientation or gender identity—must revive the Islamic quest for love that transforms.

In the Qur'an, God is named loving (wadud) and desiring (murid). *It is God who originates all things and God who calls all to return—for surely God is the One who forgives, the loving One, the possessor of the glorious throne, who enacts whatever the One desires* (Q 85:13–16). The Muslim activists presented in this book are on a journey from a dark prison of fearing to speak toward a luminous horizon of daring to love. They are moving from a position *when you were few, when you were oppressed to the ground and feared that people would carry you off by force* (Q 8:26). They are moving toward a position of strength and flexibility so that they can hear God calling them and all others to return to God's presence, for *God calls all to return—for surely God is the One who forgives, the loving One* (Q 85:14). Only in such a position of strength can they reach out to others through love. That is their ongoing struggle, their *jihad*. The journey is long and the goal is still far off. But that struggle is its own reward.

Names of Support Groups Documented

Al-Fatiha Foundation: a support group for LGBTQ Muslims in the United States, founded in 1997.

Al-Fitra Foundation: a support group for LGBTQ Muslims in South Africa, founded in 1998 in Cape Town and active under this name for a few years.

Habibi Ana, Stichting (My Beloved Society): a support group in the Netherlands for LGBTQ people of Middle Eastern ancestry (including Muslims, Jews, and Christians), established in 2005 on the platform of a gay Arab café in Amsterdam.

Imaan: a support group for LGBTQ Muslims in the United Kingdom; it began as Al-Fatiha UK in 1999 in London and changed its name in 2001.

The Inner Circle: a support group for LGBTQ Muslims in South Africa, established in 2004.

The Safra Project: a support group in the United Kingdom for Muslim women who are lesbian, bisexual, or questioning of sexuality and gender norms, established in 2001.

Salaam Queer Community: a support group for LGBTQ Muslims and their allies in Canada, founded in 2001.

Yoesuf, Stichting (The Yusuf Foundation): an education and training organization that advocates for the welfare of women, youth, and sexuality minorities from Muslim communities, established in 1998 in the Netherlands.

Names of Other Organizations Mentioned

al-Azhar: an Islamic University in Egypt which most Sunni Muslims see as authoritative.

Call of Islam: a progressive Muslim reform movement in South Africa active in the 1980s to oppose apartheid, uphold social justice, and advocate for Muslim integration into a multiethnic and religiously plural South Africa.

Center for Culture and Leisure (COC or Cultuur en Ontspannings Centrum): a Dutch organization that advocates for the rights and welfare of homosexual and transgender citizens; founded in 1946, it is the world's oldest homosexual rights organization and was formerly known as the Dutch Society for the Integration of Homosexuality.

Council of Muslim Theologians (*Jami'at al-'Ulama*) of Gauteng-Johannesburg: an umbrella organization for Muslim jurists, mosque leaders, and madrasa teachers in South Africa.

Deoband Academy: an Islamic Institute of education and law founded in India in 1860 which spread internationally through South Asian Muslim migrants; known as Dar al-Ulum Deoband.

Federation of Student Islamic Societies (FOCIS): an organization to unite all Muslim students organizations in the United Kingdom and further their Islamic allegiance; founded in 1963 and inspired by the Muslim Brotherhood.

Ikhwan (*al-Ikhwan al-Muslimun* or The Muslim Brotherhood): a modern reformist fundamentalist party founded by the schoolteacher Hassan al-Banna in the 1920s in Egypt with the goal of reordering political life of Muslims toward the Qur'an as constitution; it is very influential in Arab regions like Egypt, Syria, and Palestine, and among educated Arab migrants in the West.

Islamic Circle of North America (ICNA): an Islamic educational and social service group formed in 1968 and based in New York, initially drawing support mainly from among South Asian Muslim immigrants with links to the Jama'at-i Islami.

Islamic Society of North American (ISNA): an Islamic civic organization founded in 1982 by Muslim doctors, professionals, and students, that seeks to unify Muslims living in North America, advance their welfare, and represent their interests to the U.S. government with a more moderate agenda than ICNA.

Labor Party of the Netherlands (PvdA or Partij van de Arbeid); a mainstream political party formed in 1946 that often ruled the Netherlands and continues the left-center agenda of the Social-Democratic Workers Party originally formed in 1894.

Metropolitan Community Church (MCC): an international and interdenominational church movement for LGBTQ Christians founded in California in 1968.

Muhajirun (*Jama'at al-Muhajirun* or Those Who Leave Corrupt Society): a fundamentalist movement initiated in 1986 in the United Kingdom until it was banned as a terrorist organization in 2010; it is an offshoot of *Hizb al-Tahrir* or The Islamic Liberation Party that advocated that Muslims overthrow secular governments and implement Islamic law in Europe.

Muslim Canadian Congress (MCC): a grassroots organization that represents Muslims marginalized by other Islamic organizations in Canada.

Muslim Council of Britain (MCB): an umbrella organization for Muslim institutions in the United Kingdom, founded in 1997 with the goal of unifying Muslims and representing their concerns to the government.

Muslim Students Association of the USA and Canada (MSA): an organization founded in 1963 to establish Islamic societies on university and college campuses, funded in its early days by a Saudi charity.

Muslim Students Association of South Africa (MSASA): this outgrowth of the MYM began in 1974 to establish chapters in South African institutes of higher education.

Muslim Youth Movement of South Africa (MYM): an Islamic revivalist and reformist movement initiated at Durban in 1970 for nonpolitical revivalist activity; in 1986 its center shifted to Cape Town and the MYM adopted a more radical stance to agitate against apartheid.

Oasis of Peace: an Israeli-Palestinian experiment in conflict resolution and peaceful living in a village called *Nave Shalom* in Hebrew and *Wahat al-Salam* in Arabic.

Qibla: an Islamic revivalist movement in South Africa formed in 1981 to oppose apartheid and promote social justice.

Schorer Foundation: a Dutch institute founded in 1967 to support a mental health center for homosexual citizens which has since expanded into a research and activist organization for the prevention of HIV/AIDS and the promotion of heath and well-being for sexuality and gender minorities.

Tablighi Jama'at (Islamic Missionary Movement): a fundamentalist movement founded by the *madrasa* teacher Muhammad Ilyas in the 1920s in South Asia which seeks to reform and revive Muslim devotion worldwide; it avoids overt political activity but is deeply opposed to modern social change and secular education.

Triangle Project: the largest gay and lesbian organization in South Africa; it was established in 1981 and was named Triangle Project in 1996 and is based in Cape Town.

adab: respectful behavior.

'adl: justice—al-'Adl or "the Just One" is one of the ninety-nine names of God in Islam.

'alim: scholar—see *'ulama*.

allochtoonen: ethnic minority group members—a Dutch term for non-European immigrants as a racial minority.

Amazigh: Free People—the original population of North Africa, now predominantly Muslims, who are popularly known as "Berbers" and inhabited the region before the Romans and Arabs.

apartheid: Racial segregation—a Dutch term for the social system that enforced separate legal rights and living spaces for people based on racial classification; it was enforced by the National Party government in South Africa from 1948 (after independence from British imperial rule) until 1994 (after an uprising led by the African National Congress).

'aqd al-nikah: contract of marriage; a legal written document that includes signatures of witnesses (also called *nikah-nama* in South Asia)

'ayb: shameful act—a wrongdoing or sin.

Coloured: racial classification—in South Africa under apartheid, "Coloured" was the racial classification of Muslims of mixed ancestry; the "Coloured" community was placed above Black Africans and below White Europeans in the racial hierarchy.

dar al-ulum: religious academy—a large *madrasa* in South Asian contexts.

dars: learning—sessions of organized religious education, usually for adults as continuing education above and beyond basic *madrasa* training.

da'wa: mission work—individual or organized activity to spread Islam; many modern groups organize gatherings to missionize, like the Tablighi Jama'at, a vast international movement that began in South Asia (known as *Rijal al-Da'wa* in Arabic lands).

dhikr: remembrance—meditative chanting of the names of God or verses from Qur'an in Sufi communities.

du'a: supplication—a personal prayer or request of God on any occasion.

eid: holiday—the name of two major holidays in the Islamic calendar marked by special congregational prayers.

fahisha: immorality—transgressing limits of moral behavior; a term used in the Qur'an for a variety of sins, including those of Sodom and Gomorrah as told in the story of Prophet Lot.

fajr: dawn—the predawn prayer, the first of the five daily ritual prayers (see *namaz*).

faqih: jurist—an authority with advanced training in Islamic law or *fiqh*.

fasad: corruption—the personal quality of being a morally corrupt person.

fatiha: Opening—the first chapter of the Qur'an, called *Surat al-Fatiha*.

fatwa: legal decision—a jurist's decision about a particular problem after consultation.

fiqh: jurisprudence—legal system developed by Muslim jurists in medieval times.

firqa: sect—differences in the Muslim community based on authority, ritual, and dogma.

fitna: social disruption—refers both to political chaos and temptation to sin.

fitra: nature—especially in reference to one's original human nature.

gender dysphoria: psychic anxiety that one's ascribed gender is not in harmony with one's internal gender identity; "dysphoria" is Greek for unhappiness.

ghazal: love lyric—a genre of intensely rhyming poem about love in Persian and Urdu.

ghusl: bath—a full body bath in order to restore ritual purity after sexual intercourse, deep sleep, or contact with some polluting substance.

gyarwin: holy eleventh day—a devotional festival among South Asian Muslims on 11 Rabi' al-Thani in the Islamic calendar, in honor of the death anniversary of Sufi 'Abd al-Qadir Jilani, founder of the Qadiri Sufi order (see *tariqa*).

hadith: reports—the Prophet Muhammad's teachings and behavior written as normative text.

hakim: wise doctor—a practitioner of *unani* medicine.

halaqa: study circle—a gathering of laypeople to study Qur'an or other religious learning.

Hanafi: a legal school—one of four major Sunni legal schools (see *madhhab*) which is prevalent in South Asia.

hijra: nonman in South Asia—a person born with male sex organs and raised as a boy who identifies as female, taking on female behavior, name, and dress, and who voluntarily undergoes a ritual castration to remove both testicles and penis (compare to *khasi*).

Hudood Ordinances: the Pakistani legal decree of 1979 that stipulates the death penalty for adultery, fornication, and homosexual intercourse.

iftar: meal to break fast—the meal after a day of fasting during the month of Ramadan when Muslims fast from sunrise to sunset.

ijtihad: striving—intellectual effort and ethical discretion in the interpretation of religion.

imam: leader—one who leads communal prayer; among Shi'i Muslims, Imam (with a capital I) means a leader descended from the Prophet Muhammad's family with both religious and political authority.

iman: faith.

irba: hidden sexual desire—used in the Qur'an to describe men who "have no wiles with women" and feel no sexual attraction toward them.

Isma'ili: a number of smaller Shi'i sects whose followers have a living spiritual guide descended from Ali ibn Abi Talib.

isnad: chain of transmission—the list of people who have narrated a *hadith* report.

istinja': purification—washing after using the toilet in order to restore a state of ritual purity.

jami'a: institution of Islamic higher learning—a large *madrasa* which offers higher degrees.

janaza: funeral prayer—the last communal ritual for a deceased Muslim before burial; often Islamic leaders carry out an "excommunication" by threatening to refuse burial rites and final prayer to a member of their Muslim community.

jum'a: congregational prayer—the noon prayer on Fridays during which the whole community should gather for a sermon.

junusiyya: same-gender sexual orientation—a newly coined term to describe homosexuality in Arabic.

karamat: miracle places—tombs of holy people that are the object of pilgrimage in South Africa (known as *dargah* or *mazar* or *ziyarat* in other Islamic regions).

khalifa: responsible follower—God's vice-regent on earth as mentioned in the Qur'an; a responsible moral individual in Islamic philosophy; the political ruler in Sunni communities in the medieval era.

khasi: eunuch—person born and raised as male until castrated by removing the testicles (compare with *hijra*).

khutba: sermon—moral speech delivered by the imam at Friday congregational prayers.

kurta: tunic—a long shirt whose cloth extends to the knees worn by men in South Asia; it is often adopted as "Islamic dress" by Muslims in South Africa and North America even if they do not have South Asian roots.

Lut: Lot—the prophet depicted in the Torah and the Qur'an.

luti: sodomite—Arabic term in Islamic jurisprudence for someone who engages in same-sex anal intercourse regardless of sexual orientation.

madhhab: legal school—different systems of ritual and commercial life, each based on the Prophet's example but formulated by jurists in a different way.

maqasid: principles—a term for the essential goals of Islamic law that should guide the continuing reform and application of legal rules.

mashrab: orientation—style of religiosity and method of worship; subtle differences in approach to religion that define different Muslim communities.

mawlana: master—title for a religious scholar or respected moral leader.

mawlid sharif: noble birth—celebration of the Prophet's birthday as a devotional occasion.

minbar: pulpit—raised platform in a mosque from which the imam gives the sermon; a symbol of speaking with authority.

moffie: gay—Cape Town slang for an effeminate gay man who is assumed to take the passive role in anal sex.

mu'allim: instructor—a teacher in a religious school.

mufti: jurist with authority to a publish decision or *fatwa*.

mukallaf: a legally obligated person—in Islamic law, a person is adult, sane, and not under coercion.

mukhannath: effeminate man—those in Arab culture who are born male-bodied but act in ways that appear female in their speech, dress, and behavior.

mulla: master—title for a religious scholar or respected moral leaders; colloquial for *mawlana* in South Asian, Iranian, and Turkish lands.

murid: seeker—in South Africa, one who desires knowledge to refer to students at a *madrasa*; in Sufi orders, a disciple who seeks mystical knowledge.

murshid: spiritual guide—a spiritual elder in the Sufi tradition (see also *shaykh*).

murtadd: apostate—one who renounces the religion of Islam.

mutarrajula: woman who behaves like a man in speech, gesture, gait, or dress (compare to *mukhannath*).

na'at sharif: noble description—devotional songs of love for the Prophet Muhammad; a genre of Urdu poetry.

nabi: prophet—Islam recognizes many prophets, including Noah, Abraham, Lot, Moses, and Jesus, with Muhammad being the last and final prophet.

namaz: prayer—five daily prayers in Islam; called *salat* (in Arabic) or *namaz* (in Urdu).

nikah: marriage—acceptable sexual intercourse legalized by a contractual relationship.

niyaz: offering—making a vow or request at a saint's tomb.

niyya: intention—the intent by which any action is judged.

Qur'an: Islamic scripture—speech of God as transmitted by the Angel Gabriel to Muhammad in Arabic; originally an oral message, it was later written as a book.

ruhani: spiritual medicine—the Islamic tradition of spiritual healing that often complemented traditional medicine in Sufi communities (see *unani*).

Salafi: purist—orientation among Sunnis that believes in banning all religious innovations to return to the original way of the Prophet Muhammad's immediate followers; they tend to be reformist and polemical.

salat: prayer—see *namaz*.

shahwa: desire for sensual gratification or pleasurable consumption.

shakila: disposition—traits or characteristics that are more or less innate.

shari'a: right way—religious law based upon scripture and Prophetic example; most often applied to the Islamic system of ritual and legal norms, but each religion has a *shari'a* based upon its prior revealed scripture.

shaykh: elder—general terms of a leader or person in authority; used in South Africa to mean an imam or teacher along with *khalifa*; used in Sufi orders to mean a spiritual guide.

Shi'i: sect of Muslims who are a minority—they are officially titled "Supporters of Ali" (*Shi'at 'Ali*) and believe in following only a descendent of the Prophet Muhammad's family.

Sufi: mystic—a Muslim who strives to be in God's presence by purifying the heart, remembering God in the mind, and desisting from worldly ambition.

sunna: exemplary custom—example of the Prophet Muhammad in ritual, custom, and law.

Sunni: sect of Muslims who are a majority, officially titled "People of the Prophet's Example and Community Consensus" (*ahl al-sunna wa'l-jama'a*), believe in a leader elected by the community or a powerful leader who can enforce order.

surat: a chapter of the Qur'an—the scripture is divided into 114 chapters.

tafsir: commentary—explanation of the Qur'an's meaning.

takbir: saying "God is greater" (*Allahu Akbar*)—part of many Islamic rituals.

talaq: divorce—enacted by a husband to unilaterally terminate a marriage contract.

tanzim: organizing—ideological activism of Islamic fundamentalist organizations.

taqlid: imitation—strict following of legal decisions of the past without question.

tarawih: special prayers at night during the holy month of Ramadan.

tariqa: mystical path—designation of a Sufi order usually named after its founding saint.

ta'wiz: amulet—talisman usually worn around the neck or arm (see *ruhani* medicine).

'ulama: scholars—religious scholars who specialize in Qur'an, tradition, and law.

umma: moral community—the Islamic community as a whole.

'umra: visit to Mecca—ritual visit to Mecca at times other than the yearly *hajj* pilgrimage.

unani: Greek Medicine—traditional Islamic healing system based balancing the body's humors, analogous to homeopathic medicine (see also *hakim*).

ustad: teacher—a master teacher in religion or arts.

Wahhabi: puritan sectarians—the followers of a modern reformer who believed that Muslims must follow only a literalist reading of scripture; his followers reject other Sunnis and forcefully oppose Sufis and Shi'is, and they currently rule Saudi Arabia and other Arab Gulf kingdoms.

wa'iz: admonition—warning and advice about religion and morality

wudu': ablution—ritual washing of the face, arms, hands, feet, and ankles in preparation for prayer.

zalim: oppressor—an unjust and powerful person; a term of abuse in Islamic cultures to mean an enemy of Islam who must be opposed.

NOTES

NOTES TO THE PREFACE AND ACKNOWLEDGMENTS

1. Cleary, *The Wisdom of the Prophet*, 19.
2. Kanda, *Masterpieces of Urdu Ghazal*, 132. English translation by S. Kugle; all translations in this book of texts from Arabic, Persian, and Urdu are by S. Kugle unless otherwise noted.

NOTES TO THE INTRODUCTION

1. Asad, *Formations of the Secular*, 1–20 and 127–158.
2. Foucault, *The Uses of Pleasure*, 29.
3. Mahmood, *The Politics of Piety*, 28.
4. While writing this book, I served on the advisory board of Al-Fatiha Foundation and during its editing, I joined the *shari'a* advisory committee of The Inner Circle. Both groups are documented in this book.
5. These interviews were conducted in conjunction with writing *Homosexuality in Islam*, which did not to include bisexuality for several reasons. First, examining only homosexual and transgender issues made that book already quite long. Second, it focused on theological arguments based on the Qur'an in which I find noncondemning reference to gay men, lesbian women, and transgender persons, but do not find noncondemnatory reference to bisexual behavior. There is need for a study of bisexuality among Muslims. Such a study could be theological, sociological, or activist in orientation; the limitations of my book should not hinder others from taking up that project.
6. For a discussion of how psyche and internal disposition fit into an Islamic theological model based on the Qur'an, see Kugle, "Sexual Diversity in Islam," 136–39.
7. For an excellent introduction to the Qur'an, see Esack, *The Qur'an*.
8. For a definition of "gender dysphoria," see the Gender Identity Research and Education Society at www.gires.org.uk; and Richard Carroll, "Gender Dysphoria."
9. Changing one's sex is done through hormone therapy or sex-realignment surgery or a combination of the two.
10. The clinical terms transgender, transsexual, and intersex are to be distinguished from "transvestite." Transvestite refers to the clothes that one wears. Men may

dress in women's clothing or women dress in men's clothing without this behavior indicating anything about their gender identity or sexual orientation.

11. Castration meant cutting off testicles (though perhaps sometimes the penis was also removed). Islamic law forbids human castration, yet it was common to castrate young non-Muslim slaves, who would then have a higher value and were raised as Muslims; see Marmon, *Eunuchs and Sacred Boundaries in Islamic Society.*

12. In Arabic, the term *mukhannath* is derived from skin that is folded back upon itself, indicating inversion (like turning something inside out) and languidness— see Lane, *Arabic-English Lexicon*, 1:814 and also Rowson, "Effeminates of Medina."

13. Rowson, "Gender Irregularity as Entertainment."

14. Bouhdiba, *Sexuality in Islam* discussed these *mutarajjulat* or masculine women. I have coined a new term "emmasculine women" to parallel the more conventional "effeminate man."

15. Reddy, *With Respect to Sex: Negotiating Hijra Identity.*

16. See especially the scholarship of Andrew Yip, *A Minority within a Minority: British Non-Heterosexual Muslims,* and "Negotiating Space with Family and Kin in Identity Construction: The Narratives of British Non-Heterosexual Muslims."

NOTES TO CHAPTER 1

1. Verses from the Qur'an are written in *italics* to differentiate them from other prose; chapter and verse information is given in parentheses (with Q to indicate Qur'an, then chapter number followed by a colon and verse number). Translation of the Qur'an is by the author, with gratitude to previous translators like N. J. Dawood, M. H. Shakir, A'isha and Abd al-Haqq Bewley, and Michael Sells.

2. All quotations by Muhsin here and subsequently are from an interview with S. Kugle in Johannesburg (Nov. 1, 2005), unless otherwise specified.

3. The Call of Islam in South Africa was directed by the activist theologian Farid Esack. As the African National Congress (ANC) organized resistance to Apartheid, Muslims in the "Coloured" and "Asian" communities had to decide whether to accept favored status (above Black Africans) or to ally with the ANC. Some Muslims chose resistance and engaged in Islamic "liberation theology"; The Call of Islam was one such group and is documented in Esack, *Quran, Liberation and Pluralism.*

4. Yunus Kemp, Staff Reporter, *Cape Argus,* www.iol.co.za.

5. Kugle, *Homosexuality in Islam,* describes the theological significance of this concept; see also Kugle, "Sexual Diversity in Islam."

6. News of Gay Muslim Outreach spread through word of mouth, e-mail lists, the Metropolitan Community Church (where some Muslims congregated due to ostracism in mosques), and the Triangle Project.

7. These theological arguments are addressed in Kugle, *Homosexuality in Islam.* On the "effeminate men" in the Prophet's household, see Rowson, "Effeminates of

Medina," 64, and on eunuchs in the Prophet's household, see Stowasser, *Women in the Qur'an, Traditions and Interpretation*, 96 and 112.

8. Tayob, "The Function of Islam in the South African Political Process," 142.

9. Ibid., 57.

10. Ibid., 124.

11. All quotations by Nafeesa here and subsequently are from an interview with S. Kugle in Cape Town (March 22, 2005).

12. Kugle, *Homosexuality in Islam*, chapter 2, addresses ambiguities of interpretation in Qur'anic verses about Lot.

13. The Azzawiyah mosque complex was built in 1919 by Shaykh Muhammad Salif Hendricks (1871–1945), a Mecca-trained religious teacher in Cape Town.

14. All quotations by Tamsila here and subsequently are from two interviews with S. Kugle in London (June 14–15, 2005).

15. The minority population of Tamsila's hometown consists of Pakistani and Bangladeshi Muslim laborers and a few Afro-Caribbean families who are mostly Christian.

16. In general, see Brown, *Liberation Theology: An Introductory Guide*. On Islamic liberation theology, see Dabashi, *Islamic Liberation Theology*, and Naseef, *Liberation Theology: Islam and the Feminist Agenda in the Qur'an*.

17. Abou El Fadl, *And God Knows the Soldiers*, 108.

18. Musa, *Hadith as Scripture*, 84–97, discusses modern critics of *hadith* reports who express opinions similar to those of Tamsila.

19. Kugle, *Homosexuality in Islam*, discusses in detail Qur'an 4:15–16 and its ambiguities.

20. Kugle, *Homosexuality in Islam*, discusses adapting Islamic marriage to same-sex unions.

NOTES TO CHAPTER 2

1. Simphiwe Dana in the album *Zandisile* (Topkho Music, 2004).

2. All quotations from Nargis here and subsequently are from an interview with S. Kugle in Cape Town (March 22, 2005).

3. Tayob, "The Function of Islam," 95.

4. Ahmed, *Women and Gender in Islam*, 96–98.

5. The Inner Circle adopted study circles (*halaqa*) from the Muslim Youth Movement (MYM) which agitated against apartheid while conservative *'ulama* criticized young radicals engaging in "free interpretation" beyond the education of the *madrasa*; see Tayob, *Islamic Resurgence in South Africa: The Muslim Youth Movement*. Muhsin acted as a *naqib* or circle leader in the Muslim Students Association of South Africa (an outgrowth of the MYM).

6. All quotations by Tayyaba here and subsequently are from an interview with S. Kugle in London (June 15, 2005).

7. Tayyaba joined Kiss, a London-based support group for lesbian and bisexual women among ethnic minorities and there first befriended other Muslim lesbians.

NOTES TO CHAPTER 3

1. Cleary, *Wisdom of the Prophet*, 34.
2. All quotations by Fatima here and subsequently are from a series of interviews with S. Kugle in London (June 13–16, 2005).
3. Skovgaard-Petersen, *Defining Islam for the Egyptian State*, discusses decisions by al-Azhar authorities on cases of transgender students.
4. Fatima refers to the article "Budur tatahawwilu ila Ahmad [Budur Transforms into Ahmad]," *Zahrat al-Khalij* (Cairo, March 19, 2005).
5. All quotations by Daayiee Abdullah, here and subsequently, are from an interview with S. Kugle in Washington, D.C. (Nov. 16, 2005), unless otherwise cited.
6. From a statement by Daayiee Abdullah posted on the website of "Muslim Gay Men."
7. Robeson's black nationalist and anti-imperialist activities incited Senator McCarthy in the 1950s to single him out as a threat to American democracy.
8. Robeson, *Here I Stand*, 108.
9. Progressive Muslim thinkers concur that Imam al-Ghazali is crucial for contemporary ethics; see Moosa, *Ghazali and the Poetics of Imagination*.
10. Farah, *Marriage and Sexuality in Islam: A Translation of al-Ghazali*, 45.
11. The names of Daayiee's teachers in Saudi Arabia have been withheld at their request.
12. The tension between past decisions and universal principles is discussed with reference to homosexual intercourse in Kugle, *Homosexuality in Islam*.
13. For how Islamic marriage customs might be adapted to same-sex couplets, see Kugle, *Homosexuality in Islam*.

NOTES TO CHAPTER 4

1. Bob Dylan, *Chronicles*, 219.
2. Raymzter is the nickname of Raymond Redouan Cristaan Rensen, who is half Moroccan and half Dutch in ancestry.
3. Halbertma's defenders claimed that the insult "Fuckin' Moroccans" was a common expression since the rise of the Nationalist Party (also known as Lijst Pim Fortuyn or LPF) led by the maverick gay politician, Pim Fortuyn, who argued that Islam was not compatible with Dutch culture.
4. To compare the situation of homosexual Muslims in the Netherlands with that in Germany, see Bochow and Marbach, *Homosexualität und Islam*.
5. The Yoesuf Foundation is named after the Islamic prophet Joseph (in Arabic Yusuf or in Dutch transliteration, Yoesuf), who is the paragon of male beauty.
6. Nahas, *Homo en Moslem—hoe gaat dat samen?* 113: translation from Dutch by S. Kugle.

7. Interview for the television news program, *Nova*; transcript published in Dutch on www.novatv.nl; translation to English by S. Kugle. See also Hekma, "Imams and Homosexuality," 240–42.

8. Ibid., 240. A newspaper article in *de Folkskrant* on antihomosexual violence prompted Dutch media to interview with Imam el-Moumni.

9. The rift signaled by the El-Moumni Affair grew starker in 2004 when a young Muslim (Dutch citizen by birth of Moroccan ancestry) assassinated the filmmaker, Theo van Gogh, accusing him of insulting Islam through his made-for-TV film *Submission* which portrayed misogyny as inherent in the Qur'an and Islamic beliefs.

10. Interview on www.novatv.nl. Translation from Dutch by S. Kugle.

11. All quotations by Omar Nahas here and subsequently are from an interview with S. Kugle in Amsterdam (June 25, 2005), unless otherwise noted.

12. Nahas, *al-Junusiyya*, 21. Translation of this and all subsequent citations of this work from Arabic by S. Kugle.

13. Massad, "Re-Orienting Desire" offers the most intelligent articulation of this view, which was further developed in his book, *Desiring Arabs*; however, Massad's contentions are questioned by the autobiographical account of Omar Nahas.

14. Nahas, *Al-Junusiyya*, 21.

15. Ibid., 10.

16. Nahas, *Islam en homoseksualiteit*, 58, Translation from Dutch by S. Kugle. In this later work, Omar emphasizes that the Tribe of Lot used sex as unjust coercion more than acting against their inherent sexual orientation; on this issue, see also El-Rouayheb, *Before Homosexuality in the Arab-Islamic World*, 15–19.

17. Nahas, *al-Junusiyya*, 17.

18. Ibid., 18–19.

19. Ibid., 19.

20. Ibid., 10.

21. El Kaka and Kursun, *Mijn geloof en mijn geluk*.

22. Nahas, *al-Junusiyya*, 27–28.

23. Ibid., 29–30.

24. Ibid., 35.

25. Since Habibi Ana began as a support group, many smaller groups have also formed to fulfill the needs of more specific populations in the Netherlands and Belgium: *Stichting Nafar* in Amsterdam serves the needs of youth from North African families who have homosexual feelings, *Turks Homoloket* is an online resource for homosexual and transgender people of Turkish background in the Netherlands, *Merhaba* is a support group in Belgium for LGBTQ people of Middle Eastern and North African origins, and *Shouf Shouf* is a similar support group for LGBTQ people in the Belgian city of Antwerp.

26. Habibi Ana refers vulnerable youth to shelters like the *Veilige Haven*—Safe Haven—a shelter for minority youth opened in 2004 by the Schorer Foundation.

27. In 1912, a homosexual rights movement known as the Dutch Scientific and Humanitarian Committee (a branch of the German organization founded by the sexologist Magnus Hirschfeld) challenged laws that differentiated between same-sex and heterosexual intercourse. After World War II, the Center for Culture and Leisure (COC) formed as a social club for homosexual men, representing them to society as educated and moral citizens; see Herdt, *Same Sex Different Cultures: Exploring Gay and Lesbian Lives*, 162–63.

28. In 1962 the COC began to argue that society's patriarchal structures must be changed for all citizens to live equally with human dignity, legal rights, and healthy well-being. The COC led the reform of legal structures in the Netherlands: in 1973 homosexual citizens were allowed to enter military service; in 1993 an "equal rights" law protected homosexuals against discrimination in employment and housing; in 1998 a law defined "registered partnerships" as civil unions for heterosexual or homosexual couples with legal rights equal to those of married couples; and in 2001 marriage and adoption rights were opened to homosexual couples. These legal reforms happened earlier in the Netherlands than in other EU states, and thus set a model for progressive legislation in other nations across Europe.

29. All quotations by Rasheed here and subsequently are from an interview with S. Kugle in Amsterdam (Feb. 5, 2006).

30. Ramadan, *To Be a European Muslim*, states that it is an Islamic obligation for Muslims to be responsible citizens of the Western nation in which they reside.

31. All quotations by Osama here and subsequently are from an interview with S. Kugle in Amsterdam (March 15, 2006).

32. Teenage sex play with same-gender partners is sociologically known as "situational homosexuality" and is not in most cases a sign of homosexual orientation, but is rather a kind of sexual exploration when female partners are not available.

33. The Homo Monument was raised in 1987 and designed in the shape of a pink triangle, the sign that Nazis used to designate homosexuals before their extermination.

34. Hekma, "Imams and Homosexuality," 240. Before the El-Moumni Affair, other religious leaders created similar controversy with public statements condemning homosexuality on the basis of religious belief. The Catholic cardinal of Utrecht had previously called homosexuality "unnatural and neurotic," while a prominent Protestant member of parliament (from the conservative Calvinist community) equated homosexuality to the crime of theft; they were charged in court in an expression of public disapproval of their statements but were all exonerated from criminal charges because of the freedom of religious expression.

35. Ibid., 241.

NOTES TO CHAPTER 5

1. *Ana al-Haqq* or "I am Truth" was the statement of the radical Sufi Mansur al-Hallaj that led him into controversy and persecution. See Herbert Mason, "Hallaj and the Baghdad School of Sufism," in Lewisohn, *Classical Persian Sufism*, 72.

2. All quotations by Faisal Alam, here and subsequently, are from an interview with S. Kugle in Atlanta (Feb. 20, 2006), unless otherwise specified.
3. Kamali, *Equity and Fairness in Islam*, 25.
4. For comparable experience from a woman's point of view, one could turn to the autobiographical essay by a lesbian Muslim in the United States who worked with Al-Fatiha Foundation; see Khalida Said's autobiographical essay, "On the Edge of Belonging," in Abdul-Ghafur, *Living Islam Out Loud*, 86–94.
5. Some African American leaders uphold conservative Christian morality that is explicitly against lesbian, gay, and transgender rights. Others support the concept of a "rainbow coalition" that would let racial minorities and sexuality or gender minorities to stand together in a struggle for justice.
6. John Iwasaki, "Tolerance sets the tone at services: faithful gather for gay rights" (May 12, 2006) at http://seattlepi.nwsource.com/local/269943_gayrights12.html.
7. Barrister Arif Raza is quoted in an anonymously written article, "Muslim Canadian Congress endorses gay marriage legislation" (Feb. 1, 2005) posted at www.mask.org.za/article.php?cat=islam&id=732.
8. All quotations by Rashida here and subsequently are from an interview by S. Kugle in London (June 15, 2005).
9. The Emigrants or *Muhajirun* refers to the earliest Muslims who fled from Mecca due to persecution and settled in Medina to build a political community based on Islam. Extremist offshoots of the fundamentalist organization, The Muslim Brotherhood, use the concept of "emigration" in a different sense, meaning to reject a non-Islamic secular state and fight for the imposition of a so-called Islamic government. One such extremist group, inspired by Sayyid Qutb, formed an Egyptian militant group called "Emigration and Accusation" (*Takfir wa Hijra*) that charged the Egyptian government with being anti-Islamic and assassinated its president Anwar Sadat, whom they compared to Pharaoh. *Jama'at al-Muhajirun* takes the name of "the Emigrants" in this sense: they condemn the surrounding society, reject all legal implications of citizenship, and celebrate the license to commit violence in the name of promoting Islam. *Jama'at al-Muhajirun* was ultimately listed as a "terrorist organization" in the U.K. government's reaction to the attacks of September 11. The organization was formally disbanded and its most prominent leader, Omar Bakri Muhammad, was barred from reentering the United Kingdom, yet its many members who are British citizens continue to operate in local mosques and organizations under other names.
10. From an article by Rashida in Summerskill, *The Way We Are Now*, 154.
11. Ibid., 153.
12. Yip, "The Politics of Counter-Rejection: Gay Christians and the Church," 47–63.
13. The Qur'anic term for colors (*alwan*) refers not just to visible hues of people and plants, but also to other sensations like the "taste" of different dishes of food or aromas. For further details, see Kugle, *Homosexuality in Islam*, chapter 2.

14. The role of the Muslim Council of Britain is much like the role of South African organizations like the Muslim Judicial Council in Cape Town and The Council of Muslim Theologians in Galteng-Johannesburg.

15. Catherine Patch, "Queer Muslims Find Peace: El-Farouk Khaki Founded Salaam, Offers a Place to Retain Faith," *Toronto Star* (June 15, 2006). All quotations from El-Farouk are from this newspaper interview, unless otherwise specified.

16. Rachel Giese, "Out of the Koran: A Conference for Queer Muslims," *Xtra!Toronto* (June 12, 2003).

17. Jan Jekielek, "Canadian Muslims under Spotlight after Terror Arrests," *Epoch Times Toronto* (June 9, 2006).

18. Some asylum-seekers in Canada helped to establish Salaam Queer Community; see Marina Jimenez, "Gay Jordanian Now 'Gloriously Free': Sent to Canada to 'Straighten Out,' He Founded Support Group for Muslims in Canada," *Toronto Globe and Mail* (May 20, 2004).

19. Ibid.

NOTES TO CHAPTER 6

1. Sells, *Stations of Desire: Love Elegies from Ibn Arabi*, 72–73.

2. These verses are popular among musicians in Morocco (where Ibn Arabi lived after he left Andalusia); listen, for example, to Amina Alaoui, "Ode d'Ibn Arabi" (Album Alcantara, 1998) and Ensemble Ibn Arabi, "I Believe in the Religion of Love" (Album Chants Soufis Arabo-Andalous, 2003).

3. There were some Sufis who were outspoken in their love for a same-sex partner, such as Shah Hussain of Lahore; see Kugle, *Sufis and Saints' Bodies*, 181–220.

4. All quotations by Ibrahim here and subsequently are from an interview with S. Kugle, in London (June 14, 2005).

5. Kugle, *Homosexuality in Islam*, chapter 6, gives details of Marya the Copt and her eunuch.

6. Examples of powerful eunuchs include eminent personalities. Malik Kafur (died 1316) was a Muslim eunuch general who led the armies of the Sultanate of Delhi to conquer central and southern India; Zheng He (died 1433) was a Muslim eunuch admiral who led Chinese imperial navies on missions that were military, diplomatic, and commercial throughout the Indian Ocean all the way to the East African coast. Judar Pasha was a Spanish Muslim eunuch who led the armies of the Sa'dian dynasty of Morocco to invade the Songhay empire of West Africa. Agha Muhammad Khan was a eunuch courtier who took over the government of Iran in 1796 and founded the Qajar dynasty. For more information on the political and military roles of eunuchs, see Ayalon, *Eunuchs, Caliphs, and Sultans*.

7. The comparison that Ibrahim draws between gay men and eunuchs is echoed by the Muslim activist Faris Malik, who compiled the website www.queerjihad. com.

8. Nizam al-Din Awliya, a follower of Mu'in al-Din Chishti, taught that service to the needy is better than ritual worship, emphasizing a hadith of the Prophet

Muhammad: "All people are God's family, and the most beloved of people are those who do most good for God's family."

NOTES TO THE CONCLUSION

1. This report is recorded in the collections of al-Bukhari and Muslim ibn Hajjaj.
2. Kugle and Stephen Hunt, "Masculinity, Homosexuality and the Defense of Islam: A Case Study of Yusuf al-Qaradawi's Media Fatwa," *Religion and Gender* 2/2 (2012): 254–79.
3. Wadud, *Inside the Gender Jihad*, 177–86.

BIBLIOGRAPHY

Abdul-Ghafur, Saleemah, ed. *Living Islam Out Loud: American Muslim Women Speak.* Boston: Beacon Press, 2005.

Abou El Fadl, Khaled. *And God Knows the Soldiers: The Authoritative and the Authoritarian in Islamic Discourse.* Lanham, Md.: University Press of America. 1997.

Ahmed, Leila. *Women and Gender in Islam.* New Haven: Yale University Press, 1992.

Asad, Talal. *Formations of the Secular: Christianity, Islam, Modernity.* Stanford: Stanford University Press, 2003.

Ayalon, David. *Eunuchs, Caliphs, and Sultans: A Study of Power Relationships.* Jerusalem: Magnes Press, 1999.

Bochow, Michael, and Rainer Marbach, eds. *Homosexualität und Islam: Koran, islamische Länder, Situation in Deutschland* [Homosexuality and Islam: the Qur'an, Islamic Countries, and the situation in Germany]. Hamburg: Männerschwarm-Skript, 2003. In German.

Bouhdiba, Abdelwahab. *Sexuality in Islam.* London: Saqi Books, 1998.

Brown, Robert McAfee. *Liberation Theology: An Introductory Guide.* Westminster: John Knox Press, 1993.

Carroll, Richard. "Gender Dysphoria and Transgender Experiences." In Sandra Leiblum, ed. *Principles and Practice of Sex Therapy.* New York: Guilford Press, 2007.

Cleary, Thomas, trans. *The Wisdom of the Prophet: The Sayings of Muhammad.* Boston: Shambhala Press, 2001.

Dabashi, Hamid. *Islamic Liberation Theology: Resisting the Empire.* New York: Routledge, 2008.

Dylan, Bob. *Chronicles: Volume One.* New York: Simon and Schuster, 2004.

El Kaka, Imad, and Hatice Kursun, eds. *Mijn geloof en mijn geluk: Islamitische meiden en jongens over hun homoseksuele gevoelens* [My Faith and My Fate: Islamic Young Men and Women on Their Homosexual Feelings]. Amsterdam: Schorer Boeken, 2002. In Dutch.

Esack, Farid. *Qur'an, Liberation and Pluralism: An Islamic Perspective of Interreligious Solidarity against Oppression.* Oxford: Oneworld Press, 1997.

———. *The Qur'an: A Short Introduction.* Oxford: Oneworld Publications, 2002.

Farah, Madelain, trans. *Marriage and Sexuality in Islam: Translation of al-Ghazali's Book on Etiquette of Marriage.* Salt Lake City: University of Utah Press, 1984.

Foucault, Michel. *The Uses of Pleasure. The History of Sexuality*, vol. 2. New York: Vintage Books, 1990.

Hekma, Gert. "Imams and Homosexuality: A Post-Gay Debate in the Netherlands." *Sexualities* 5/2 (2002): 237–48.

Hendricks, Pepe (ed.). *Hijab: Unveiling Queer Muslim Lives*. South Africa: African Minds, 2009.

Herdt, Gilbert. *Same Sex Different Cultures: Exploring Gay and Lesbian Lives*. Boulder, Colo.: Westview Press, 1997.

Jama, Afdhere. *Illegal Citizens: Queer Lives in the Muslim World*. No place: Salaam Press, 2008.

Kamali, Muhammad Hashim. *Equity and Fairness in Islam*. Cambridge: Islamic Texts Society, 2005.

Kanda, K. C. *Masterpieces of Urdu Ghazal from the 17th to the 20th Century*. New Delhi: Sterling, 1992.

Kugle, Scott Siraj al-Haqq. *Homosexuality in Islam: Critical Reflection on Gay, Lesbian, and Transgender Muslims*. Oxford: Oneworld, 2010.

———. "Sexual Diversity in Islam," in Vincent J. Cornell, Virginia G. Blakemore-Henry, and Omid Safi, eds. *Voices of Islam*. Westport, Conn.: Praeger Publishers, 2006, vol. 5 subtitled *Voices of Change*.

———. "Sexuality and Sexual Ethics in the Agenda of Progressive Muslims," in Omid Safi, ed. *Progressive Muslims: On Gender, Justice and Pluralism*. Oneworld Press, 2003.

———. *Sufis and Saints' Bodies: Mysticism, Corporeality, and Sacred Power in Islam*. Chapel Hill: North Carolina Press, 2007.

Kugle, Scott, and Stephen Hunt, "Masculinity, Homosexuality and the Defense of Islam: A Case Study of Yusuf al-Qaradawi's Media Fatwa," *Religion and Gender* 2/2 (2012): 254–79.

Lane, Edward. *Arabic-English Lexicon: Derived from the Best and Most Copious Eastern Sources*. Cambridge: Islamic Texts Society, 1984; original printing, London: Williams and Norgate, 1863–93.

Lewisohn, Leonard, ed. *Classical Persian Sufism: From Its Origins to Rumi*. London: Khanaqahi Nimatullahi Publications, 1993.

Mahmood, Saba. *The Politics of Piety: The Islamic Revival and the Feminist Subject*. Princeton, N.J.: Princeton University Press, 2005.

Manji, Irshad. *The Trouble with Islam: A Muslim's Call for Reform in Her Faith*. New York: St. Martin's Press, 2003.

Marmon, Shaun Elizabeth. *Eunuchs and Sacred Boundaries in Islamic Society*. Oxford: Oxford University Press, 1995.

Massad, Joseph. *Desiring Arabs*. Chicago: University of Chicago Press, 2007.

———. "Re-Orienting Desire: The Gay International and the Arab World," *Public Culture* 14/2 (2002): 161–185.

Moosa, Ebrahim. *Ghazali and the Poetics of Imagination*. Chapel Hill: University of North Carolina Press, 2005.

Musa, Aisha. *Hadith as Scripture: Discussions on the Authority of the Prophetic Traditions in Islam*. New York: Palgrave Macmillan, 2008.

Nahas, Muhammad Omar. *Homo en Moslem—hoe gaat dat samen?* [Homosexual and Muslim—how to reconcile that?] Utrecht: FORUM Institute voor Mutliculturele Ontwikkeling, 2005. In Dutch.

———. *Islam en Homoseksualiteit* [Islam and Homosexuality]. Amsterdam: Bulaaq, 2001. In Dutch.

———. *Al-Junusiyya: nahwa namudhaj li-tafsir al-junusiyya* [Homosexuality: Toward a Method for Interpreting Homosexuality from the Perspective of a Muslim Homosexual Man]. Roermond, NL: Arabica, 1997. In Arabic.

Naseef, Omar. *Liberation Theology: Islam and the Feminist Agenda in the Qur'an*. Bloomington, Ind.: AnchorHouse, 2007.

Ramadan, Tariq. *To Be a European Muslim*. Leicester: Islamic Foundation, 1999.

Reddy, Gayatri. *With Respect to Sex: Negotiating Hijra Identity in South India*. Chicago: University of Chicago Press, 2005.

Robeson, Paul. *Here I Stand*. Boston: Beacon Press, 1971.

El-Rouayheb, Khaled. *Before Homosexuality in the Arab-Islamic World, 1500–1800*. Chicago: University of Chicago Press, 2005.

Rowson, Everett. "The Effeminates of Early Medina," in Gary D. Comstock and Susan E. Henking, eds. *Que(e)rying Religion: a Critical Anthology*. New York: Continuum, 1997.

———. "Gender Irregularity as Entertainment: Institutionalized Transvestitism at the Caliphal Court in Medieval Baghdad." in Sharon Farmer and Carol Braun Pasternack, eds. *Gender and Difference in the Middle Ages*. Minneapolis: University of Minnesota Press, 2003.

Sells, Michael. *Stations of Desire: Love Elegies from Ibn Arabi and New Poems*. Jerusalem: Ibis Editions, 2000.

Skovgaard-Petersen, Jakob. *Defining Islam for the Egyptian State: Muftis and Fatwas of the Dar al-Ifta*. Leiden: Brill, 1997.

Stowasser, Barbara Freyer. *Women in the Qur'an, Traditions and Interpretation*. Oxford University Press, 1996.

Summerskill, Ben, ed. *The Way We Are Now: Gay and Lesbian Lives in the 21st Century*. London: Continuum, 2005.

Tayob, Abdulkader. "The Function of Islam in the South African Political Process: Defining a Community in a Nation," in Abdulkader Tayob and Wolfram Weisse, eds. *Religion and Politics in South Africa: From Apartheid to Democracy*. Waxmann Verlag, 1999.

———. *Islamic Resurgence in South Africa: The Muslim Youth Movement*. Cape Town: University of Cape Town Press, 1995.

Wadud, Amina. *Inside the Gender Jihad: Women's Reform in Islam*. Oxford: Oneworld, 2006.

Whitacker, Brian. *Unspeakable Love: Gay and Lesbian Life in the Middle East*. Berkeley: University of California Press, 2006.

Yip, Andrew. *A Minority within a Minority: British Non-Heterosexual Muslims.*
Research Report for a Project Funded by the Economic and Social Research Council, 2003.

——. "Negotiating Space with Family and Kin in Identity Construction: The Narratives of British Non-Heterosexual Muslims." *Sociological Review* 52/3 (2004):
336–49.

——. "The Politics of Counter-Rejection: Gay Christians and the Church," *Journal of
Homosexuality* 37/2 (1999): 47–63.

INDEX

Terms from Arabic (and other Islamic languages) are given in italics.

Abou El Fadl, Khaled, 49, 106
Aboutaleb, Ahmed, 135
abuse, 33, 45, 73, 142, 168; sexual, 65, 67, 142; of religion, 47; of alcohol, 29, 120, 214. *See also* rape and sexual molestation
activism, 7, 12, 44, 101, 147, 149, 163, 164, 173, 175, 189, 213–215, 220–222, 224; mode of, 2–4, 8, 22, 43, 53–54, 56, 69, 76, 79, 80, 82, 113, 116–117, 136, 150, 151, 153, 158, 185, 190–191, 194, 196, 204, 216–218, 221; related to Israel-Palestine, 142–143, 145, 190
activist, viii-ix, 1–2, 3, 4, 8, 11, 14, 23, 50, 56, 113, 117, 121, 138, 147, 152, 156, 161, 175, 185, 194, 217–218, 229; contrasted with advocate, 202, 218
adapting religious politics, 3, 5, 46, 80, 81–114, 138
adjusting secular politics, 3, 54, 114, 115–117, 121–122, 127, 131, 135–136, 138, 149–153, 191, 196, 221. *See also* secularism: secular politics
adultery. *See* fornication
Africa, 222. *See also* East Africa and Tanzania; ethnicity: African American or black; North Africa and Morocco; South Africa, Democratic Republic of
agency, 5–6, 10, 14, 43, 45, 68, 111, 122, 132, 147, 181, 198, 218, 220; abdicating, 86, 178; *khalifa* as exemplar of, 32, 112, 157–159. *See also* choice; ethics
AIDS and HIV, 29, 147–148, 204, 214. *See also* disease, sexually transmitted
Al-Alwany, Taha Jabir, 99
Alam, Faisal, 157–171, 172, 190
Al-Azhar, Islamic University, 96, 147, 244n3
Al-Fatiha Foundation, 44, 98, 107, 158–159,

163–172, 241n4, 247n4; Al-Fatiha Canada, 164, 186; Al-Fatiha UK, 171–174, 178, 214
Al-Fitra Foundation, 22, 25, 30–31, 202
Al-Ghazali, Abu Hamid, 102–103, 105
Al-Qa'ida (International Islamic Front for Jihad against Jews and Crusaders), 174
Ali B (Dutch-Moroccan hip-hop singer), 133
'Ali ibn Abi Talib (Imam 'Ali), 195
'alim (religious scholar, plural *'ulama*), 14, 24, 33, 42, 127, 184, 199–201, 243n5
Amnesty International, 163
Amsterdam, 1, 126, 129–130, 134, 150; support organizations in, 128, 134, 150
An-Naim, Abdullahi, 157
apartheid, 24, 26, 28–29, 32–33, 55, 69, 197–198, 204, 243n5
apostasy (renouncing Islam), 41, 52–53, 69, 74–75, 130, 146, 168, 174, 223
Arab countries. *See* Middle East region
Arabic language, 14, 28, 30–31, 51, 84, 96, 102–103, 117, 121, 123–125, 143, 171; as language of Qur'an, 107, 129, 176–177; and literature, 122, 178
Asad, Talal, 5–6
assimilation and integration, 70, 117, 119–120, 133, 135
asylum, 146, 190, 248n18
Atlanta, 164, 165

Belgium, 117, 125, 245n25
biology 2, 6, 47–48, 234, 245–46, 248, 305n15. *See also* diversity; nature: diversity in
bisexuality, 9, 15, 44, 50, 124, 186, 241n5
Black Muslims and Nation of Islam in the United States, 98, 100
Blair, Tony, 189

prayer (*salat* or *namaz*), 3, 12, 24–25, 36, 41,
43, 71–72, 86–88, 96, 129–130, 140, 176–177,
182, 212–213, 219, 226; at dawn, 66, 87,
159, 216, 217; desisting from, 62, 77, 143,
146, 159, 168; at funeral, 158–159, 201; with
homosexual partner, 203, 216; ; at Kaʿba,
94, 95; learning method of, 27, 86, 159,
168; not understanding what is recited in,
31, 129
Progressive Islam, 32–34, 49, 53–54, 75, 99,
102, 105–107, 112–114, 183, 189–190, 201–
202, 223, 244n9
prophets before Muhammad, 21, 31, 39, 210;
Jesus, 43; Joseph, 244n5. *See also* Lut
prostitution, 39, 49, 142
psyche, 16, 27, 83, 85, 92, 96, 122–123, 126,
195–196, 241n6
psychiatry and psychology, 10, 15, 56, 95–96,
122–126, 137, 142, 144–145, 148, 178, 188,
194–195, 196–203, 217–218, 221. *See also*
therapy and counseling
puberty, 10, 18, 25–26, 27, 35–36, 72, 100, 123,
129–130, 139, 160, 186, 211
purity, 27, 66, 206; and pollution, 130

Qibla (anti-apartheid organization), 34
queer, 8, 13, 19, 37, 186, 190
Qurʾan, 8, 22, 24, 27, 31, 33, 54, 72, 75, 77,
86, 93, 118, 161, 163–164, 177–182, 241n6;
condemns corruption, 38, 122; definition
of 14, 47; as open text, 106, 187; political
views of, 135; related to marriage, 78, 177,
180; study of, 69, 87–89, 99, 103, 139, 160,
176, 187, 198
Qurʾan interpretation, 14, 31–32, 39, 43,
48–49, 53–54, 63–64, 71, 76, 88, 98, 122,
124, 168, 177–181, 202, 222, 241n5, 247n13;
importance of context in, 48, 77, 178, 222;
of metaphorical or ambiguous verses,
110–111, 122, 183; under new social conditions, 31, 69, 105–106, 243n5; principles of,
31, 32, 49, 106–107, 228; terms for homosexuality in, 161, 163, 208; translation as,
161, 163, 177–178
Qurʾan quoted, 21, 25, 32, 33, 53, 56, 93, 103,
111, 122, 180–181, 187, 218, 229

Rabiʿa of Basra, 68
racism. *See* ethnicity: discrimination on the
basis of
Rahman, Fazlur, 105

Ramadan (month of fasting), 25, 41, 86, 94,
188
Ramadan, Tariq, 135, 246n30
rape and sexual molestation, 31, 65, 187. *See
also* sibling: sexual abuse by
Raymtzer, Raymond Redouan Cristaan
Rensen, 115–118, 133
reconcile Islam and homosexuality, viii, 2,
9, 12, 22–23, 29, 30, 48, 70, 83, 161–162,
199, 205–206; through dialogue, 122, 127,
130–132, 166, 174–175, 184–185; inability
to, 61–62, 67, 74–75, 166–167, 171–172,
201; through intuition, 42, 98, 135, 181,
208–209, 216; through jurisprudence, 103;
through therapy, 201, 203; resistance to,
107, 118, 168, 210
reform, 13, 36, 49, 52–53, 105–107, 113–114,
119, 151, 157, 183, 189, 221, 224–226
religion. *See din*
religious pluralism, 45–46. *See also* marriage, heterosexual: interreligious
reproduction, 92–93, 103, 120, 227. *See
also* health and healing: sexual and
reproductive
rights, 2, 4, 5, 10, 12, 28–29, 45, 52, 119, 135,
136, 147, 149–150, 156–157, 165, 166, 189,
221, 223–224, 227; of Muslim women, 99,
109, 117, 119, 224–226; movement for civil,
98–101, 107–108, 114, 165; movement for
gay, 82, 101, 108, 113 114, 121, 131, 186, 189,
223–224, 227
Robeson, Paul, 101
role model, 11, 101, 103, 133–134. *See also* father:
as role model; mother: as role model
Rotterdam, 118, 147

Safra Project (support group in UK), 44, 49,
51–52
Said, Edward, 4–5
Salaam Queer Community (support group
in Canada), 164, 185–190
Salafi, 46, 106, 113, 210, 212
salvation and paradise, 20, 82, 86–87, 181, 217
San Francisco, 102, 164
Saudi Arabia, 73, 160, 182; studying Islam in,
102–106; supporting conservative movements abroad, 46, 99, 102, 106, 233
Schorer Foundation (in Netherlands), 148,
245n26
secularism, 2, 3, 5, 13, 29, 107, 130, 160, 182,
209; in Netherlands, 116–117, 119–120,

Scott Siraj al-Haqq Kugle is Associate Professor in the Department of Middle East and South Asian Studies at Emory University. His previous books include *Rebel between Spirit and Law: Ahmad Zarruq, Sainthood and Authority in Islam*; *Sufis and Saints' Bodies: Mysticism, Corporeality, and Sacred Power in Islam*; *Sufi Meditation and Contemplation: Time-less Wisdom from Mughal India*; and *Homosexuality in Islam: Critical Reflection on Gay, Lesbian, and Transgender Muslims*.